FLORIDA STATE
UNIVERSITY LIBRARIES

AUG 27 1997

TALLAHASSEE, FLORIDA

CRISIS, URBANIZATION, AND URBAN POVERTY IN TANZANIA

A Study of Urban Poverty and Survival Politics

DR. JOE LUGALLA

UNIVERSITY
PRESS OF
AMERICA

Lanham • New York • London

Copyright © 1995 by
University Press of America,® Inc.
4720 Boston Way
Lanham, Maryland 20706

3 Henrietta Street
London WC2E 8LU England

All rights reserved
Printed in the United States of America
British Cataloging in Publication Information Available

Library of Congress Cataloging-in-Publication Data
Lugalla, Joe
Crisis, urbanization, and urban poverty in Tanzania : a study of urban
poverty and survival politics / Joe Lugalla.
p. cm.
Includes bibliographical references.
1. Urbanization—Tanzania. 2. Urban poor—Tanzania.
3. Tanzania—Economic conditions. I. Title.
HT384.T34L84   1994
307.76'09678—dc20   94-32954 CIP

ISBN 0–8191–9741–6 (cloth : alk. paper)

 The paper used in this publication meets the minimum requirements of
American National Standard for Information Sciences—Permanence
of Paper for Printed Library Materials, ANSI Z39.48–1984.

Dedicated to
Mary Makungu Lugalla

Contents

Abbreviations	ix
Tables	xi
Acknowledgments	xiii
Introduction	xv

Chapter 1
Colonialism and the History of Urbanization in Tanzania — 1

- Colonialism and the Colonial Economy — 1
- Colonialism and Industrialization — 8
- Urbanization During Colonialism — 10
- The Physical and Social Structure of Colonial Towns — 13

Chapter 2
The Post-Colonial State and the Urbanization Process: 1961-1993 — 19

- Introduction — 19
- Rates of Urban Growth — 20
- Factors Responsible for Urban Growth — 22
- Employment and Unemployment in Urban Areas — 25
- The Post-Colonial State Policies on Urban Development — 27
- Decentralization of Urban Growth: The Growth Pole Strategy — 28
- The Relocation of the Capital City from Dar-Es-Salaam to Dodoma — 33
- Ideology and Urban Planning — 37

Chapter 3
The Problems and Politics of Urban Housing — 41
Introduction — 41
The Magnitude of the Problem — 42
The Shortage of Housing — 42
The Growth of Squatter Settlements — 43
The Housing Conditions (Quality of Housing) — 44
The Housing Policies of the Post-Colonial State (1961-1988) — 49
    The Institutional Approach — 50
    The Project/Program Approach — 54
Problems, Constraints, and Analysis of Housing Policies — 57
Urban Housing, Class, and Status — 69

Chapter 4
Squatter Settlements and the Politics of Urban Poverty in Dar-Es-Salaam: A Case Study of Three Settlements — 73
Introduction — 73
The Research Site — 74
Physical Characteristics of Housing — 75
Income, Poverty, and Housing — 78
Social and Political Organization — 82
    The Social Dimension — 82
    The Political Dimension — 87
The Social Networks — 88

Chapter 5
The Crisis in Urban Civic and Social Service Facilities and Urban Poverty — 95
Introduction — 95
The Nature of Urban Civic Facilities and Services — 97
    The Social Service Facilities — 97
        Health — 97
        Education — 99
        Recreation — 102

The Physical Infrastructure	103
Electricity and Water Supply	103
Sanitation and Drainage	106
Bank, Postal, and Telephone Services	109
Urban Transportation System	110
Usafiri Dar-Es-Salaam (UDA) Dar-Es-Salaam Transport Company	112
The "Dalla-Dalla" Buses	114
Other Means of Transportation in Dar-Es-Salaam	114

Chapter 6
Urban Poverty and Survival Politics   119
Introduction	119
The Reality	120
Urban Social Classes and Their Consumption Patterns	126
The Informal Sector and the Urban Poor	129
The Street Boys and Girls	137
Living or Surviving from Begging	141
Problems Encountered by Informal Sector Operators	144
The Sector of Illicit Activities	146
Corruption	147
Prostitution	148

Chapter 7
The State and the Urban Poor   155
Introduction	155
The State's Attitude Toward the Urban Poor	155
The State's Policies on Urban Poverty (1961-1993)	161
The Human Resources Deployment (*Nguvu-Kazi*) Act of 1983	166
The Act	166
Background Ideas to the Act	169
The *Nguvu-Kazi* Act in Practice	170
Analysis	175

Chapter 8
Conclusion: How Tanzania Should Proceed From Here 181

Notes 191
References 203

Abbreviations

BNI	Basic Needs Income
BRU	Building Research Unit
CCM	Chama Cha Mapinduzi (Revolutionary Party)
CDA	Capital Development Authority
CHS	Center for Housing Studies
CRDB	Cooperative and Rural Development Bank
DCC	Dar-Es-Salaam City Council
EEC	European Economic Commission
ERB	Economic Research Bureau
ERP	Economic Recovery Program
IDA	International Development Agency
ILO	International Labor Organization
IMF	International Monetary Fund
JGAT	Journal of Geographical Association of Tanzania
KCU	Kagera Cooperative Union
NBC	National Bank of Commerce
NDL	National Distributors Limited
NESP	National Economical Survival Plan
NHC	National Housing Corporation
NIEO	New International Economic Order
NMC	National Milling Corporation
NSSS	National Sites and Services Schemes
NTC	National Transport Corporation
NUWA	National Urban Water Supply Authority
PHFCT	The Public Housing Finance Company of Tanzania
ROB	Registrar of Buildings
RRA	Rent Restriction Act
SAP	Structural Adjustment Plan
SCP	Slum Clearance Program
SIDO	Small Scale Industrial Organization
SUDECO	Sugar Development Corporation
SUP	Squatter Upgrading Program
TALIRO	Tanzania Livestock Research Organization
TANESCO	Tanzania Electric Supplying Company
TANU	Tanganyika African National Union

Abbreviations

TARO	Tanzania Agricultural Research Organization
THB	Tanzania Housing Bank
TISCO	Tanzania Industrial Studies and Consulting Organization
TNR	Tanzania Notes and Records
UDA	Usafiri Dar-Es-Salaam (Dar-Es-Salaam Transport Co.)
WHO	World Health Organization

Tables

1.1 Towns/Cities and their Economic Activities in Tanzania
2.1 Urban Population and Growth Rates Since 1948
2.2 Total Urban Population of Tanzania and Dar-Es-Salaam City
3.1 Percentage of Construction Material and Toilets Used in Houses, 1969 and 1977
3.2 Distribution of Wage Income by Area and Percentage of Wage Earners in Dar-Es-Salaam and Dodoma in 1971 and 1976
3.3 Proportion of Tenant- and Owner-Occupied Houses in Dar-Es-Salaam in 1980
3.4 National Sites and Services and Squatter Upgrading Projects in Tanzania
3.5 Twenty Years of NHC Performance and Employment Trends, 1962-1982
4.1 Occupations of Household Heads in the Three Settlements
4.2 Distribution of Levels of Living
5.1 Modes of Urban Passenger Transportation in Dar-Es-Salaam
5.2 Breakdowns of UDA Buses
6.1 Respondents by Type of Residencial Area
6.2 Critical Problems Experienced by Urban Dwellers
6.3 Estimated Monthly Basic Necessary Income (BNI) for a Family of Five Members in Urban Areas in Tanzanian Shillings (Tshs.) in 1988
6.4 Sources of Extra Income
6.5 Employment in the Informal Sector by Activity Category
6.6 Hawkers, Peddlers, and Street Vendors by Activity, Gender, and Percentage
7.1 Legal and Illegal Businesses in 1983
7.2 Detention of the Unemployed in Dar-Es-Salaam Campaigns: Two Sample Days

Foreword

It is with great pleasure that I have agreed to the request of Dr. Lugalla to write this foreword for a job well done by a fellow East African on a book that covers a lot of my own scholarly interests, mainly urbanization and its related problems in Sub-Saharan Africa.

Research and books on the topics the author addresses have been published before, albeit in piecemeal form, but this is the first work, to my knowledge, by a native Tanzanian who has grown up in rural Tanzania and has come to the city of Dar-Es-Salaam. This means that he has firsthand experience with the process he describes; he has witnessed the rural-urban migration of his own family and friends and has also acquired the western tools of sociological analysis to be able to bring this work in the form it is in now.

This book addresses important issues current in our times and of particular concern to those interested in Africa's development. The author's focus on the effects of structural adjustment policies as advocated by the World Bank to be followed by most countries in Sub-Saharan Africa shows how they have hit poor Tanzanians even harder than before and this is conspicuously more so among the urban poor. Whereas rural poverty also abounds, urban poverty tends to be more visible, especially being juxtaposed with affluence which among the elite groups which is usually just a stone's throw away. The author has also wisely discussed the urbanization problem as one that goes back to the colonial times when the cities were clearly planned without the concerns or interests of the Africans. This has continued into the post-colonial period when meager resources at the national level and poor planning has continued to be unfavorable to the urban poor.

The book clearly outlines the problems of urbanization, singling out housing, the politics of poverty, and survival strategies for the low-income groups. The readers are not left thinking that the urban poor are a desperate group of people waiting for solutions from above or "manna from heaven" as the biblical story tells. We learn from the author that the poor in Dar-Es-Salaam and other Tanzanian cities have been busy trying to make their own makeshift houses in squatter settlements as a way of providing their own housing. As a partial solution they also have engaged themselves in the informal sector, albeit in very low-income

Foreword

survival activities as the author describes. The poor are, to say the least, not a desperate group but one with a potential that could be nurtured by more positive state policies and programs.

This is a book that will be relevant to students of urbanization in the Third World countries and also to planners and donors concerned with the fate of the majority poor in developing countries. The Tanzanian planners and policymakers will surely find useful hints from reading this book.

> Kinuthia Macharia
> Assistant Professor of Sociology
> Harvard University, Cambridge
> June, 1994

Acknowledgments

Since I began the studies that led to the writing of this book, I have accumulated a debt of gratitude to several institutions and individuals. First, my thanks go to the University of Dar-Es-Salaam in Tanzania which has been granting me a variety of paid study leaves that enabled me to spend some time in the Federal Republic of Germany, Austria, and the United States of America. The research material for this work was collected in Tanzania. The data analysis as well as the writing began in Germany, crystalized in Austria, and concluded in the States. Because of this, my sincere thanks should go to all institutions which financed my stay in these countries. Specifically, many thanks should go to the German Academic Exchange Service Organization which financed my doctoral studies in Germany between 1984 and 1989, the Austrian Academic Exchange Service Organization which sponsored my stay in Vienna in 1992, and the Carnegie Scholarship Foundation which supported my ten months' stay as a Visiting Fellow at the Harvard Medical School where the final product of this work was realized.

I have benefited from ideas of a lot of individuals, friends, and colleagues from these places. First, many thanks should go to Professors Michaela Von Freyhold, Hartmut Haussermann, Rainer Mueller and Dr. Dietrich Milles of the University of Bremen who read and commented on the earlier drafts of this work. While in Germany, I also enjoyed illuminating ideas of Professor Gottfried Mergner of the University of Oldenburg. Socially I felt as if I was at home because of the warm hearts of sympathy and kindness of Elizabeth Sittig, Hilke and Helmut Hoffman's family. While I was in Vienna, the ideas of Professor Talos and Manuela Delpos assisted me in putting some of my views on the right track. Harvard Professors Kris Heggenhhougen, Byron Good, and Mary-Jo Good and Mrs. Anne Fitzgerald-Clark of the Department of Social Medicine have also been of great help. This is without forgetting the moral as well as social support which I always got from my visiting fellow colleagues Dr. Noah Ndosi, Dr. Lucy Muchiri, and more particularly Dr. Christina Mwangi who always inspired me with a sense of humor and encouragement.

Back home my many thanks should go to my fellow colleagues in the Department of Sociology at the University of Dar-Es-Salaam and in particular Cuthbert Omari, Christopher Comoro, Sethy Chachage, Patrick

Acknowledgments

Masanja, Felician Tungaraza, John Sivalon, Abu Mvungi, and Abunuwas Mwami. These and my undergraduate as well as postgraduate students in the department have assisted me a lot in reformulating some of my subjective statements. This work would not have come out in its present form without the moral and material support of my family, in particular, Sapi, Huruma, Wende, Monica, and Edda. My wife, Mary, and our two sons, Tumaini and Imani Ushindi, endured my absence during the initial stages of this work. They stayed in Tanzania alone when I was in Germany laying down the groundwork of this work. I therefore owe them a lot. Unfortunately, Mary passed away unexpectedly on July 8, 1989 before experiencing the fruits of her tireless efforts. This work is dedicated to her and our two sons.

Introduction

Tanzania, which is among the poorest nations of the South, has an area of 945,000 sq. km., of which 59,000 sq. km. is made up of lakes and inland waters. There are also 800 km. of coastline along the Indian Ocean. The country lies between 1 to 11 degrees South and between 29 to 39 degrees East. The country is bordered by Kenya and Uganda in the North, Zaire, Rwanda, and Burundi in the West, Malawi and Zambia to the Southwest, Mozambique to the South, and the Indian Ocean to the East. At present, Tanzania's total population is estimated to be around 26 million people of which 85% live in the rural areas and 15% are urban.

After being under colonialism for a total of 75 years (30 and 45 years of German and British colonialism respectively), the country attained her political independence on December 9, 1961.

The country is essentially characterized by a predominantly agricultural-based economy whose contribution to GDP is about 60%. Besides subsistence farming, which is the main preoccupation of the people in the countryside, Tanzania's major agricultural exports include coffee, cotton, sisal, tobacco, cashew nuts, tea, and pyrethrum.

Socially, the country is a multicultural society with about 125 different ethnic groups with different languages, customs, folklore, and myths. The postcolonial state has been unable to evolve a true homogeneous Tanzanian nationalism. The question is, "What holds Tanzania together?" The Swahili language and its culture have played and continue to play a major role as a unifying factor. Swahili became the only official national language immediately after independence and therefore became the medium of instruction in primary schools. All these changes, together with TANU's and later CCM's promise to eradicate poverty, inequality, and exploitation via a variety of policies inherent in the Arusha Declaration, which aimed at building a socialist society, have played a crucial role in holding Tanzania together.

Politically, Tanzania is divided into 20 administrative regions which are, in turn, divided into districts which are again subdivided into divisions, then wards, and finally villages. Since the early years of independence, Tanzania has been a one-party state. In 1967, via the Arusha Declaration, the country decided to adopt the socialist path of

Introduction

development based on the principles of "Ujamaa" (Socialism). Social and economic development policies based on this ideology have been dominant in Tanzania at least until early 1991 when, via the Zanzibar Declaration, the Central Committee of the ruling party CCM denounced most of the major policy directions inherent in the Arusha Declaration. In the meantime, the country is involved in bringing in a variety of social, political, and economic reforms. Attempts are being made to introduce political pluralism and the dominance of free market economy. The multi-party general elections are due to take place in 1995.

Although Tanzania did record significant economic growth coupled with social and economic development during the early years of independence until the late 1970s, the period beginning with the 1980s has been very difficult as far as Tanzania's economy and social development is concerned. This period has been characterized by a severe social and economic crisis which has contributed a lot toward a falling standard of living and quality of life for the majority of the population. The crisis has been characterized by GDP growth rates which have not been corresponding with rapid population growth rate and poor performance of the agricultural sector leading not only to food shortage, but also to a tremendous decline of the export sector output. This has, in turn, led to a shortage of foreign currency and to declining export revenues, as well as a low and decreasing capacity of the government to save, an increasing rate of budget deficits, and a negative balance of payments. This has intensified the rate of external dependence and the situation of indebtedness in budget financing.

A variety of factors, both internal and external, seem to have been responsible for the current crisis. Externally, the first and the second round of the oil price increase in 1973 and 1979 and the sharp decline in international terms of trade since the end of the coffee boom in 1977 must have triggered the financial position of Tanzania. To these one should also add the collapse of the East African community in 1977 which necessitated substantial new investments to provide services that were formerly rendered by the community using facilities located in Kenya and Uganda, and finally the Tanzania-Uganda war imposed on Tanzania by Amin's invasion, whose cost is estimated to have been 500 million dollars. These events met Tanzania in unaware situation and affected its plans. Internally, the crisis has been caused by the kind of

Introduction

policies Tanzania has adopted since independence toward the agricultural sector. These policies have been suppressing agricultural sector producer prices and have destabilized the stable rural settlements and forms of social organization and institutions through the introduction of preplanned and adhocly implemented forced villagization. These policies set in motion the preconditions for the start of the agrarian crisis Tanzania experiences today.

Clearly there might be more factors than the ones mentioned above but these other factors are not the subject matter of this book. What is important to note is that the present crisis is an acknowledged fact. The net result of the crisis has been the deterioration of the standard of living of the majority of the population. The crisis has also eroded the social and economic development achieved during the first one and a half decades of independence and continues to threaten the remaining but dilapidated social economic and physical infrastructure.

In its attempt to deal with the crisis, the government has, since 1981, adopted a variety of adjustment policy measures. These have included "The National Economic Survival Plan" (NESP) of 1981, "The Structural Adjustment Program" (SAP) of 1984, "The Economic Recovery Program One/Two" (ERP1/ERPII) of 1986 and 1989 respectively, and "The Economic and Social Action Plan" (ESAP) and "The Priority Social Action Plan" (PSAP), both of 1989. The objectives of these policy measures have been to attain macroeconomic balance by bringing national expenditure into line with national income, to attain greater efficiency in resource allocation involving resource switching across economic sectors, to reduce inflation, to reduce foreign exchange constraints by increasing exports and encouraging the use of locally available raw materials, and finally, the mobilization of resources over the long term in order to raise rates of economic growth and living standards, for the majority poor in particular.

It has now been more than a decade since both the crisis and the accompanying adjustment policy measures have been dominant in development processes of Tanzania. However, social and economic hardships persist and have multiplied rather than decreasing. Why is this so? How has the crisis affected different social groups in Tanzania? How do different social groups cope with the situation? What are their coping mechanisms? What does the state do and how does it react toward

Introduction

people's initiatives? My curiosity about these questions inspired me to conduct a study in Tanzania which could lead to answering some of them.

What I basically attempt to present in this book is a brief account and analysis of the history as well as the politics of the process of urbanization in Tanzania in the wake of social economic crisis and the politics of structural adjustment programs. I focus on what has been the impact of the crisis in urban areas in Tanzania. How has this crisis affected the process of urbanization and what type of social groups suffer most and how? An attempt is made throughout the work to expose the impact of the crisis upon urban dynamics on the one hand, and how this shapes both the situation of poverty and the politics of poverty. As a result of this background, I invested a lot of effort in studying how the majority urban poor fared in the urban system, how they were being affected by the crisis, and how they coped with it. The book is therefore an analysis of the politics of urban poverty and survival tactics in Tanzania.

In order to put the whole work in its proper theoretical and historical context, I start with a discussion of the impact of colonialism on the process of urbanization. In Chapter 1 I show how the politics of colonialism influenced and shaped the nature and pattern of urban development in Tanzania. In Chapter 2 I analyze the nature of the postcolonial state policies on urban development and how these have contributed to the pattern of urbanization experienced in Tanzania today. I also link here the colonial and postcolonial policies on urbanization and argue concretely that in a way the latter are a legacy of the former and hence the postcolonial policies have been unable to institute radical reforms in order to alter the pervasive nature of the process of urbanization in Tanzania. Since the process of urbanization is a fragment of the national fabric, it captures, undoubtedly in a heightened form, basic elements of both continuity and change in a society. It is important to appreciate its societal context in order to understand well the internal dynamics inherent in this process. It is on this basis that I find Chapters 1 and 2 necessary since they link the macropolitics operating at the societal level and micropolitics surfacing at the urban level. One of the most serious problems confronting urban Tanzania is the problem of urban housing, discussed in Chapter 3. Besides exposing the magnitude of the problem in this chapter, I also identify and analyze Tanzania's

Introduction

urban housing policies to locate both their strengths and weaknesses. In brief, this chapter looks at how the state has been grappling with the urban housing question.

Chapter 4 looks at people's local initiatives in solving the urban housing problem. This is done through an indepth study of the social economic conditions of life in three squatter settlements in Dar-Es-Salaam. What comes out of this study is the fact that, contrary to the state's conventional wisdom that these settlements are a menace to proper urban development and that they must be cleared, squatter's initiatives reveal people's own struggles in trying to solve their urban housing problems. The study also reveals that squatters are the most needy segment of the urban population but the least assisted.

In Chapter 5 I look at the impact of the crisis upon urban civic and social services like health, education, urban transportation, electricity, water supply, drainage, and other urban sanitation facilities. This is done by assessing quality and adequacy of these services and how different social groups suffer as a result. Chapter 6 is devoted to the politics of poverty and survival tactics. I show the different kinds of strategies which people are adopting in order to survive given the current social and economic hardships. As a result of this, I highlight a variety of economic activities of the informal sector and other legal as well as illegal *cum illicit* activities. In this chapter I also discuss the fate of street children and some humiliating income generating activities like begging and prostitution.

If people are reacting towards the crisis as well as the social economic hardships of life in the way described in the preceding chapters, how is the state reacting? What kind of policies has it adopted in order to confront the problem of urban poverty? Have these policies succeeded? I attempt to answer these questions in Chapter 7, looking at the relationship between the state and the urban poor. Finally, in Chapter 8 I suggest some long term solutions which Tanzania has to consider implementing to solve the urban crisis as well as the problem of urban poverty.

1
Colonialism and the History of Urbanization in Tanzania

Colonialism and the Colonial Economy

After the 1884 Berlin Conference of the "scramble and partition of Africa", Tanzania became a German colony known as *Deutsch Ostafrika* or German East Africa. In 1918, after World War I, Tanzania was placed under the British Mandate and remained a trusteeship territory of the League of Nations until it achieved its independence in 1961. The Germans stayed in Tanzania for a period of 30 years and the British for 45 years. During each of these periods, as I shall argue later, the colonial economy was geared toward the production of raw materials for industrializing Europe. The colonial economy was molded in such a way that it accomplished this objective. In Tanzania the production of cash-crops, i.e., coffee, sisal, and cotton, was introduced during the German period and remained the main preoccupation of the colonial economy even during the British period.

The German colonial economy consisted broadly of two main types of production. First, individual peasants produced cash-crops and second, plantations were worked by forced waged labor. Initially, the Germans seem to have wanted to establish a predominantly plantation economy, but as things worked out, individual peasant production became at least more important than plantation economy. Rather than the settler plantation economy, which depended solely on the government's loans and the colonial state's protection, the colonial state realized that peasant cash-crop production was administratively cheap and easy. As the days passed, the Germans used three main ways of organizing their economy, namely, white settler farming, plantation farming operated by foreign companies, and small scale peasant cash-crop production.

Setting this colonial economy in motion necessarily involved a "redirecting" of the means of production within the colony's interests and demands. Most affected was the pre-colonial social structure including land and labor. It was this " redirecting" of the indigenous labor power that had important consequences on the social structure, and since then the basic economic structure is still a neo-colonial one.[1]

The colonial state imposed taxation (a hut tax of 3 rupees to be paid in cash) and the first taxation ordinance was enacted in 1897. During this period, raising money was not a simple task for the Africans, but because of the demand of the colonial state, they had to raise money through one of the two following ways.

1. They could sell something like food, an animal, or a cash-crop such as cotton, coffee, or tea grown specifically to earn money, or
2. They could work as laborers in the transportation and communications network that physically got the crops from the fields on their way to the ports, work in European-run plantations, or they could be forced to work in the colonial state bureaucracy that oversaw the whole process of rural exploitation.[2]

Africans had to migrate to other rural areas to seek employment in export-crop plantations, and those who engaged in peasant cash-crop production stayed more or less in their own rural areas. Those who joined the colonial state bureaucracy had to migrate to the urban areas where most of the government offices, railway stations, ports, and warehouses were concentrated. Those who joined the tertiary sector activities, i.e., working in hospitals, courts, schools, army camps and police, migrated to both rural and urban areas although the tendency was to cluster more in the latter.

Most of the job opportunities in the colonial bureaucracy required Africans to have minimal education. To achieve this end, the colonial state introduced a formal education system. It is through this colonial education that the African culture was distorted. In other words, while cash-crop production distorted the traditional economic structure on one hand, colonial education on the other hand had an adverse impact on the socio-cultural structure of the Tanzanian society. Sabot (1979) argued that educated rural Africans tend to migrate to the urban areas in search of employment more often than the uneducated ones.[3]

As for the involvement of Africans in the cash-crop economy, Coulson (1982) while quoting Redmond (1972) provides some interesting figures from the Songea region:

> In 1899, the first year in which tax was collected, 1651 rupees were paid in cash, 706 rupees in kind, and 21,209 rupees representing the labor of more than 7,000 men were paid in labor. By 1903 the cash-payment was 38045 rupees.[4]

Between the years 1903 and 1911, the value of export products in rupees was 291,450 for rubber, 44,900 for ivory, 179,620 for copra, 14,130 for livestock, 226,600 for sisal, 92,250 for cotton, 85,150 for coffee, 13,960 for sesame, and 151,750 for hides.[5]

All cash-crops that were grown on large estates and plantations (sisal, for example) required a substantial amount of labor. As a general rule (though there could have been exceptions) those rural areas that had peasant cash-crop production (coffee and cotton) did not supply labor to the plantations. By 1910, there were 54 sisal plantations exporting about 20,000 tons a year.[6] Although the price fell somewhat before World War I, sisal became the most valuable export product, a position that was to be reinforced in the 1920s and 1930s, and survived even after independence.[7]

In order to minimize costs, the colonial economy used migrant labor in the plantation economy. It was originally planned that laborers would come from the surrounding areas, and for this reason, areas of "native" reserve were left between and near the plantation areas. But because the plantations did not grow their own food, most of the farmers in these reserves found that by growing and selling food to the laborers who worked in these plantations they could make sufficient money to pay tax without submitting to irksome conditions on the states. So instead, migrants came from far away — basically from Njombe, Songea, Burundi, Rwanda, and Kigoma (Iliffe 1971).[8]

Of central importance in establishing the colonial economy was the infrastructure of transportation, commerce and administration. The Germans built telegraph lines, put steam engine boats on the great lakes, and most importantly (from an economic standpoint) built roads and railways. In fact, until the recent (1970) Chinese-built Tanzania-Zambia Railway Line (TAZARA), the country's railway system was essentially what the German colonial administration left behind.

The location of the railways was determined solely by German considerations of their economic aspirations. Their functions were twofold:

1. To link up export-crop-producing areas with the coastal ports of Tanga and Dar-Es-Salaam, and
2. To facilitate the rapid movement of troops to defend the country's borders if necessary during the war. The Germans knew that the British would attack them from Kenya. Hence with the railway system they designed, they could thus move the troops within 24 hours (Brain 1979:44).

Thus, the colonial transportation and communication network was essentially outward-oriented. The network was not built in order to link up areas of the rural main population, or the southern poor part of Tanzania with the relatively rich northern part. In any way, this network was not designed to expand the internal domestic market, and in reality, having an internal self-sustaining economy was never the goal of the Germans. Unfortunately, "development" in Tanzania has, to a very considerable extent, continued to run along the lines laid out by German colonialism.[9]

It took the Germans approximately 20 years (1885-1906) to "pacify" the whole country.[10] What German colonialism did in Tanzania in an extraordinarily short amount of time, had and still has an adverse impact on the present Tanzanian social and economic structure. The cash-crop production brought the rural population into the sphere of influence of petty commodity production. Towns were set up and became part and parcel of this mode of production.[11]

These changes were not the results of the internal social and economic forces but rather results of an impulse coming from social and economic forces located elsewhere.

After World War I, Tanzania became a British mandate territory. In essence, the British colonial policy was not different from that of the Germans. Considering the fact that, at least by 1914, a balance had been achieved between plantation agriculture, white settler farming, and small scale peasant production, the British did not want to institute major policy changes to what was already set in motion by the Germans.[12] This is clearly noted from the statement in 1926 from the British Governor, Sir Donald Cameroon, who said that

> The first object of the government is to induce the native to become a producer directly or indirectly, that is to produce or to assist in producing something more than the crop of local foodstuffs that he requires for himself and his family.[13]

Thus the structure of the economy remained the same, and emphasis on cash-crop production continued unabated. Until 1938 sisal remained the largest export in terms of value, followed by rubber which suffered severe competition from production in Southeast Asia; then came hides and skins, copra, groundnuts, and beeswax, all largely produced by peasants, with coffee some distance behind.[14]

The British were not interested in investing heavily in Tanzania because of her mandatory, and later on, trusteeship status. The more farsighted British colonial officials recognized that independence was inevitable with only the timing in question. Much of their investments were done in Kenya. However, this did not preclude their active participation in economic exploitation and plundering of the rural economy.

From the mid-1930s to mid-1950s, the British believed that force was necessary to make small farmers change their agricultural techniques. In 1937 they amended the Native Authorities Ordinance to allow bylaws to be passed for the enforcement of soil conservation measures and other agricultural practices (Coulson 1982: 52). This meant that anyone who "offended" could be taken to a Native Authority Court at which the chief presided, and be fined or imprisoned. (ibid.)

Several agricultural development schemes which combined attempts to prevent soil erosion with other agricultural aims were adopted during this period. For example, the Sukuma Development Scheme of 1947 was started in order to increase cotton production. The Mbulu Development Scheme involved a cattle census followed by compulsory reductions in the numbers of animals, and the Iringa Dipping Scheme involved compulsory dipping of cattle for a small fee to be paid for each dipping. Other schemes intended to protect soil on steep slopes of Uluguru, Usambara, and Pare mountains were started. In these areas, peasants were forced to build bench terraces.[15]

Various studies have already shown that African farmers adopted these new agricultural schemes with tense resistance. By the mid-1950s it was clear that the application of force and compulsion was counterproductive; therefore, a new approach was sought. Few rich African farmers or villages labelled by the British as "progressive" were identified and resources like fertilizer, machinery, and extension services were concentrated to them. Other agricultural policies, e.g., "The Transformation and Improvement Approaches" were also adopted by the colonial state during this period. With these policies in operation, the British initiated an open espousal of differentiation. The British logic behind these policies can be well understood when one reads the 1950 Annual Report of the Department of Agriculture which said

> Agricultural extension work in Africa frequently finds itself up against a brick wall of peasant conservatism, sometimes strengthened by political misconceptions. . . . It becomes necessary to withdraw the effort from some portions and to concentrate resources on small selected points, a procedure which has come to be known as the 'Focal Point Approach'. Under this method limited areas or progressive individuals are chosen for initial attack. . . . Once success has been achieved and appreciated at these points, it is then a comparatively simple matter to spread outwards from them.[16]

The British labelled those African farmers who resisted to adopt new agricultural methods as stubborn, lazy, ignorant, conservative, and uncooperative. As Coulson (1982) has argued, there was no recognition that logic often lay in the refusal to do what the extension staff advised.

Most of these schemes had a negative impact on the African way of agriculture. For example, Collinson (1963), noticed that the Sukuma land tie-ridging system, while it undoubtedly resulted in soil and water conservation and so raised yields in dry years, it was nevertheless an intensive method in its use of labor at a critical time of the year, and therefore reduced the total area which could be cultivated by a given labor force.[17] Saylor (1970) has shown that farmers who accepted the recommendations for cotton spacing suffered losses varying from 55 kg. per hectare in the Mwanza district to 85 kg. per hectare in the Shinyanga district. Saylor found also in 1969 that it made no significant difference in which month cotton was planted — quite contrary to the recommendations of the extension service to plant early.[18] The difficulties arising from attempts at improving the cattle economy were also similar. Coulson observes that dipping is only beneficial if it is carried out regularly for the whole life of an animal. But if it ceases (as well it may if the distribution of chemicals and maintenance of the dip and water supply depend on government bureaucracy) then the animals will be more susceptible to disease than if they had never been dipped and had achieved a resistance.[19] Similarly the idea to destock cattle to an individual is useless if grazing is communal, unless all cattle owners destock together, and even then the poor suffer proportionally more than the rich.[20] Thus Parkipuny (1976:147-8) is probably right when he claims that destocking will never be acceptable until there is a more even distribution of cattle. This calls for revolutionary changes in most parts of Tanzania.[21]

Rural-class formation became the agenda through these colonial agricultural policies. Labor-hiring peasants or small rural capitalists or *Kulaks* (the word often used in the Tanzanian literature), soon came to be found in every part of the country. These people bought and claimed large areas of good land.

In two areas these *Kulaks* played a particularly conspicuous role. One was in the Ismani area, not far from Iringa town. A study conducted in this area by Awiti (1972) showed that in 1972, 9% of the farmers held 53% of the land under cultivation, owned 96% of capital equipment, and contributed nearly 70% of the maize that was marketed.[22] The other area was Mbulu in the Arusha region. Here, African wheat farmers began by hiring tractors and combine harvestors from settlers and finally became rich and purchased their own new equipment. By the end of the 1960s, about 150 African farmers were not only cultivating large areas of wheat, but were also providing an efficient hire service for about 4,000 in the area.[23]

A similar situation was happening almost throughout the country. Until independence, the capitalist mode of production had found its roots in rural Tanzania. This capitalism underdeveloped the rural sector in a variety of ways. By redirecting the Africans from subsistence food production to export-crop production, the Tanzanian farmers became dependent on the forces and dictates of a world capitalist system outside their own will. Since then, Tanzanian farmers have not succeeded in fighting against this force, and the impact of this force upon the African social economic structure continues to be negative. By introducing policies which encouraged and fostered rural differentiation, colonial rural capitalism divided the rural people into poor, middle, and rich peasants. These classes continue to exist now and their relations have continued to be exploitative and contradictory rather than harmonious. By identifying specific areas for cash-crop production and others for mere provision of a migrant labor force, the colonial economic system led to the emergence of uneven regional development. By introducing an economy which does not serve the internal market, colonialism initiated a systematized process of rural surplus appropriation. It is this process that created and continues to enforce rural poverty and underdevelopment. Surplus which is produced from the rural areas is not reinvested in the same areas, but is invested partly in luxurious service structures in urban areas and the rest is taken outside the country. In general, the colonial economy has had an adverse impact on Tanzania's social formation. On the one hand it has created and widened the gap between towns and the countryside (rural-urban inequality) and on the other hand, it has created special urban forms which perform specific functions.The section on colonial economy and urbanization in this chapter deals with this issue in detail. Suffice it to say that it is this concrete situation which the post-colonial state inherited immediately after independence and (as I argue later in this work) the post-colonial state's policies that have tended to exacerbate this situation.

One crucial point has to be noted at this point.The history of the process of urbanization, rural underdevelopment, rural poverty, and rural-urban migration in Tanzania cannot be understood outside the framework of the nature of the colonial economy which I have outlined above. The discussion which follows from now on cannot be understood if the analysis presented so far is left out. Equally important in the colonial economy and closely linked to the nature and form of the urbanization process in Tanzania is the process of industrialization. The section that follows deals with this issue in brief.

Colonialism and Industrialization

Not much can be said about industrialization under colonialism because it was almost non-existent. The position of the colonialists concerning this was negative. This is confirmed by the Secretary of State's statement in 1935 which reads

> It is undesirable to accelerate industrialization of East Africa which must for many years to come remain a country of primary produce.[24]

The British believed that industrialization would bring ruin to the tribal society that Cameroon and his administrators were trying to rediscover and retain (Coulson 1982).They held the belief that the African worker "detribalized" in the towns was dangerous. His place was in the village or working for short periods on European plantations (ibid.).

The kind of industries which were encouraged were only those which conformed with the colonial economy of agricultural raw materials. Most of them were for processing the agricultural raw materials such as cotton ginneries, sisal decortication industries, and coffee curing. Other import-substitution industries (for consumer goods) which forced the African to join cash-crop production in order to get money which could enable them to buy these European manufactured goods were also encouraged.

Indeed, by 1920, competition from mass-produced imports had already destroyed most of the traditional craft skills in Tanzania (Coulson 1982). In 1921 the list of industries in Tanganyika included 12 ginneries, four flour mills, six soap or oil mills, 14 jewelry manufacturers, two printers, two furniture makers, three soda water factories, one tobacco factory, two manufacturers of salt, one of pottery, and two of lime, coming to a total of 49 factories in all (ibid.p.71). Some coffee processing and eight sisal factories should probably be added to the list, but by any standard the industrial sector was minute (ibid.). The tobacco factory employed 102 workers, and the two salt-works employed 300 people between them (ibid.). The remaining factories were no more than small workshops, and almost all had been in operation before World War I.

Most of the industries established between 1914 and 1945 continued to be purely agricultural, import-substitution-consumer goods and service-oriented in nature. Although the resource base was sufficient for balanced industrialization (coal fields near Lake Nyasa, iron ore deposits in Liganga, and power generated from water), the colonial state decided not to industrialize. By 1945, the only factory of any size depending on imported inputs was a beer factory. Most of the other factories were either processing agricultural products that could not otherwise be exported, or they were processing for local markets on a very small scale. Most of these industries were concentrated in urban areas and therefore had a comparative advantage. For example, in 1945 there were 103 grain mills and 72 oil mills and soap factories for a total urban population of less than 150,000.[25] In all 761 establishments existing by then, only less than 15,000 people comprised the total labor force.

World War II had very little impact on industrial development in Tanganyika. Goods that could no longer be imported from Britain were imported from Kenya instead. In fact, Tanganyika's imports from Kenya and Uganda rose from 7.5 million shillings in 1939 to nearly 25 million shillings in 1945 (Honey 1974).[26]

The British policy towards industrialization was also racist in character. In some instances they discouraged non-British investors even if it meant that what they would have produced would have to be imported from Kenya. Although this attitude did not survive for a long time, the pace of industrialization remained slow and dependence on Kenya continued to increase. The main difference between the list of factories at the end of 1955 and that of 1945 lies in the number of factories involved in maintenance and repair of trucks, cars, agricultural machinery, and boats. In the sphere of manufacturing, a tin-manufacturing plant (metal box) employing 218 workers, a paint-mixing plant (Robiallac) employing 51 workers, and Tanganyika Meat Packers employing 800 workers were established in 1955.[27] Some textile and weaving factories also came to the fore. By 1958 there were still only about 300 enterprises with more than five employees in manufacturing (as distinct from processing export) with just 20,000 workers mainly in the food and furniture business.(IBRD 1961).

So although the period nearing the year of independence (1961) showed slight progress, for most of the colonial period industrialization was really almost non-existent. As long as those few industries established remained concentrated in urban areas, they acted as pull factors for rural-urban migration on the one hand, but failed to provide the urban migrants with employment opportunities on the other. Most of the people who got employment in urban areas worked in the service sector. The nature of industrialization was unbalanced in the sense that it depended solely on the performance of the agricultural sector, and provided nothing in return in order to revolutionize and develop the agricultural sector. Again, this situation intensified the process of rural-surplus appropriation on the one hand, and facilitated the emergence of "parasitic" urban nodes on the other, a structural relationship still persisting in Tanzania today.

In brief, it is important to argue that the nature of this industrialization is significant in our analytical work because it offers us parameters within which we can understand the mode of urbanization, rural-urban inequality, rural-urban migration and both rural and urban poverty in Tanzania. The following section examines the nature of the urbanization process during the colonial period. This analysis can only be well understood if one has grasped the politics of the colonial economy discussed in the previous sections.

Urbanization During Colonialism

During the colonial period, the process of rural-urban migration was very insignificant.The majority of the rural people migrated to other rural areas to seek employment in the plantation economy. Whereas many African governments today face the problem of overabundant urban labor, during colonialism employers were troubled by the scarcity of wage labor (Berg, 1965, Mason, 1958).[28] The current stress on unemployment and underemployment is (for reasons which will emerge later) a post-independence phenomenon. However, this is not to argue that the unemployment problem was non-existent during colonialism. The colonial state set up strict laws which restricted African urban migration. One of these laws was the Colonial Labor Utilization Ordinance of 1923. The question then is, How did the organization of the colonial economy lead to the emergence of urban settlements? What was the nature of these settlements?

Most of the towns emerged in political administrative centers of the colonial state. Dar-Es-Salaam and most of the other towns with regional headquarters developed as a result of this process. Other towns emerged at railways and crossroads like Dodoma, Morogoro, and Tabora. Some of them developed in areas where either cash-crop production (Arusha, Tanga, and Moshi) or mining (Shinyanga for diamonds in Mwadui, Mwanza for gold in Geita) was dominant. Besides other factors, Mwanza, Tanga, Kigoma, Dar-Es-Salaam, and Mtwara developed also as important ports for export and import trade. Some defensive forts which were established during the German colonial period in strategic positions for the surrounding countryside became the basis for the development of some new towns. Iringa and Mbeya towns were developed this way. At least until early 1915, these military forts and posts had become administrative capitals of various districts in which they were situated. More than half of all Tanzanian towns grew in this way, and later commercial functions came too to dominate the economic life of these towns.

These towns were not industrial ones. Apart from petty commodity production, industry was small to non-existent in them. As Brain (1979) argues, their *raison d'etre* was administrative, and commercial functions which they performed were in relation to the surrounding countryside. Institutions for policing, taxing, and generally monitoring and administering the rural colonial economy were set in them. They also held institutions for collecting and buying cash-crops from the countryside, providing cheap goods for peasants to purchase (salt, sugar, knives, bicycles, etc.), and providing more expensive goods and more sophisticated entertainment if there were white settler farmers in that vicinity (Brain, 1979: 45). Brain is probably right when he says that

> industrial capitalism in Germany needing an ensured source of supply of certain tropical raw-materials, produced in her new colony an essentially capitalist rural economy, urban only to the extent that the infrastructure necessary to service this rural economy tended to cluster at common points which became towns. (ibid.)

Hence, there is no doubt that the main aim of the colonial towns was to service the colonial agricultural economy. It is no wonder to note that in Tanzania, each main town can at least be identified with a particular cash-crop. Table 1.1 below provides a summary of this congruence.

TABLE 1.1
Towns/Cities and Their Economic Activities in Tanzania

TOWN/CITY	ECONOMIC ACTIVITY
Dar-Es-Salaam	Capital City (up to 1973), Main Port
Morogoro	Cotton, Sisal, Crossroad and Railway Station, Sugar
Dodoma	Crossroad, Railway Station
Tanga	Port, Sisal, Tea, Railway Station
Moshi	Coffee, Sugar, Tourism, Railway Station
Arusha	Coffee, Tourism, Railway Station
Mwanza	Port, Cotton, Gold, Railway Station
Shinyanga	Cotton, Diamond, Gold, Railway Station

Source: Lugalla, J.L.P. "Conflicts and Politics in Urban Planning in Tanzania", African Study Monographs, Volume 9 Number 4, 1989.

It is clear from Table 1.1 that each major town in Tanzania is associated with an export-oriented economic activity. However, besides the importance of these towns to the colonial economy, rural-urban migration remained insignificant during colonialism and urban growth was very slow.

If one adopts the definition of the Tanzania Bureau of Statistics of an urban area, which defines an urban area to be that settlement with a population of more than 10,000 people, then only 2% of the total population of five million lived in urban areas in 1914 (Brain, 1979:47). The remaining 98% lived in the rural areas. By 1948, the total population had reached 7.5 million, but the urban population was only 3% (ibid.). The rate of urban growth remained at 3% per year between 1900 and 1948, and by 1948 the following towns had these populations: Dar-Es-Salaam (69,200), Tanga (20,600), Arusha (5,300), Mwanza (11,300),

Tabora (12,800), Dodoma (9,400), and Mbeya (3,100) (Sabot, 1979:44). It is interesting to note here that the population of Dar-Es-Salaam City alone was greater than the combined total for the other six towns (62,500). This, as Sabot argues, implies that with the same rate of natural increase in the capital and regional centers and the same average length of stay of migrants, the absolute magnitude of net migration to Dar-Es-Salaam was growing faster. This means that as an administrative capital, chief industrial center, and primary port, Dar-Es-Salaam had reinforced its position at the top of Tanzania's urban hierarchy (Sabot,1979).

Although the African urban workers were also migrants from the rural sector, their migration cycle tended to be longer than that of the rural plantation workers. Sometimes their stay in urban areas lasted for a whole working lifetime before they returned to their rural areas as old men (Brain,1979). Urban Africans were required to live in specifically defined areas and hence colonial towns acquired a distinct urban form and structure which necessarily reflected the nature of the social structure which had been created by colonialism. This is an issue to which I now turn.

The Physical and Social Structure of Colonial Towns

The primary concern of this section is to examine the effect of the colonial social economic structure upon the physical built structure of the Tanzanian towns, and to link the symbiotic relationship of this physical layout of the urban areas with the urban social structure. In order to achieve this I will start by highlighting the nature of the colonial urban social structure. I have already showed how various colonial policies lead to the process of class formation in the rural areas. Colonialism had the same impact in the urban areas. A nascent working class comprised of Africans was formed. A few Europeans who worked as administrators in the colonial state and others who worked in other foreign companies became urban-based. Merchant capitalism, which was also urban-based, was mainly dominated by Asians. This exchange merchant capitalism was not independent but instead was incorporated into and subordinate to metropolitan capitalist economies. The merchant capitalists were also divided into classes of the poor, middle, and rich. The same division applied to Africans who lived in urban areas. While Europeans occupied jobs of higher status followed by Asians, the Africans occupied jobs of lower cadre, such as dockworkers, garden (*Shamba*) boys, messengers, low grade clerks and hotel waiters. In general, there was a very close relationship between race and class, occupation and income.

Since the towns were an essential part of the colonial economy, their physical structure also reflected the logic of colonial mentality and development. Since each colonial economic undertaking was essentially a planned one, the towns too were a product of that planning. The planning was done by and for the Europeans. Towns were designed in such a way that their physical layout reflected the social distances of hierarchical colonial social organization.[29] Racial and class segregation were dominant in these towns. Europeans lived in essentially attractive suburbs. Their houses were large and well-built and set in expensive spacious gardens. Streets in these areas were maintained and had lights. Houses were supplied with water, electricity and modern sewage connections. Golf courses, social clubs and other recreational facilities surrounded these luxurious residential areas of the whites. The best examples of these areas are Oyster Bay in Dar-Es-Salaam, Kijengi in Arusha, Isamilo and Capri-Point in Mwanza, Mlimani in Dodoma, Loleza in Mbeya, and Gangilonga in Iringa. During colonialism these areas were called *Uzunguni*, a Swahili word which means "a European area." Most of the houses in these areas were built in low density plots. Next to the *Uzunguni* area was the *Uhindini* area, an area of residence for people of Asian origin which, in several towns, housed shops and was the central area for trade business and commerce. This was the next favored area in terms of provision of urban social services, and the majority of the houses were built on medium density housing plots. Upanga and houses along the present Samora Avenue in Dar-Es-Salaam are a case in point. In Dodoma, houses on the southern part of the railway station simply support this point. Africans were left to reside in areas of high density, sometimes in unplanned residential settlements without piped water, electricity, street lights, or a modern sewage system. Residential segregation was also accompanied by segregation in the provision of social services like hospitals and schools.

In summary, the facilities and living areas of the towns were different for each of what were seen as three racial communities, African, Asian, and European. Each of these had its own schools, churches, clubs, hospitals, bars, and so on.[30] This was considered to be equality from the point of view of colonialism. The colonial idea of equality, as Brain has argued, is interestingly illustrated by an episode in 1955 when an education grant worth 3.6 million pounds was allocated "equally" to European, Asian, and African education. As Nyerere pointed out at that time, with 21,000 Europeans, 80,000 Asians, and 8 million Africans in the country, this worked out at approximately 720 shillings to each European, 200 shillings to each Asian, and two shillings to each African.[31] In several towns it was quite unusual and, in fact, forbidden for Africans to wander aimlessly in designated European residential areas. Africans likely to be seen in these areas were house servants, gardeners, watchmen, golf-ball boys, and sometimes cocktail waiters.[32]

From the above analysis, it should be clear by now that these descriptions of high, medium, and low density residential areas were mere technical terms used in colonial urban planning in order to camouflage or conceal the terms "African", "Asian", and "European" housing whose application would seem to be more racist.

In his analysis of Dar-Es-Salaam, Iliffe (1979) has argued that in order to prevent intermingling, the Germans began in 1912 to divide the town into three racial building zones. The British completed the scheme after 1918, and located the African zone west of the commercial center of Kariakoo which used to be a camping site for their carrier corps.[33] It is in this area that Africans leased plots and built their own houses for rental and owner occupier purposes. According to Iliffe's description, most of these houses were single story structures with mangrove-pole frames, mud walls, and palm-frond roofs.[34] In most cases the owner occupied one room and rented out the other. This landlord was usually called a *Fadhahausi* (father of the house) in Swahili slang.[35] I really believe like Iliffe that this is how African landlordism began developing in urban areas in Tanzania.

As the city continued to grow, typical settlements for Africans became located far away from the city center. Ilala, which became a new African settlement next to Kariakoo, grew under this principle. The conditions of the African residential areas were appalling since most of the Africans who lived in them were either unemployed or received very low incomes. An investigation conducted in 1939 showed that 60% of the employed Africans earned less than 15 Tanzanian shillings (Tshs.) a month.[36] Another survey revealed that one African man in three was unemployed, malaria increased with distance from the city center, while tuberculosis, the scourge of the world's slums went almost unchecked.[37] Only 24 street lights and 16 water kiosks served the African townships by July of 1944, but by then, the African population had already increased from 25,000 in 1939 to 56,765 in 1948.[38]

Iliffe has argued that it was this pressure of population growth which changed the whole character of Dar-Es-Salaam. Lack of housing lead to the emergence of shanty housing settlements on the one hand, while the same situation forced the colonial government to start providing official housing on the other. The Magomeni Quarters northwest of Kariakoo and designated for African residence were built out of this necessity and policy. Even though, it has been estimated that only 15% of African households lived in publicly owned homes in 1950.[39] Of the 500 plots at Magomeni, 150 were acquired by people who owned houses elsewhere. Thus, as Iliffe argues, it is through this process that Kariakoo's urban capitalism was exported to the new suburbs. Rickshaws disappeared in the streets and urban buses replaced them in the late 1940s.[40] Few industries started developing in the Pugu industrial area, and the majority of migrants got employment in the construction industry and industry in general as opposed to the usual trend of being employed as domestic servants. There were other Africans who continued to work as domestic servants, and others in the commercial sector. But according to the law of segregation they had to live in their African township area.

Most of the Africans preferred to live on the eastern part of Kariakoo since this area was bordered by *Mnazi Mmoja* grounds and was very close to working places and service centers like the post offices, railway stations, and others. Access to this area was determined by income, and in this respect, it only accommodated better paid Africans, most of whom were the African elites. Since it is the elites who started developing political consciousness, it is no wonder that the New Street (commonly known today as *Lumumba*) which is very close to this area became the organizational center of the nationalist movements and later the Tanganyika African National Union (TANU) (Iliffe, 1979).

As years passed, Dar-Es-Salaam grew and became too big, too diverse, too shifting in composition, too secular, and eclectic in culture for religious leaders to dominate.[41] Some townsmen accepted no authority at all. The presence of unemployment forced some youths to collect scraps and sell oranges, and others sat on the pavement waiting for the chance to unload a truck or thronged the dock gates at dawn when the harbor was crowded.[42] Violence started developing and police questioned any African found on the streets after 10:00 p.m., and those who failed to provide satisfying information concerning their place of residence and type of employment were detained and later repatriated back to their rural homelands (Iliffe, 1979).

Iliffe has described the form of social organization of these settlements as follows. It ranged from that one which was purely political in nature to one more ethnic in form and content. There emerged tribal associations which performed several functions like assisting the new migrants in securing employment and housing and assisting fellow tribesmen in matters concerning funeral and marriage ceremonies. Earlier on, the Germans had established a regulation which forced tribes to bury their tribal mates dying in hospitals.[43] This laid down the foundation for the urban social networks of affiliation and assistance which are now dominant in urban areas in Tanzania.

Interest in sports, especially football, intensified. The presence of football clubs like Sunderland (now Simba Sports Club), Young Africans (Yanga), and Cosmopolitan became very famous and contributed to dividing the urban residents into specific zones which associated them with a particular football club, and influenced the way people dressed and their favorite colors. Such division has been maintained up to now. For example, the Msimbazi Street area in Dar-Es-Salaam is an urban sports interest zone for the members and fans of the Simba Sports Club, while Jangwani Street is under the monopoly of the Yanga Sports Club. While the colors of red and white are identified with the Simba Club, the Yanga Club identifies itself with green and yellow.

It is this kind of complexity and composition which the post-colonial state inherited during the eve of independence on December 9, 1961 in the case of Dar-Es-Salaam. Other urban areas experienced a similar kind of "development" trend. These trends have continued to surface to date.

In brief and in conclusion, it is now clear how colonialism distorted the self-sustaining pre-colonial social and economic structure. The colonial economy not only distorted the traditional African social and economic structure, but also brought in rural and urban capitalism, an economic system which was based on commodity production and was outward oriented. Through direct and indirect methods of coercion, Africans came to adhere to the laws of motion of the colonial economy. Some joined cash-crop production, and others found waged employment. In some areas this involved rural-rural migration, and in others rural-urban migration. In both patterns of migration the main reason for one to migrate was economic.

It is also clear now how the colonial economy created new settlements called towns. The role of these settlements was to service, monitor, and administer or supervise the colonial economy, and their major functions remained thus administrative and commercial. Since the employment structure of these towns was almost wholly in the tertiary sector, the towns did not themselves directly produce economic surplus.

Their survival depended on the performance of the agricultural sector. Therefor, my conclusion is that Tanzanian colonial towns were "parasitic" rather than "generative". Since they have continued to perform the same role up to now, then the same argument applies to the nature of urban areas in post-independent Tanzania.

I have also shown in this chapter how the physical spatial structure of colonial towns reflected the nature of the macro-social class structure. This is, indeed, concrete evidence of the impact of the politics of colonialism in urban Tanzania.

Throughout the colonial period, and especially by the late 1940s, there was increasing African political activity. From 1954 onward, Africans (via the umbrella of TANU) started crying for a single objective. That was *Uhuru,* which means freedom or independence. As Brain (1979) has commented, this objective was more appealing to the masses than detailed explanations. Until *Uhuru* was achieved, it was not necessary to define it or what would come after it.[44]

Considerable discontent of the African masses in both rural and urban areas, and occasional rioting against colonial regulations throughout the 1950s spurred the development of nationalist consciousness. TANU the political party set itself up against the colonial authority and finally Tanzania achieved her independence in December 1961.

What major changes were brought by independence? Did independence alter the already established colonial social and economic structure? What was the impact of the post-colonial state's policies on the process of urbanization? The following chapters will address these issues.

2
The Post-Colonial State and the Urbanization Process: 1961-1993

Introduction

I have argued in Chapter 1 that the colonial heritage of Tanzania was the backdrop against which its existence as a newly independent country developed. By then the economy of Tanzania had already been shaped to respond to the needs of its colonial rulers and the world capitalist system in general. It is now clear how colonialism shaped and determined the process of urbanization in Tanzania and the kind of regulations and legislations that were adopted in order to confront the urban question.

This chapter seeks to explain what has happened during the post-colonial period in Tanzania in terms of urbanization. It describes in brief the rates of urbanization and discusses the nature and magnitude of this urban growth. Also described in this chapter are the problems of urban employment and unemployment and outlined are some of the urban planning polices which have been adopted by the post-colonial state since independence in matters pertaining to, for example, housing, rural-urban migration, town planning, and an attempt to control the rapid urban growth. The urban housing problem is among one of the intra-urban policies which have received much attention in Tanzania. For this reason this problem will be discussed separately in chapter three.

Rates of Urban Growth

Tanzania is one of the African countries with a high rate of urban population growth from 9.2% to 12% per year. Table 2.1 below shows this trend of population growth since 1948.

TABLE 2.1
Urban Population and Growth Rates Since 1948

Census	Total Population	Urban	%Urban	Urban Annual Growth Rates
1948	7,480,400	197,300	2.6	-
1957	8,788,500	364,100	4.1	6.8
1967	11,958,6544	685,092	5.7	6.3
1978	17,036,499	2,257,921	13.3	10.8
1988	22,485,625	4,043,684	17.9	-

Source: Bureau of Statistics. Data for Tanzania mainland only.

The table shows that the total population was 7,480,400 in 1948, of which 197,300, or 2.6%, were living in urban areas. The second national population census of 1957 recorded a total population of 8,788,500, of which 364,100, or 4.1%, were urban dwellers. The first post-independence population census of 1967 revealed that the total population was 11,958,654 while the urban one was 685,092, or 5.7%. The census of 1978 recorded a total population of 17,036,499, of which 2,257,921 or 13.3%, were urbanites. The most recent census of 1988 recorded a total population of 22,485,625, of which 4,043,684 lived in urban areas. While the annual growth rate of the total population increased from 3% between 1947 and 1957 to 3.1% between 1957 and 1967, and to 3.3% during the 1967-1978 period, that of the urban population declined from 6.8% over the 1948-1957 period to 6.3% between 1957 and 1967 and rose considerably to over 10.8% between the 1967-1978 period. There is no doubt that it must have increased by now.

This data, together with other data collected from the Bureau of Statistics, show that the urban population growth rate is faster than the rate of growth of the total population. They also show that the share of urban population in total population has more than doubled between 1978 and 1988. There is no data to justify that the trend must have reversed by now. Throughout this period, Dar-Es-Salaam has accounted for almost 34% of the urban population. Since colonialism, Dar-Es-Salaam has firmly established itself as the most urbanized region in the country. It has accommodated over one third of all urban dwellers in the country over the last three decades.[1] (See Table 2.2.)

The other key towns which seem to have attracted urban population concentration recently are Mwanza, Tanga, Mbeya, Morogoro, and Tabora. These towns, together with Dar-Es-Salaam, accommodated 1,187,014 in 1978, which was 52% of the total urban population of 2,257,921.

TABLE 2.2
Total Urban Population of Tanzania and Dar-Es-Salaam City (DSM)

Year	Total Urban Population	Population of DSM	%
1948	197,300	51,000	25.8
1957	364,100	128,742	35.4
1967	685,092	272,821	39.8
1978	2,257,921	769,445	34.1
1986	3,877,000	1,409,382	36.3
1987	4,151,000	1,512,041	36.4
1988	4,443,000	1,623,238	36.5
1989	4,755,000	1,741,943	36.6
1990	5,087,000	1,869,126	36.7
1991	5,636,396	2,052,300	36.4
1992	6,245,126	2,253,425	36
1993	6,919,599	2,474,260	35

Source: Figures for 1948, 1957, 1967, 1978, and 1988 are from the population census. Figures from 1986 to 1993 are estimates.

These estimates have to be treated with caution. This is precisely because data from the Dar-Es-Salaam city council indicate that the actual population of Dar-Es-Salaam had already reached nearly 2 million in 1987. Surprisingly, the 1988 census data only show a population of 1.4 million.

The reasons for urban population concentration in Dar-Es-Salaam City are obvious. First, Dar-Es-Salaam has been the capital city of Tanzania since the colonial period up to 1973 when a decision was made to transfer the capital city further inland to Dodoma. Second, Dar-Es-Salaam is a major port in Tanzania with modern port facilities, and therefore an important outlet/inlet city for import and export trade. Compared to other urban centers as a capital in both colonial and post-colonial states, Dar-Es-Salaam has enjoyed official investments in various socioeconomic and political infrastructure like roads and other communication network systems, security, and political buildings. These factors, together with other advantages of economies of scale, have always tended to attract industries to Dar-Es-Salaam. Thus it is no wonder that 52.89% of the 220 industries employing more than 10 people inherited by the post-colonial state from the colonial state at the time of independence were in Dar-Es-Salaam.[2]

According to the 1978 industrial census published by the Bureau of Statistics, there were 293 establishments in Dar-Es-Salaam (23%) and 1267 establishments throughout Tanzania which employed more than 10 people. The city accommodated 48,292, or 44%, out of the total 109,772 persons who were engaged in these establishments. The city spent 550,215,000 Tshs. (or 61% of the total production cost of 904,054,000 of these establishments) but also contributed 61% to the total value of these establishments.

Factors Responsible for Urban Growth

There are several factors responsible for the rapid population growth in the urban areas. Besides the changes in geographical boundaries of urban areas leading to an incorporation of former rural designated areas or villages into urban milieu, the following factors seem to be predominant.

1. Increased life expectancy due to increased medical facilities and health education;

2. A high birth rate accompanied with a declining rate in infant mortality rates, again due to better distribution and availability of medicare and hygiene education;
3. Better nutrition, availability of clean water, and relatively satisfactory national food distribution plans which have almost wiped out the danger of starvation; and
4. Rural-urban migration

The most effective factor toward rapid urban growth has been that well-known process of rural-urban migration, which in Tanzania has been a result of various "pull" and "push" factors. About 70% of the urban population are rural-urban migrants. Why is this so?

There is a growing consensus of research findings that rural to urban migration is primarily motivated by economic factors even when other reasons such as family ties and pursuit of education and vocational training may initiate the first move.[3]

In his study of rural-urban migration in Arusha and Moshi towns, Mlay (1974) observed that

> One of the most important factors influencing initial urbanward migration is the need for regular cash earnings occurring from wage employment, and that even in subsequent moves many inter-urban migrants are seeking to improve their conditions or to better their job prospects. Furthermore, the propensity to migrate is strongly influenced by the impact of education and by discontent arising from both limited opportunities and unfulfilled expectations with the rural economy.[4]

The presence of relatively higher per capita incomes and standards of living that most of the rural dwellers think to be existing in urban areas also tend to motivate migrants.

Green (1979), while commenting on the rapid growth of urban population in Tanzania, has argued that

> with urban wages and purchasing power continuing to rise faster than those in rural areas, and the urban-rural gap in terms of access to education, health, and water continuing to widen, rising rural-urban migration has been inevitable.[5]

To this must be added the negative impacts of villagization, general rural stagnation, decline and underdevelopment. One has to include also the effects of educational expansion. Concurrent with this expansion in primary schools which increased from 9,947 schools in 1981 with an enrollment of 3,531,000 students to 10,396 schools with an enrollment of 3,373,000 students in 1990 and that of secondary school students which increased from 64,192 in 1978 to 132,409 students in 1989 (according to the Bureau of Statistics), has been the constant rethinking and restructuring of the aims and goals of primary education. But in spite of the changes in the curricula and the restatement of the educational aims, the legacy of an educational system removed from the basic needs of a rural and underdeveloped society continues to influence, in varying degrees, both the content and the output of all the educational institutions.[6]

Although the Education for Self-Reliance (ESR), which was introduced in 1967 as a follow-up policy of the Arusha Declaration at the level of the ideology, intended and still intends to prepare primary school graduates for life in the rural agricultural sector, psychologically the aspiration for non-agricultural activities and even urban employment is still fostered by the education received and the prevailing conditions in rural areas. First, the incentives for primary education to recipients and their parents are the prospects of further education and certainty of regular wage employment outside farming. Primary education is seen as a stepping stone toward secondary education, which is, in turn, a bridge toward waged employment *in the urban areas*. One can clearly notice this by the rapid increase in self-help constructed Parent Secondary Schools (*Sekondari za Wakulima*) in every district. Together with normal government and private secondary schools, these schools increased from 155 to more than 200 in 1989.

While there has been a reasonable expansion of secondary education, only three technical colleges are available in the whole country to teach secondary school graduates various technical skills which might be suitable for urban and rural life. These are in Dar-Es-Salaam, Arusha, and Mbeya. Although some of the secondary schools are teaching technical subjects, still about 75 % of all secondary schools in Tanzania teach general subjects.[7] Their curricula have remained theoretical for several years and therefore academic, according to the Ministry of Education. Attempts to make these schools more practical and geared toward the needs of rural life have been futile. Hence, the kind of education students get is totally divorced from the realities of their rural environments where the majority of them live. At the same time, graduates are viewed as having failed if they have to turn to the farm for a livelihood after seven years of primary education. Despite the state's discouraging the use of the negative term "failure" for those who do not get admission to public secondary school, and replacing it with the seemingly polite Swahili term, *Kutochaguliwa*, which means "not being selected", the idea that education automatically results in a "successful" life, i.e., waged employment and life in an urban area, is usually an illusion. Even so, it is the secondary school graduates who turn to the urban areas more than the primary school graduates. These come to town not because they have the educational certificates but because they stand a better chance of being employed in the urban economy. In general, it is for the planners that rural-urban migration is a problem. But to the migrants it is an escape from a miserable life in rural poverty.

It is now evident that, even if the skills acquired in schools in Tanzania were relevant for rural living, the prospects of putting many of them to good use are remote as long as traditional methods of production and marketing persist.[8] Thus Sabot, in his 1971 study of urban migration in Tanzania, observed that the educated rural inhabitants tended to migrate more to urban areas than the less educated or uneducated.[9] The proportion of the male urban population 20 to 24 years old with five years or more of education throughout Tanzania in 1967 was 57%. The proportion of the rural males in the same age group with five years or more of education was 20% according to the 1967 census. The large difference between the two population groups is due partly to the fact that more and more of the educated people from the rural areas find their livelihood in the towns.

Education achievement is an important qualification in the urban labor market. Mlay (1977) has acknowledged that education was one of the largest determining factors in the differential drift to the towns.[10]

Rural-urban migration has caused severe problems in the urban areas in Tanzania. Overpopulation of urban areas has created several problems in government planning and has almost brought to a halt adequate provision of employment, civic facilities, social services, and housing.

Employment and Unemployment in Urban Areas

Available employment and unemployment statistics are sketchy. Such data is always derived from one of two sources. First is the annual survey of employment and earnings conducted by the Bureau of Statistics, and second is the annual manpower report to the president prepared by the Ministry of Manpower Development. These sources are unreliable for several reasons. First, they suffer from a high nonresponsive rate because they usually depend on mailed questionnaires. Second, they do not include wage earners employed in small holder agricultural enterprises in the informal sector and employees in private households. Apart from this lack of comprehensive accurate recording of employment, there is also the problem of seasonal fluctuation in large employment rates. This occurs both at regional and urban levels depending on the existence of activities which employ large numbers of people seasonally such an construction, coffee picking, and sugarcane cutting. Such fluctuational statistics are not always recorded in these two sources.

The other problem is that, due to financial problems caused by the economic crisis, these surveys are not conducted every year as they used to be because of their high costs. There are also delays in printing and distribution.

The most recent employment and earnings data available is provided in the 1991 Statistical Abstract produced by the Bureau of Statistics. This data show that the unemployment rate in rural areas is 2.2% while in urban areas it is 10.6%. The underemployment rates in rural and urban areas are 3.8% and 5.5% respectively. The unemployment rate for males age 10 and older is 2.1% in rural areas and 6.7% in urban, while for women of the same age it is 2.3% in rural and 15.5% in urban. This suggests a greater number of unemployed women in urban areas than men. The rates for underemployment are 3.6% for males in urban and 8% for women. Both levels of wage employment and unemployment differ between rural and urban centers and between different towns. This is precisely because of the tendency to concentrate development in certain towns which increasingly absorbs an increasingly large percentage of national expenditure and investments, especially in industrial development, social services, and related infrastructure.

In general, rapid rates of urban population growth and the uneven distribution of such growth, accompanied by a low growth rate (or for that matter, stagnation) of wage employment simply support the argument that the pressures they have created are enormous. With the current policies of structural adjustment (which insist on retrenchment and hiring freezes even for university graduates because of the severe financial crisis confronting the government) one would think that unemployment rates must have increased terribly. While these events have been happening, it does not mean that the state has been on vacation, leaving this pervasive development to operate unabated. Various policies have been announced or adopted since independence in order to arrest the polarization of urban development. The section below reviews some of these policies.

The Post-Colonial State Policies on Urban Development

Until late 1960, Tanzania, like many other post-colonial African countries, did little to define its urban development policy. The development of towns and cities was to continue more or less along the path already laid down by the colonial state. No attempts were made at the beginning in order to question the ideological background and content of the urban policies of the colonial state.

Thus, Dar-Es-Salaam City was to continue growing and developing along the lines suggested and recommended by Sir Alexander Gibb in the 1948 master plan for Dar-Es-Salaam. This is what happened until 1968 when the post-colonial state hired a Canadian consulting firm called The Project Planning Associates of Toronto Canada (PPAL) to prepare a new master plan for Dar-Es-Salaam.

Immediately after independence, the post-colonial state abolished all colonial laws and regulations which restricted the flow of Africans into urban areas. Hence, the African population in urban areas grew very fast. In Dar-Es-Salaam there had been an average rate of increase of 9% per year from 1948 to 1957, but this shot up to 14% between the 1948 and 1967 censuses. High rates of growth for the Africans and predominantly low income population were also notable in other smaller towns.[11]

The first major post-colonial state's approach to urban development throughout the 1960s was the control and allocation of land by the state. All land was declared national property, and under a series of acts and regulations beginning in 1963, all freehold land was converted to government leasehold, and the previous owners were then obliged to pay land rent.[12] Conditions for development were laid down for the use of all urban land, with the details agreed upon by the Town Planning Division and the Lands Division.[13] The zoning policy of the colonial government which divided residential urban land into low, medium, and high density areas continued to operate. Residential segregation by race was also abolished. At the beginning, emphasis on plot allocation and provision of services was shifted from the former European areas to the high density and low-income African areas.[14] There were also some efforts to construct low-cost housing. However, as I shall demonstrate later on, this approach never met its objectives.

In general, the period between independence and that of the Arusha Declaration in 1967, did not only witness the perpetuation of most of the colonial urban policies, but also the unequal regional distribution of resources which led to unequal regional development, housing problems and the problems of unemployment. The policies adopted to confront these urban problems were ad-hoc and patchy.

Immediately after the announcement of the Arusha Declaration as a blueprint for Socialist Construction on February 5, 1967, a new emphasis began to appear in Tanzanian urban policies. Because the post-colonial state had vowed via the Arusha Declaration to abolish inequality and exploitation and was aiming at building a country based on principles of socialism (*Ujamaa*) it became necessary for the state to device strategies to arrive at such objectives. At the level of urban development the state was confronted with the problem of rapid urban growth and its concomitant effects one the one hand and the unequal regional development on the other. Along with this also came the problem of rural-urban inequality and the fear that urban areas were exploiting the rural areas.

In order to avoid and solve these problems, the post-colonial state identified one major policy on urban development. This was introduced in 1969 and its main objective was to decentralize urban growth through the dispersion of industrial investments in designated "Growth Pole Centers". The other minor approach adopted and, in fact, related to the above one was the enaction of bylaws and regulations aimed at restricting rural-urban exodus or at repatriating all loiterers in urban areas to their rural home areas.

Decentralization of Urban Growth: The Growth Pole Strategy

The Post-Arusha Declaration period saw Tanzania political philosophy extending no further than a mild and pragmatic "anti-urbanism" or, more precisely, pro-ruralism as can be revealed in various statements of former President Nyerere and also in the 1967 Arusha Declaration. In his booklet, *Socialism and Rural Development,* Nyerere argued,

> We must not forget that people who live in towns can possibly become the exploiters of those who live in the rural areas. All our big hospitals are in towns and they benefit only a small section of the people of Tanzania. Yet if we have built them with money from outside Tanzania,

it is the overseas sale of the peasants' produce which provides the foreign exchange for repayment. Those who do not get the benefit of the hospitals thus carry the major responsibility for paying for them. Tarmac roads, too, are mostly found in towns and are of special value to motor car owners. If we have built those roads with loans, it is again the farmer who produces the goods which will pay for them. What is more, the foreign exchange with which the car was bought also came from the sale of the farmers' produce. Again, electric lights, water-pipes, hotels, and other aspects of modern development are mostly found in towns. Most of them have been built with loans and most of them do not benefit the farmer, but will be paid for by foreign currency and by the sale of his produce. We should always bear this in mind. (Nyerere, *Freedom and Socialism*, 1968, pp. 242-243)

Prefacing the second Five Year Plan, which sought to emphasize rural development, Nyerere stated,

There are now in this city Dar-Es-Salaam many who come to look for work but cannot find any, and many others without houses. It would be better to spread to other parts of the country the attractions now concentrated in the capital. (Second 5 Years Development Plan: 1969-1974, page XVIII)

Elsewhere, Nyerere stressed that the basis of Tanzania's success must be self-reliance and that farmers and peasants were not helped by increasing parasitism in the towns.[15] In carrying out this line, minimal resource allocations of public investment for urban infrastructure were made during the 1970s, further reinforced by the rural bias of major and substantial foreign investments.[16] However limited the success of its rural development push, urban control policies and campaigns can be interpreted as a corresponding and anti-urban line which was already growing in the TANU Party (Tanganyika African National Union) and later, Chama Cha Mapinduzi (CCM), which was well known for its early attempts to resist rapid concentrated industrialization and uncontrolled urbanization.[17]

The major policy which aimed at decentralizing industrialization in order to disperse the spillovers of this industrialization into other urban centers was announced in 1969 through the second Five Year Plan (1969-1974). This plan, among other things, identified nine other towns other than Dar-Es-Salaam throughout the country which were to become "New Growth Pole Centers". Any further industrial development was to be located in these towns. They were Morogoro, Dodoma, Mbeya,

Mwanza, Mtwara, Tabora, Tanga, Moshi, and Arusha. According to this policy, moves were to be taken to decentralize certain government functions, and to locate new industries "where possible" away from Dar-Es-Salaam. This was the backbone of the longterm policy toward urban development. It was argued that such a policy was necessary if

1. Urban development was to act as a stimulus and a complement to rural development;
2. Unacceptable urban social conditions were to be avoided;
3. Cities were not to become an increasing drain on the country's financial and physical resources[18]

Thus, the policy recognized several issues. First, it regarded urban areas as agents of social change, and in this case they had a role to play in enhancing rural development. However, the policy did not spell out clearly how this was going to be done. Nor did it explain how complementary to the rural areas the towns were supposed to be and vice versa. Second, the policy realized that there were some social conditions in urban areas which it considered as "unacceptable" and "undesirable". These were to be avoided in future development. But the policy neither identified concretely the undesirable social conditions, nor went further in diagnosing the factors leading to such undesirable social conditions. The policy also did not define, for example, "unacceptable" and "undesirable". Thus, this vagueness left a loophole through which the state could take advantage and declare at any time that some social conditions in urban areas were unacceptable. This loophole has always been used to criminalize the unemployed urban poor and informal sector operators. Third, by avoiding cities that drain the country's financial and physical resources, the policy was considered progressive for recognizing the parasitic nature of the Tanzanian urban areas. But by posing the question of exploitation geographically and not as a social relation, the approach had an adverse effect on implementation, and in a way contributed toward its failure. The basic stated objectives of this policy were

1. To restrain the overall rate of urban population growth;
2. To distribute that growth among various urban centers in order to avoid the primacy of Dar-Es-Salaam, and to disperse total urban population to other urban centers in order to maximize development impact in rural areas;

3. To maintain a general level of well-being in towns in harmony with the requirements of an equitable urban-rural balance and satisfactory work performance by the urban community.[19]

The only articulate policy implemented to achieve this was the Industrial Location policy. In it, all new industrial investments and establishments were to be concentrated in the nine identified growth-pole-centers. The industrial dispersion policy rose from the assumption that the creation of industry would lead to subinvestments and therefore provide markets for rural produce and finished products for the rural population.[20]

The implementation of this policy can best be evaluated by what actually happened to Morogoro and Arusha. Both towns have potential for industrial development. Their hinterlands are well endowed with resources. There are a lot of food crops grown and there is plenty of water. The supply of electricity from Nyumba ya Mungu Dam (for Arusha) and Kidatu Dam (for Morogoro) is abundant. Transportation from these towns to the ports is accessible by both roads and railway. During colonialism, only the Meerschaum soft drink factory, the Tanganyika extracting company, and some coffee curing plants existed in Arusha. Later, as a capital of the East African Community (EAC), Arusha benefitted from the location of Phillips Radio Factory in 1968 and the General Tyre Factory in 1969. In Morogoro there was the Tobacco Curing and Processing Company established in 1968 and several sisal decorticating plants. In 1967, the urban population of Arusha and Morogoro was 30,961 and 38,224 people respectively.[21]

The plan stated clearly that 9% of all new industrial establishments had to be located in Arusha. It is not clear what percentage had to be in Morogoro. By 1975, Arusha had 35 new industrial establishments, and Morogoro had 23. Two main industrial estates were established in Arusha, namely, Unga Limited and Themi Industrial Estates. These estates accommodated new industries like Kilimanjaro Textile, Sunflag, Tanzania Breweries, Alfi, and others. In Morogoro, a new major industrial estate known as Mazimbu developed between 1970 and 1980. This industrial estate accommodated the following famous new industries: The Multi-Purpose Oilseed Producing Company (Moproco), Tanzania Seed Company, Tanzania Tanneries Factory, and the Morogoro Shoe Company. It also was the site of Morogoro Leather Factory, Canvas Mill, Ceramic, Cotton, and Polyester Industry in the far north of this estate very near the Morogoro Dodoma highway. Available data indicate that in Arusha, industrial development grew at the rate of 214% between 1965 and 1970, and at the rate of 71% between 1971and 1975.[22] In Morogoro the rate was 25% between 1965 and 1970 and 53% between 1970 and 1975, and 152% between 1975 and 1980.[23] By 1983, Arusha had 52 industrial establishments while Morogoro had 58. (Gambishi 1983:37). Close proximity to the sea outlet, availability of both good roads and railroad facilities from both the Central Line and the Tanzania-Zambia Railway Authority (TAZARA) and the Tanzania Zambia Highway (TANZAM) give Morogoro an advantage over Arusha. Statistics show that the urban population of Morogoro had gone up by 59% (from 38,224 in 1967 to 60,782 in 1978) and that of Arusha went up by 78% (from 30,961 in 1967 to 55,223 in 1978).[24]

If you compare population increase and employment statistics, the general trend is that employment has been increasing with time. Recorded waged employment for all sectors increased from 44,171 in 1979 to 48,673 in 1982, an increase of 10% in Morogoro, and 41,929 to 46,045 or 11% in Arusha.[25] If you compare the rate of change in employment in industries and other sectors, it is evident that the rate of growth in industrial employment has been fast. For Arusha, the rate has been 1.5%, and for Morogoro industrial employment increased by twice as much.

As far as these towns, as well as Mwanza and Mbeya, are concerned, the new industrial locational policy has been successful. What is more crucial, however, is whether this strategy has succeeded in dispersing industries away from Dar-Es-Salaam in order to limit its primacy. The trickle-down effects these industries have had on the development of the rural hinterlands are not clear.

The employment opportunities that have opened up in these towns clearly present a positive effect of the policy. However, two negative issues are also evident. First is the uneven regional development which exists between some of the privileged "Growth Pole Centers" and other towns like Songea, Lindi, Singida, Kigoma, and Sumbawanga. Second is the number of rural-urban migrants these industries have attracted in these towns. The towns are now failing to accommodate the urban influx, and the result is the proliferation of abject poverty and squalor. Large numbers of squatter settlements have emerged in these towns, including Msamvu and Kichangani in Morogoro, Unga Limited in Arusha, Nyakato and Mbuyuni in Mwanza, and Mwanjelwa in Mbeya. These settlements are indeed a product of this policy. At the same time, the primacy of Dar-Es-Salaam has not been reduced either. Industries and other investments have continued to relocate to Dar-Es-Salaam. Of the 265 new industrial establishments between 1969 and 1979, 129, or 46.8%, were located in Dar-Es-Salaam. As a result, the process of overurbanization of Dar-Es-Salaam has continued unabated. Figures collected from the Statistical Abstract of 1991 show that 36.3% of persons engaged in manufacturing in 1988 were in Dar-Es-Salaam, and by 1990 the city was accommodating 39.7% of electricity consumers throughout the country. This shows that in total this policy has been a failure.

Besides the Growth Pole Strategy as a complement policy to urban development, perhaps, as Stren (1979) has argued, the most dramatic policy decision in the 1970s was the announcement of the relocation of the capital city from Dar-Es-Salaam (DSM) to Dodoma.[26] The section below deals with this policy decision.

The Relocation of the Capital City from Dar-Es-Salaam to Dodoma

The decision to relocate the capital was made in October of 1973. Although the project was known to be costly for a poor country like Tanzania, President Nyerere, while announcing this decision, stressed that the cost factor was a short term burden but the new capital of a country was a permanent thing. He said,

> If we decide that the capital shall remain in Dar-Es-Salaam or moved to Dodoma, we shall be making a permanent decision. Therefore, the reasons on which we are to base a decision ought to be permanent reasons. We shall not use short term reasons to make permanent decisions. (*Daily News Paper*, February 10, 1973)

Two major arguments were advanced in favor of the relocation program. One was geographical and the other was political or ideological. Geographically, it was argued that Dodoma was situated at the center of Tanzania. Therefore, by moving the capital from Dar-Es-Salaam (the periphery) to Dodoma (the center and heart of Tanzania), Tanzania was correcting a geographical imbalance. Politically or ideologically, it was asserted that, apart from other security reasons, Dodoma would symbolize the socialist ideals of Ujamaa City. And because the state was concentrating on rural development, it was more plausible to situate its headquarters in a rural environment. Hence, Dodoma would be a rural socialist city close to the people whom it was determined to serve.

Thus, it was clear from the beginning that it would be profitable to have Dodoma as the new capital of an aspiring socialist nation. The city was also meant to be the model of socialism. In the context of what Tanzania had already embarked on, the decision to relocate its capital was a progressive one. In terms of urban development policies, the decision has to be seen in the context of the 1969 Growth Pole Strategy.

In October of 1973, immediately after the relocation decision, President Nyerere established two organizations to actually carry it out. An independent Ministry for Capital Development (MCD) and a parastatal organization called Capital Development Authority (CDA) were established. The role of MCD was "to provide political and national capital perspective, and interrelating the capital development program with the overall national plans and policies."[27]

In other words, the MCD was to act as a go-between, or middleman, between the party on one hand and the government on the other in matters concerning the development of the capital city. The CDA had several roles:

1. To implement the decisions of transferring the capital city from Dar-Es-Salaam to Dodoma;
2. To prepare plans for the development of Dodoma as a capital city;
3. To advise and assist in the orderly transfer of the government headquarters to Dodoma;
4. To acquire and hold land and immovable property subject to the direction of the president; and
5. To provide necessary facilities to carry out the transfer of the capital city.[28]

Three foreign firms were invited to submit their master plan proposals for the new capital. These were the Project Planning Associates International Limited of Toronto Canada (PPAL), Doxadis Associates of Greece, and Engineering Consultancy Firms Associates of Japan. A firm called Planning Development Consultants of West Germany submitted their master plan proposals without invitation.[29] The proposals were examined by a jury of other foreign consultants appointed by the government. These were R. Lacrois of Arthur D. Little, Professor R. Mitchell, and T. Saaty of the United Nations Environmental Program (U.N.E.P.) based in Nairobi. UNEP and the government of Tanzania endorsed the PPAL proposals.[30]

As Doherty (1975) foretold, PPAL was undoubtedly going to produce a technically competent and attractively written plan, just as it had produced the 1968 master plan for Dar-Es-Salaam. The result was the New Capital Master Plan for Dodoma (NCMP). The new capital was planned for a population of between 350,000 and 400,000, which it is expected to reach in 1995 when all the government offices will be in Dodoma. In brief, the NCMP planned enough space for service sectors, housing, government offices, community services, and for service industries. Behind the plan is the hidden concept of the development of a "man-centered city". There is an articulation of a number of different land uses and spatial patterns in the city. It is clear from the plan that people will be arranged in residential communities. Each urban area will have differential type of housing in terms of low, medium, and high density. Each residential community will have its school, medical care facilities, parks, playgrounds, shops, and small farms. Also provided in the plan are open areas for every family's water and plumbing. Pedestrians and cyclists will have their own road system, as will cars and public transportation. The logic behind such a planning system is that it will reduce traffic jams and congestion, and therefore increase efficiency.

The NCMP shows that there will be special urban centers which will be focal points for surrounding residential communities so that people can have access to services like shops, markets, banks, community social facilities, bus stops, and post-primary education facilities. These so-called "Center A" areas will be downtown, serving the whole city. Hotels, movie theaters, transportation terminals, parastatal organizations, and other business offices will be located in this area. Polluting industries will be located in the western, downwind part of the city. It is argued in the NCMP that Dodoma is supposed to be a man-centered city where an ordinary Tanzanian will feel at home and at ease, whether he is working or relaxing. The plan promises that the "ivory towers" so characteristic of other city centers and therefore inconvenient to office workers will be absent in Dodoma. Squatters will not be welcome in Dodoma.

In summary, that is the general content of the NCMP prepared by PPAL. A critique of the weakness of such a plan will be discussed in the section where I examine the nature of town planning in Tanzania. What I want to examine now is whether the capital transfer program has been successful. As I have argued, the Dodoma project was, among other things, proposed as a counterweight to the development of Dar-Es-Salaam. As such, the project was designed to bring about the development of backward areas of the country through massive investments in the form of a new city.

It has now been 20 years since that decision was made. 40% of the government work was supposed to be stationed in Dodoma by 1981, and the whole transfer program was only supposed to take ten years.[31] Unfortunately, this has not been the case. By July of 1993 (nearly 20 years since the decision was made and 10 years after the anticipated relocation deadline of 1983) only two government ministries had their headquarters in Dodoma. These are the Prime Minister's office and the Ministry of Minerals. The development pace of the transfer program has been very slow. Why is this so?

Indeed, it sounds very reasonable and logical to blame the slow pace of the capital transfer program on the present economic crisis. Even so, it was quite clear that Tanzania alone could not have afforded the cost of the project. Several factors even suggest that perhaps the government is not serious about the transfer program. First, although the presidential state house complex in Chamwino Village (30 km from Dodoma) was officially opened on July 27, 1981, the office of the president is still in Dar-Es-Salaam. All important official meetings, state banquets, and other national ceremonies still take place in Dar-Es-Salaam. Although some sessions of the *Bunge,* or National Assembly, have been taking place in Dodoma since 1973, most of the political and government administration are still being conducted in Dar-Es-Salaam. Moreover, the government itself continues to build important official buildings in Dar-Es-Salaam rather than in Dodoma. For example, while the headquarters of the Ministry of Minerals is housed in a dilapidated building in Dodoma, the Ministry of Minerals, Energy and Water recently built a 5-story building in Dar-Es-Salaam instead of in Dodoma. The Ministry of Health moved its headquarters from Ocean Road Street to Samora Avenue in Dar-Es-Salaam, only half a kilometer from its old location. The headquarters of the Tanzania Bureau of Standards (TBS), built in the early 1980s, is located in the Ubungo area and not in Dodoma. While it is stated in the NCMP that Dodoma will have a University specializing in Geology and Engineering, several extension projects in the Faculty of Engineering and Science are already underway at the old university in Dar-Es-Salaam, while surveying and designing of Dodoma University have yet to begin. In fact, a new and very modern Geology building was opened in 1986 at the University of Dar-Es-Salaam. These examples portray the attitude of the state toward the capital transfer program. Thus it is clear that, while the economic crisis may have contributed toward the slow pace of the development of Dodoma, the fact that the state itself is not serious about the project overrides the economic factor. By behaving in that way, the state is purposefully holding back the development of Dodoma on the one hand, and enhancing the growth of Dar-Es-Salaam on the other.

Ideology and Urban Planning

Attempts to provide town or city plans in Tanzania are not old. Since the introduction of the first Master Plan for Dar-Es-Salaam in 1948 by Alexander Gibb, several attempts have been made to provide town plans with clearly differentiated land use patterns and, subsequently, substantial resources spent on them.

Most of the ideals of modern town planning in post-independent Tanzania came to the fore in 1968 through the Dar-Es-Salaam Master Capital Plan, prepared by the Project Planning Associates of Canada (PPAL). The 1976 New Capital Master Plan (NCMP) for Dodoma was prepared by the same planning consultant, and subsequent towns plans were prepared by foreign planning consultant firms or by local Town Planning Division personnel at the former Ministry of Lands Housing, and Urban Development.

Through these master plans, comprehensive spatial designs for cities and towns have been prepared. Land has been zoned to accommodate specific areas for housing, commerce, recreation, industry, and a variety of other purposes identified through detailed physical, demographic and socioeconomic surveys, thus grouping some activities together while segregating others. Transportation networks have been designed to link these different zones, and public utilities such as water supply, electricity, and sanitation have sometimes been provided. Through these master plans, land use has been controlled through legislation and the creation of administrative procedures for issuing building permits. In this way, "orderly" and "planned" development, it is argued, has been encouraged. Through these procedures and techniques, town planners for Tanzania claim that they analyze urban needs and problems scientifically and seek to deal with them through the rational allocation of resources, a process which has been seen as purely technical, and thus neutral from ideology.

By analyzing the master plans of Dar-Es-Salaam and Dodoma, it can be argued that town planning in Tanzania has been completely divorced from the ideological aspiration of the state. Thus the plans have ended up perpetuating the colonial legacy of town planning. By doing so, the plans have acted as ideological instruments of neo-colonialism, and have ended up benefitting the minority on one hand and undermining the majority on the other.

The first post-independent Master Plan (MP) for Dar-Es-Salaam was published in 1968, twenty years after the former plan produced by Sir Alexander Gibb in 1948, eight years after independence, and one year after Tanzania had decided to build up socialism.[32] The delay of eight years demonstrates the low priority and cursory treatment urban development received and continues to receive in national development plans.[33]

The MP for Dodoma was published in 1976. It very closely resembled the MP for Dar-Ed-Salaam in several ways. First, they were both prepared by the same company and this was after Tanzania had decided to build socialism. Therefore, it is surprising to note that urban planning consultants from socialist countries were not invited to prepare the plans. Both plans have proved to be expensive and Tanzania has been unable to implement them successfully.

In both MPs one can notice the colonial legacy. Both recommend western models of city planning. However, it is in their planning of residential areas and provision of housing that the ideologies of these planning consultants are most clearly revealed.[34] They both identify three types of residential areas in the city. The DSM MP defined terms like *high standard, medium standard*, and *low standard* in the following ways:

1. **High Standard Areas**
   Should contain high-priced private and National Housing Corporation houses, paved roads, and street lighting. Each house should have adequate water and power supply and should be linked to a central sewage system.
2. **Medium Standard Areas**
   Should have residential areas with medium priced NHC and private houses, paved roads, and power and water connections. Houses should be connected to a septic tank.
3. **Low Standard Areas**
   Residential area with self-built houses. Houses should be occupied by many families and local roads should be unpaved. Houses should have pit latrines or septic tanks and power should be provided in the collector streets only.

The product of this plan has been the development of the affluent residential areas of Msasani, Masaki, Mikocheni, and Mbezi Beach as high standard areas, Sinza and Tabata as medium, and Buguruni, Kiwalani, Vingunguti, and Ubungo Kisiwani as low standard areas.

The Dodoma MP, not wanting to adopt these offensive standard terms, opted for technical terms that seemed more polite. This MP called them Low, Medium and High Density Areas. But these were to set up to develop with the same standards identified in the MP for Dar-Es-Salaam. Analytically and in practice, these technical terms stand for Rich High-Income Class, Medium-Income Class, and Poor Low-Income Class.

Seen in this context, it can be argued that both plans recognize, identify and plan for the perpetuation of existing class division in the society. While identifying this pervasive situation, the plans actually maintain the status quo. The MPs go beyond the plans of Alexander Gibb, recommending the controlling of squatters. They recommend their removal and the use of police in this process.

Although it is stated in the MP for Dodoma that the city is supposed to be a stimuli for socialist rural development, it is, however, not clear on how this is to be carried out. From the layout of the plan it is clear that Dodoma will be a purely administrative city and therefore more "parasitic" to the rural hinterland than "generative".

The two MPs have left a neo-colonial legacy in town planning in Tanzania. All other town plans prepared by Tanzanian town planners continue to follow this pattern of urban planning. They use more or less the same concepts, techniques, and ideologies. As a result, they have provided less of an advantage to the urban poor. If development is to focus on man as Nyerere has always argued, then urban plans, like any other development planning operation, ought to focus, among other things, on the interests and needs of the marginalized urban majority. Closely related to the problem of urban planning is the provision of urban housing. Chapter three deals with this issue in depth.

3
The Problems and Politics of Urban Housing

Introduction

One serious problem now confronting Tanzania in urban areas is the provision of housing. When Tanzania obtained independence in 1961, the post-colonial state abolished the colonial system of providing housing on the basis of race. Tanzania promised to provide good and decent housing to all citizens, and placed housing among the three basic human needs, which are *food, clothing,* and *housing*.[1] However, Tanzania has not been in a position to solve the problem of urban housing in general, and the housing problem of the majority low income earners in particular.

Although rapid urban population growth is said to be the major cause of the present housing problems, several other factors have also contributed towards this problem, including[2]

1. Inappropriate policies and strategies;
2. Poor and weak policy management, especially at the district and local levels;
3. General poverty among the majority urban dwellers;
4. The inability of the government to provide low-cost conventional housing;
5. Strict enforcement of inappropriate, colonial, and outdated planning and building codes and standards. Most of these have been adopted wholesale from advanced capitalist countries where they were adopted under a particular defined cultural orientation and economic base; and

6. The economic crisis which has resulted in the poor performance of the institutional approach to the provision of housing.

This chapter examines the policies and strategies which have been adopted and implemented by post-colonial Tanzania since independence in order to solve the housing question. The chapter begins by assessing the magnitude of the problem.

The Magnitude of the Problem

In Tanzania the problems facing urban housing can basically be described at two levels. At one level is a shortage of housing units in urban areas (quantity). At another level is the fact that most of the dwelling units already existing in the urban areas are not in good conditions (quality). At the same time it has to be clear that when we talk of the problem of urban housing in Tanzania, our main interest in this context is in the low-income family.

The Shortage of Housing

I have shown in Chapter 2 that growth of the urban population has been very rapid. Such population growth has always surpassed the ability of the government to provide adequate housing units for that population. Hence, at present, a wide gap exists between the demand for housing and the supply of housing (availability) in the urban areas.

It has been estimated that at the end of the first Five Year Plan (1964-1969) there was a shortage of 37,000 housing units in urban areas.[3] According to this plan, 25% of these units were supposed to be built by private individuals. The National Housing Cooperation (NHC) which was established in 1962 was supposed to build 27,800 housing units.[4] By the end of the plan in 1969, the NHC had built only 6,327 units, out of which 4,678 were in Dar-Es-Salaam. But because 70% of the housing units built in Dar-Es-Salaam had been under the slum clearance program, the net addition to housing stock was minimal and the gap was almost 21,000 housing units.

In the second Five Year Plan (1969-1974) it had been realized that 8,000 housing units per year were needed in urban areas. However, only

50% of the targeted goals were reached by the end of the plan in 1974.[5] Due to the rapid growth of urban population during this period, the gap between demand and supply of housing shot up to 25,000 units at the beginning of the second Five Year Plan. Recent data indicate that the shortage of housing had already reached 300,000 units in 1982.[6]

The Growth of Squatter Settlements

Reliable data documenting the extent of urban squatter development is not available. A comprehensive count carried out in 1969 showed that there had been 14,720 squatter houses, and the number increased to 27,981 in 1972.[7] In 1975 a study of squatter housing in 13 major towns indicated that 72,500 squatter houses existed by then within a population of 1,650,000.[8] This study revealed that 44% of the total population of Dar-Es-Salaam were squatters.[9] Recent estimates show that 70% of the total urban population live in settlements of this type. 70% of the total population of Dar-Es-Salaam are squatters.[10] Information collected from the Directorate of Housing in the Ministry of Cooperatives and Local Government show that squatters developers are constructing a minimum total of 10,000 dwelling units per year in urban areas.[11]

In Dodoma, squatter settlements have grown very fast in peripheral areas of the city since the 1973 decision to make it the new capital. On November 25, 1984, the government-owned paper *Sunday News* revealed that areas of Chang'ombe, Maili Mbili, and Chaduru hosted a lion's share of illegal settlements.

Recent information reveal that at least 40% to 50% of the total urban population of Dodoma are squatters.[12] At the same time, Mlimwa West, Area "C", and some parts of Kilimani have been developed officially as residential areas for the affluent groups.

In Tanzania the growth of squatter settlements has created severe planning problems since services must somehow be organized on the basis of irregular settlement patterns. Most of the squatter areas are poorly serviced and are, in most cases, occupied by the urban poor. A survey carried out in the early 1970s showed that, in comparison to non-squatters, squatters in Dar-Es-Salaam were generally poorer, had significantly less formal education, and were more heavily engaged in the non-wage sector of the urban economy.[13] However, it is wrong to assume that in Tanzania slums or squatter settlements are populated only by people who have low incomes. Squatters are not a homogeneous group. Some are better off than others, but it is the poorest who are the most disadvantaged. They are forced to live on the outskirts of the cities and towns, well away from the employment opportunities and urban services. Frequently, environmental health conditions in these areas are appalling.

The Housing Conditions (Quality of Housing)

Whether a particular type of housing is good or bad is a decision which is subjective and value-laden. In the context of this study, it does not matter whether people live in cement-block, corrugated iron roofed rectangular houses, or in cone-shaped mud and grass thatched houses. What matters is whether their dwelling units are compatible with cultural and environmental phenomena and needs. But at the same time, it is far more important to me that there are certain universals in regards to needs, universals that we should probably assume and which are, of course, later subject to empirical tests. Among these universals I count the following things:

1. It is better to be healthy than sick;
2. It is better to be housed in a dwelling that offers protection from weather than in a temporary shelter that needs to be repaired regularly and offers no real protection;
3. It is better to have more space than less space; and
4. It is better to have facilities that promote hygiene than to lack such facilities.

In my opinion these kinds of consideration apply anywhere, to anyone, regardless of cultural orientation or tradition. This is my bias.

The data from 1967 census show that the residential areas for the affluent social class, i.e. Oyster Bay and Regent Estate, maintained their low-density status as suggested by Gibb with 6.3 persons per acre. The ethnic composition of these two areas was 75% Europeans for Oyster Bay and 63% for Regent Estate. African people hardly resided in these areas during this period. (Schmetzer 1982). 82% of these people living in the medium density areas were Africans with an exception of Eastern Kinondoni area where 29% of the residents were European.The high density residential areas had an African population of more than 95%.

The data provided by 1978 population census shows that the situation worsened instead of improving especially to the majority of African people living in high density and overcrowded areas.

While the average density per acre increased from 6.3% people to 8.1% in low density areas, and from 41.8% to 42.4% in medium density areas, the average density in high density and overcrowded areas increased from 85.9% to 106.0% and from 137.8% to 158.3% respectively.

This information provides the quantitative side of the problem and does not tell us anything in depth about the conditions of the housing units or residential areas occupied by different social groups.

In order know what kind of housing is used by different social groups, it is important to examine the conditions of these residential areas and their housing units, and the way they are integrated into the urban service system.

In their analysis of 1967 census report, Egero and Henin (1973) revealed that only 34.8% out of a total 83,431 households available in Dar-Es-Salaam were considered to be in permanent structures. 57.4% were in semi-permanent structures, and 5.7% were in other structures, and 2.1% were undefined.[14]

The surveys which provide the basic information about the housing conditions in Tanzania are the Household Budget Surveys(HBS). Only three of such surveys have been carried out in Tanzania since independence. The first one was in 1969, the second in 1977 and the most recent one was carried out in 1991/92.I have borrowed some data from these HBS in order to examine the conditions of housing in Tanzania.

Table 3.1 gives a clear picture of the housing conditions in both rural and urban Tanzania. Improvements have taken place in the use of corrugated metal sheets for roofing, in foundations and in concrete-cement or stone floorings, the use of poles, branches and grass declined while that of poles and mud and of mud blocks had increased. A very significant improvement took place in the use of toilet systems. The percentage of pit latrines increased from 23% to 56% while the number of houses without toilet facilities declined from 50% to 22%.

The data presented in Table 3.1 is general. Therefore, it does not give us a clear picture of housing conditions in urban areas.

The 1991/92 HBS shows that in the rural areas about 84% of the households have poor floors. In Dar-Es-Salaam is about 10%. 34% of the households in Dar-Es-Salaam have no electricity and about 40% of the urban population in the whole of Tanzania live in overcrowded houses.Only 41% of the population of Dar-Es-Salaam have water piped in housing units and 83.1% of the population in the whole country use pit latrines. The situation is appalling in squatter settlements and other high density residential areas.

TABLE 3.1
Percentages of Construction Material and Toilets Used in Houses, 1969 and 1977

Wall Materials	1969	1977
Mud and Poles	43	45
Poles, branches, grass	36	32
Mud blocks or mud	15	16
Burned bricks	2	02
Stone, sand-cement, concrete	03	03
Other	01	02
Roof Materials		
Grass or leaves	70	61
Metal sheets	17	26
Mud	11	11
Other	02	02
Foundation Materials		
No foundation	90	73
Stones in sand mortar	-	16
Stones in mortar	02	-
Stones loosely laid	07	04
Concrete, cement, bricks	01	06
Other	-	1
Toilet Systems		
No toilet construction	50	22
Private pit latrine (or bucket)	23	56
Shared pit latrine (or bucket)	26	17
Other	1	5

Source: I.L.O. (1982), *op.cit.*, page 122.

TABLE 3.2
Distribution of Wage Income by Area and Percentage of Wage Earners in Dar-Es-Salaam and Dodoma in 1971 and 1976

Wage Group per month in Tanzania Shs.	Dar-Es-Salaam 1971	Living in Squatters in DSM	Dodoma 1976	Living in Squatters in Dodoma
000-099	3.8	05.6	00.00	01.1
100-199	17.5	23.1	01.3	02.6
200-299	33.8	38.4	03.1	61.3
300-399	18.5	18.3	56.3	27.7
400-499	06.4	05.4	17.1	04.8
500-599	04.3	2.7	04.6	01.0
600-699	03.5	02.1	02.8	00.4
700-799	02.4	01.4	01.9	00.2
800-899	01.1	00.6	01.5	00.6
900-999	01.0	00.4	03.4	00.2
1000-1499	03.8	00.4	05.1	00.2
1500+	04.1	04.1	01.6	00.05

Source: Skutsch, M.C. *Urban Housing in Tanzania*, Department of Urban and Rural Planning, Ardhi Institute, Dar-Es-Salaam, Page 15.

It is clear that the urban housing conditions still leave much to be desired. Bearing the fact that the majority of the urban population (70%) live in squatter settlements, it remains obvious that most of these settlements are of low quality, and reflect conditions of abject poverty and squalor. As of 1988, at least 90% of the urban population were already living in areas or houses which did not merit the present required official and legal standards.[15] In most cases, the required standards are beyond the ability of the urban poor, and do not reflect the socio-cultural reality of the local situation. The International Labor Office study of 1982 noted that about 90% of urban housing was constructed on a self-basis. The plots were very small and in most cases did not conform with building regulations (ILO 1982). Thus, only about 10% of the houses were built by constructors and most of them were on large surveyed areas. If 50,000 of such houses needed major repairs, as it was estimated in 1982 by the Ministry of Economic Planning, one can imagine the magnitude of the problem in the unsurveyed-self-help urban housing sector (ibid).Table 3.2 (on the previous page) shows who lived where in Dar-Es-Salaam and Dodoma in 1971 and 1976 respectively.

The table shows who earns what and stays where. Thus in 1971, 84.3% of the wage earners in Dar-Es-Salaam got wages not more than 599 Tshs., and 93.5% stayed in the squatter settlements. In Dodoma, 82.4% of the urban wage earners had salaries not exceeding 599 Tshs., and 97.4% of these were staying in squatter settlements. This means that the majority of the urban dwellers in both Dar-Es-Salaam and Dodoma were low income earners, and most of them lived in squatter type settlements. In other words, there was a strong correlation between income and area of residence, and there is no reason to think that the situation has improved now. Table 3.3 shows in brief who lives where and owns what.

TABLE 3.3
Proportion of Tenant- and Owner-Occupied Houses in Dar-Es-Salaam in 1980

Area	Tenants	Owners	Total
Squatter Areas	50.7%	20%	70.7%
Planned Areas	24.8%	4.5%	29.3%
Total	75.5%	24.5%	100%

Source: Ndjovu, C.E.K. *The Housing Market in Dar-Es-Salaam*, Ardhi Institute, DMS 1980, Page 35.

The following conclusions can be derived from the above table. That is, about 70.7% are squatters in Dar-Es-Salaam city. Only 20.3% are owners of the houses where they live and the biggest proportion, 50.7%, live in squatter settlements as tenants. Tenants in planned areas are 24.8% while owner occupiers are only 4.5%. Certainly, the majority of the urban dwellers are not owners of their own dwellings precisely because most of them are either low income earners or are unemployed. Indeed, it is this section of the urban population which has suffered most in terms of the urban housing problems.

Given the present rapid rate of urban population growth which is taking place at the time when Tanzania is experiencing a severe economic crisis, there is no sufficient data to prove that the problem of urban housing may be solved in the near future. It is within this background that the government has been formulating a variety of policies with the aim of both improving the standard of the existing stock of houses and constructing new dwellings in order to catch up with the ever increasing demand.

The Housing Policies of the Post-Colonial State (1961-1988)

At the beginning of this chapter it was argued that the first step taken by the post-colonial state in regards to housing was the abolishment of provision of housing in terms of race. Although the government has taken several steps since independence to encourage the construction of houses, and has been constructing houses for its employees, the main thrust of its housing policy implicitly rests on the premise that housing is the responsibility of the people themselves. The first three years development plan (1962-1964) spelled out the housing policy which was to be adopted by the post-colonial state. In summary, the policy read as follows:

> The policy with regard to housing is to provide low cost housing for renting in areas where private enterprise does not meet the demand, to encourage urban dwellers to own their houses by means of an experimental tenant purchase scheme, to assist houseowners by means of loans, improve their houses by the construction of roof in permanent materials.[16]

In trying to achieve the above objectives, Tanzania applied various methods, policies, and strategies including political campaigns such as *Operesheni Nyumba Bora* (Operation Better Housing). The government also established several housing institutions and cooperatives and implemented site and service scheme projects. Basically, one can summarize the Tanzanian housing policies into the following three broader policies:

1. **The Institutional Approach**
   This entails the establishment of housing institutions like the National Housing Corporation (NHC), Tanzania Housing Bank (THB), and the Registrar of Building (ROB).
2. **The Project/Program Approach**
   This involves adopting projects like the National Site and Service Schemes, Squatter Upgrading Projects, and the Slum Clearance Programs.
3. **Legislation Method**
   This method works by enacting laws and regulations dealing with housing matters such as the Rent Restriction Act of 1984.

While the first two approaches can be considered *developmental*, the third one has been adopted for *regulatory* purposes. For example, housing tribunals have been established from headquarters to regional and district levels, municipal by-law, building codes, and other various official directives have been set and announced in order to regulate housing matters. I will start by examining the first two approaches. The nature of the legislation/regulatory method will become clear as the general discussion on housing and urban poverty continues.

The Institutional Approach

With this approach Tanzania has been able to establish several housing institutions such as The National Housing Corporation (NHC), The Permanent Housing Finance Company of Tanzania (PHFCT), The Building Research Unit (BRU), The Registrar of Buildings (ROB), the Center for Housing Studies at the Ardhi Institute of Dar-Es-Salaam, and the Tanzania Housing Bank (THB).

NHC was established in 1962 by an Act of the Parliament Number 45 in order to perform the following functions.

1. To lend or grant money to a local authority for the purpose of an approved housing scheme to be undertaken by the local authority;
2. Subject to the provision of section 6 and 10, to make loans or guarantee loans made to any person or body of persons, corporate or unincorporated, for the purpose of enabling such a person or body to acquire land and construct thereon

approved houses or other buildings or to carry out approved housing schemes; and
3. To construct houses or other buildings, and to carry out approved housing schemes.[17]

However, since 1973, the Tanzania Housing Bank (THB) has assumed the first two responsibilities, and at present NHC is mainly dealing with the construction of houses for rental purposes. During the first five-year development plan (1964-1965), NHC was given the task of building 1,000 housing units per year in Dar-Es-Salaam, and 70% of these houses were to be built under the slum clearance program.[18] During this period, NHC constructed 4,678 houses in Dar-Es-Salaam, of which 4,292, or 91.7%, were low-cost houses, and 186 units were medium-cost houses. During the second five-year development plan (1969-1974), a total of 5,000 low-cost houses were built in Dar-Es-Salaam, 60% of which were under the slum clearance program. Another 1,131 units were built by NHC on a tenant purchase basis in different urban areas. However, as I have already argued, the net addition of housing units was minimal because most of the new units were just replacing those units which have been demolished under the slum clearance program.

By 1980, the total housing stock under the management of NHC was 18,319 housing units, which means that NHC had by then managed to construct an average of 743 units per year during the 18 years of its operation.[19] Since then the performance of NHC has been slow, while the urban population has been growing at an average rate of 250,000 people per year.[20] Among the factors which have contributed to the low performance of NHC are shortage of funds, shortage of building materials, and lack of adequate vehicles for transporting materials.[21]

The Permanent Housing Finance Company of Tanzania (PHFCT) was established in 1968 following the recommendations of the Commonwealth Development Corporation. The company was established in order to provide mortgage lending. It operated on the basis of commercial credit at 8.5% annual interest (Chachage 1982). The company provided loans for owner-occupant housing costing between 30,000 and 100,000 Tshs. (ibid). However, its market was limited to the provision of "luxury" houses and therefore attracted only 4,000 potential borrowers before it was abolished.[22]

The 1967 announcement of the Arusha Declaration, which was a blueprint for socialist construction in Tanzania, brought in slight changes in the Tanzanian housing policy. The emphasis now was on the mobilization of self-help efforts, establishment of a financial institution for constructing houses, and the provision of site and service schemes. The second five-year development plan stated clearly that:

> The rapid growth of urban population can claim huge investments in infrastructure. This may lead to a conflict between different objectives. On the one hand, shelter must be provided for urban population, while on the other hand the government is committed to redressing the imbalance between urban and rural areas. A sound policy must therefore harmonize this apparent conflict. This will be done if as many town dwellers as possible took to themselves, singly or jointly in groups, to provide housing with only a minimum of necessary assistance from the state. This is the essence of Self-Reliance.[23]

The aftermath of the Arusha Declaration culminated in the creation of the following institutions. In 1970, the Building Research Unit (BRU) was established following the recommendations of the Economic Commission to the Cabinet. The aim of BRU was

1. to clear and solve the problem of housing construction and its technology;
2. to support national organizations in terms of research on housing and housing construction; and
3. to coordinate various research activities on housing, putting much emphasis on the application of cheap resources which were locally available in the country.[24]

One has to note here that it was not clearly known how the first aim of BRU was going to be achieved. It is therefore clear that BRU was established purely as a research organization.

A year after the establishment of BRU, Tanzania, via a 1971 Act of the Parliament Number 13, called the "Acquisition of Buildings Act" established an autonomous parastatal organization called the Registrar of Buildings (ROB). Under this new act, all rented buildings worth 100,000 Tshs. were nationalized and acquired by the state. ROB acquired the interests and assets of these buildings and assumed the right of occupancy. This was one of the significant post-Arusha Declaration developments at the level of urban housing. Until February of 1985, ROB owned 8,463 housing units of this type throughout Tanzania.[25] Like NHC, ROB has also engaged itself in the construction of houses for rental purposes, and by 1980, ROB had already constructed 379 housing units.[26]

In 1972, partly due to the failure of PHFCT, and mainly as a follow-up policy of the Arusha Declaration, the government via Act Number 34 of 1972 established the Tanzania Housing Bank (THB). THB succeeded PHFCT and started its operations in January of 1973. The objectives and functions of THB are

A. To mobilize local and external resources for housing development
B. To promote housing development by:

1. making available loans or equity financing for housing to any person;
2. making available technical and financial assistance for site and service facilities;
3. rendering technical, financial and other assistance for promotion and implementation of owner-occupied schemes;
4. rendering technical, financial and other assistance to Ujamaa Villages in preparation and implementation of building programs;
5. rendering technical, financial and other assistance for the establishment and administration of institutions, cooperatives and other organizations engaged primarily in housing development for the benefit of the people of the United Republic of Tanzania; and
6. making loans or guaranteeing loans made by others or any person or body of persons, corporate or un-corporate for the purpose of enabling such persons or bodies to carry out housing development.[27]

In order to achieve these objectives, THB's operations are governed by the following five principles.

1. THB finances only those projects which are economically viable, socially desirable, and technically feasible.
2. In making loans, THB must satisfy itself that adequate provisions for the enforcement of repayment of the loan and repayment of interest exist. THB must also determine the type of value of collateral or security to be pledged by the potential borrower.
3. The bank must be satisfied with the expected ability of the borrower to repay the loan without undue hardships.

4. The borrower is required to provide the bank with all necessary and relevant information and to allow inspection of the books and records during the time the loan remains outstanding.
5. The bank must taken all necessary measures to protect its interest.[28]

Another institution worth mentioning here is the "Center for Housing Studies". This center was established as a result of the consultation between the government of Netherlands and the Ministry of Lands, Housing and Urban Development (on behalf of the government of Tanzania). The Center for Housing Studies (CHS) is an affiliate organization of the Ardhi Institute of Dar-Es-Salaam and operates under its umbrella. Its responsibility is to conduct short local and international courses and seminars on housing matters in the Third World. The center also carries out research studies on housing matters in Tanzania. Hence, the center is both a teaching and a research organization whose objective is to provide the government and other relevant bodies with input information which may help in one way or another in understanding and solving the problems of housing in Tanzania.

The Project/Program Approach

The Slum Clearance Project (SCP), the National Site and Service Schemes (NSSS), and the Squatter Upgrading Program (SUP) are typical strategies which have characterized this approach.

The SCP started immediately after independence as part and parcel of the NHC operations. This strategy came as a result of the President's call to remove old thatched houses in urban areas. As a result, houses of this type were demolished and new houses of "better" quality with materials loaned by the government were erected. The slum clearance approach was abolished in 1969 after realizing that the net increase of housing stock was minimal. The approach also created various social problems and frustration resulting from the displacement of the slum dwellers.

In 1972, following the recommendation of the Economic Commission of the Cabinet Number 81 on the National Housing Policy, and Number 106 of the same year on National Sites and Service Schemes, and also the recommendations of the World Bank and the International Development Agency (IDA) with their willingness to provide a "soft" loan, the government of Tanzania was lead to adopt the National Site and Services Schemes (NSSS).

In this approach, the government provided already serviced new plots with infrastructure and necessary community facilities like water, roads, drainage system, social centers, markets, schools, and health facilities. The idea is that the people who get these plots have to build their own houses by either applying for housing loans from THB, or through their own resources.

So far, this project has been implemented in two phases. During the first phase of the project (1974-77) 8,932 serviced plots were provided in three major towns, namely, Dar-Es-Salaam in Sinza, Mikocheni and Kijitonyama areas (Mbeya in Mwanjelwa area) and Mwanza in Nyakato area (See Table 3.3). In Dar-Es-Salaam, the first phase ended up with construction of new four urban dispensaries, seven primary schools, and six "modern" markets.[29]

Phase two of the project started in 1977, and involved the survey of 18,985 plots in Dar-Es-Salaam, Morogoro, Tanga, and Iringa towns. It was expected that this phase could benefit more than 350,000 people which would be 50% of the squatters in 1977.[30] Table 3.4 below presents the actual performance of both phases of the NSSS.

The NSSS started with very high hopes precisely because of the money provided by IDA. IDA alone provided a loan of 16.7 million dollars with 3% annual interest.[31] 65% of the total budget of NSSS was financed by foreign organizations. The Ministry of Lands, Housing and Urban Development became so ambitious that they established a separate department responsible for the NSSS and a Project Manager was appointed. At present, the project performance is declining, and, in fact, the second phase which was supposed to end 1981 is yet to be completed because of the financial problems. The foreign assistance is no longer forthcoming.

TABLE 3.4
National Sites and Services and Squatter Upgrading Projects in Tanzania

Location	Phase I (1974-77)		Phase II (1977-81)	
	Serviced Plots	Upgraded Areas	Serviced Plots	Upgraded Areas
Dar-Es-Salaam	6,182	7,600	14,150	9,138
Mwanza	1,900	-----	------	-----
Mbeya	850	1,200	------	-----
Iringa	-----	-----	1,770	1,088
Morogoro	-----	-----	810	2,069
Tabora	-----	-----	925	2,278
Tanga	-----	-----	1,330	732
Totals	8,932	8,800	18,985	15,811

Source: World Bank: Tanzania: Second National Sites and Services Project, Annex 1, Table 3; Washington DC.

Closely linked to the NSSS and, in fact, part of it was the government's adoption of a new policy towards squatters. It was decided that all squatter areas were to be officially recognized and accepted, and that a procedure was to be adopted in order to upgrade them. This involved the recognition of squatters as they are, and to upgrade them by providing roads, street lights, piped water, electricity, and, if possible, the drainage system. In addition, schools, health facilities, and markets were also envisaged in the plan of upgrading. The upgrading exercise also got the financial assistance of the World Bank.

Since 1974, some 7,600 housing units in the Manzese area (the biggest squatter area in Dar-Es-Salaam) have benefitted from this program. In addition, special credit facilities were made available for house owners in Manzese in order to enable them to improve their houses. The THB introduced a special system for house improvement loans in which a loan applicant could receive up to a maximum of 10,000 Tshs. for the purpose of structural improvement of his house.[32] However, as Schmetzer (1980) has argued, this THB scheme had a very slow take-off due to lack of sufficient publicity on behalf of THB.[33]

Brain (1979) has praised this approach of upgrading squatters because of the following advantages it had.

1. The community was left intact, most of the houses were not demolished, and in most areas their location remained the same.
2. Unlike the resettlement approach or the slum clearance and the national sites and services approaches, this approach required less government money.
3. The squatter upgrading approach potentially easily mobilized the energies and efforts of the squatters themselves.[34]

Table 3.4 shows that a total of 8,800 housing units were upgraded during the first phase of the project between 1974-1977. During this phase, only Dar-Es-Salaam and Mbeya towns were included in the project. The second phase of the project involved 15,811 housing units in Dar-Es-Salaam, Iringa, Morogoro, Tabora, and Tanga.

Problems, Constraints and Analysis of Housing Policies

One of the major bottlenecks to housing development in Tanzania is the acute shortage of financial resources, both internal and external.[35] As it has already been argued in the previous chapters that the lack of foreign exchange has affected the entire economy and the production capacities of domestic industries has been severely curtailed.[36] This situation has affected the housing sector since even the low-income housing has a 25% dependence on locally-produced materials such as iron sheets, cement, and nails. In the case of corrugated iron sheets (whose demand has been and is quickly increasing), its production in 1980 was only 50% of that in 1977.[37] Production of cement has also not kept pace with the demand, and it is estimated that the supply gap increased by 64% between 1975 and 1980.[38] Moreover, the prices of these building materials have been rising continuously. As of 1993, a 50 kg. bag of cement cost 2,500 Tshs., which is 50% of the minimum pay. A corrugated iron sheet of good quality sells at 5,000 Tshs., which is, in fact, equivalent to one month's minimum salary.

While the prices have been increasing by more than 100% annually, the peoples' cash income has been increasing at an average rate of 5% per year (Tibaijuka, 1987). At the same time, one has to bear in mind that inflation has been eroding away the value of wages. For example, the 1985 minimum wage of 810 Tshs. had less than 40% of the purchasing power of the 1974 minimum wage, and less than 30% of the 1964 minimum wage.

The housing bank does not operate in favor of the poor. In order to get a housing loan from the bank, THB requires a borrower to:

1. prove that he is credit worthy;
2. open a special account with the bank with a deposit of not less than 5% of the expected loan;
3. be less than 55 years old, and attach three passport size photographs to the application;
4. submit a copy of a land title and the right of occupancy of a long lease; and
5. submit a copy of the house plan and building permit from either the city or town council[39]

The client is also obliged to pay the valuation fees to the Tanzania Legal Corporation which prepares the mortgages. The sum of these expenses may amount from between 850 Tsh to 2000 Tshs.[40] Indeed, such procedures are beyond the ability of the majority urban poor.

Related to the bank problem is the shortage of plots in urban areas. There is a chronic shortage of surveyed building plots, and the procedures one has to follow in order to acquire a plot are cumbersome, long, and expensive. For example, in Dar-Es-Salaam the households increased by 42,200 between 1967 and 1972 and the plots surveyed and distributed were only 6,042, with a deficiency of about 36,158 plots.[41] In 1979, there were 3,000 applications for building plots in Dar-Es-Salaam. However, only 1,059 plots were available, 794 plots in the high density residential areas, 199 plots in the medium density area, and 66 in the low density area.[42] At present, Dar-Es-Salaam alone requires some 10,000 new house plots per year in order to keep pace with its annual population increase, but the city has so far managed to survey only between 500 and 800 plots per year over the past eight years.[43] Similarly, other urban areas in Tanzania have the same backlog in the provision of plots.

In order for one to apply for a loan from the bank, he must own a building plot in an officially surveyed area and must have the right of occupancy and a certificate of land title. Even where the few plots of land which are available have been located, it takes between one or two years to obtain a land title deed without which no loan can be applied for. Sometimes it may take a much longer time depending on where the client is. This is precisely because of the fact that all title deeds throughout Tanzania (with the exception of Dodoma) have to be issued by the Principal Secretary of the Ministry of Lands which is based in Dar-Es-Salaam. Ten squatters living in the Unga Limited area in Arusha town informed me during my research visit there that they have been waiting for their title deeds for the past five years. Finally, they had to sell their plots to other people because they were unable to build the houses with their own financial resources. They could not apply for a loan from THB because they had no title deeds for their plots.

Another problem is that all loan applications have to be forwarded to the THB headquarters for approval. This process alone can take another one to two years. This means that the whole procedure of getting the title deed, and finally the approval of the loan by the bank may take between two and four years. Worse is the corruptive tendency of the bureaucracy. In order to make sure that both the title and the loan are processed quickly and smoothly, the applicant (hereafter referred to as the client) has to provide the so called *chai* (tea) or *chakula* (food) or *Lazima kuvaa shati ya mikono mirefu* (The client has to put on a long sleeved shirt). In simple terms, it means that the client has to bribe or corrupt the officers concerned at all levels. Thus, the whole procedure is not only time consuming, but also very expensive. What does this mean to the urban poor? First, it means that they cannot dare to apply for a building plot in a surveyed area because they are unable to handle the costs involved in the whole process, which automatically excludes them from applying for a loan from THB because they will not have the title deed. Secondly, those who are lucky enough to own plots in planned surveyed areas normally hesitate to apply for loans from THB because either they do not have the 5% down payment or they cannot afford to repay the loan, or the THB considers them not credit worthy.

It is obvious that the bank helps the high income earners. This is indeed contrary to the first objective of the bank. Related to that is the fact that such a practice contradicts the desire of the Tanzanian state of pursuing a socialist discourse based on the equality of men by men. Recently, the bank argued that its major aim now was to inculcate in borrowers the ideas of depending more on their own efforts than on the Bank (*Daily News Paper*, 10/18/84). However, such being the case, the Bank does not justify why it should continue to exist.

One more serious problem which has developed in Tanzania concerns the corruptive behavior of the land officers during the allocation of plots. My findings from both Dar-Es-Salaam and Dodoma where I interviewed 500 households in 1987 indicate the following: 240 respondents (48%) had applied for surveyed plots (40 of them in Dodoma and the remaining 200 in Dar-Es-Salaam) since 1983. Only 10 (4.1%) from Dar-Es-Salaam and all from Dodoma had been allocated plots by the end of June, 1987. But none had so far received the certificate of land title, a situation which is delaying some of them from applying for the THB loans. The remaining 260 (or 52%) argued that they were unwilling to apply for these official surveyed plots because of the expense involved. Although the official fee for a plot in a high density area was between 4000 Tshs. and 6000 Tshs., the respondents complained that land officers demanded between 50,000 and 100,000 Tshs. in Dar-Es-Salaam, and between 20,000 and 50,000 Tshs. in Dodoma as a bribe.

The National Housing Corporation (NHC) and the Registrar of Buildings (ROB) do not seem to have managed to solve the problems of the urban poor either. The two organizations have very high overhead costs due to personnel management, lack of forward planning, poor bookkeeping and stocking procedures, and extravagance.[44] The NHC and ROB are typical bureaucratic parastatal organizations with many of their employees underemployed. Table 3.5 shows the performance and employment trends of NHC.

The data from the table shows the contradictions inherent in the NHC, and the underemployment of NHC employees. It is clear from the table that the number of housing units constructed per year by NHC has been diminishing, investment in housing has been fluctuating, but very surprising is the fact that the number of the NHC employees has been increasing. It is due to these overhead costs that rents always go up.

The Building Research Unit (BRU) is purely a research organization. BRU does not finance housing construction. BRU builds demonstration houses in rural and urban areas so that people can adopt the plans while building their own dwellings. The weakness of BRU lies in terms of the way it views the housing problem in general and the urban areas in particular. Implicitly, BRU sees the problem of housing in Tanzania in terms of the *ignorance* of the people in using the "right" and "simple" building materials and technology, and not in terms of the inability of the people which is a result of urban poverty.

TABLE 3.5
Twenty Years of NHC Performance and Employment Trends, 1962-1982

Year	Total Investment in Housing, Infrastructure, and Equipment	Houses Constructed	Number of Employees
1962/63	23.0	51	10
1963/64	5.0	11	120
1964/65	17.0	1010	250
1965/66	17.0	1220	380
1966/67	18.0	1210	510
1967/68	19.0	1500	660
1968/69	18.0	2400	760
1969/70	22.0	870	860
1970/71	31.0	1340	910
1971/72	28.0	2060	970
1972/73	24.0	1240	1020
1973/74	23.0	1240	1120
1974/75	12.0	310	890
1975/76	27.0	450	1090
1976/77	14.0	150	810
1977/78	5.0	180	970
1978/79	12.0	290	1050
1979/80	5.6	100	1027
1980/81	----	100	1070
1981/82	12.4	----	1070

Source: *Daily News Paper*, August 6, 1982.
Note: The amount of money is in million Tanzanian Shillings.

BRU and CHS perform more or less similar activities. They are even stationed quite close to one another, and they could probably operate well and more efficiently if they were merged together. Given the current economic crisis, this would probably minimize costs, and avoid the duplication of tasks and responsibility, a problem which is common within the two institutions. This would probably enhance the quality of research work. The fact that there exists a duplication of tasks, research work, and seminar contents between BRU and CHS confirms the problem of lack of coordination of activities between various institutions and organizations in Tanzania.

As far as the "Project" or "Program" approach to urban housing problems, the following shortcomings have so far been noted. Zakaria's 1982 study on housing in Dar-Es-Salaam revealed that the National Sites and Service Scheme Project (NSSS) ended up benefitting the high income earners.[45] The first phase of the NSSS project defined low income earners as those people earning less than 750 Tshs. per month. The second phase of the project increased this level to 1,000 Tshs. The present high quality housing, and even flats built on many of the plots under this project, indicate that the owners of these houses are definitely not the target group. That is the low income earners. For example, most of the houses built in Sinza and Mikocheni area in Dar-Es-Salaam are in the 120,000 to 500,000 Tshs. cost range, which is, in fact, beyond the reach of the low income households.[46] How has this happened?

There are three main reasons why the project has ended up benefitting the high income earners:

1. The initial mis-allocation of some plots to persons wealthier than the target groups. This is either due to lack of clear allocation procedures, corruptive behavior of some officials responsible for the allocation of plots, or both;
2. The pooling of housing resources by family groups larger than the plot applicant's own households; and
3. Unofficial changes of plot holder after plot allocation.[47]

Kulaba (1985) has noted that over 70% of the sites and services plots provided in Dar-Es-Salaam have been taken up by middle or high income families, thus erecting very expensive buildings.[48]

At one level, this tendency illustrates the difficulty of ensuring that only low income families benefit from such projects, if at the same time the needs of the wealthier families are not being met. At another level, this is a result of the scarcity and very expensive building materials which the low income families cannot afford, and the present building codes enforced in the sites and service areas. One has to add also the already mentioned institutional procedures of getting a building permit, and loan applications, procedures which I have argued are cumbersome, costly and time-consuming. Very often these procedures are not clearly known to the public, and neither are the fees charged at each state. Such procedures have proved to be very prohibitive to the urban poor. That is why even those who were lucky to have been allocated plots in the sites and service areas have ended up selling their plots to prospective and wealthy individuals who have the ability to build houses in these surveyed areas. Most of them use the money which they get after selling their plots to build residential units in squatter areas. They would rather build in the squatter areas precisely because, in these areas,

1. they are free, and are not bound by any city or town council building codes and regulations;
2. they have the choice of the squatting area they want;
3. they are not subjected to pay land rents or other charges;
4. they can avoid all regulations imposed on official surveyed plots; and
5. they can enjoy investment opportunities (like small gardening, poultry keeping and others) which might be prohibited in planned areas

Sometimes due to the above factors, even the wealthy people have preferred to squat rather than apply for an official surveyed plot. Indeed, one can observe the following squatter settlements in Dar-Es-Salaam which are basically residential areas of the better-off section of the urban population: The Mlalakua and Savei areas, most of which are occupied by university professors and lecturers, Kimara, some parts of Ubungo-Kibangu, Kimara Stop-Over, Kimara-Mavurunza, and some parts of Ukonga and Gongo La Mbotto. One can draw two conclusions from this. One is the fact that in Tanzania, given the current economic crisis, a squatter settlement is not necessarily synonymous with poverty. There are squatter areas for the urban poor like Buguruni, Kiwalani, Kipawa, Shimo La Udongo, Mtoni Kwa Azizi, Keko-Mwanga, Keko-Machungwa, Keko-Magurumbasi, and Vingunguti in Dar-Es-Salaam. At the same time one has squatter settlements for the better-off. Second is the fact that there are apparent reasons compelling people to resort to squatter settlements. While the shortage of plots might be a compelling reason for the well-to-do individuals, the advantages of squatter areas in terms of the possibility for one to operate a project in order to supplement income given the current economic crisis is another compelling factor. Therefore, to the urban poor, it is poverty which forces them to squat while to the well-off the economic advantages of squatter areas play a dominant role.

A recent survey conducted in the Sinza and Mikocheni areas revealed that most of the plots under the NSSS which were yet to be developed (since 1977) belonged to the low-income earners.[49]

My interview in 1987 with the Project Manager of the Sites and Services project, Ndugu Majani, revealed that more than 70% of the low-income earners who were allocated surveyed plots in both phases of the project were no longer owners of the houses built on these plots. Most of them had to sell their plots to other people.

The program of upgrading squatters by accepting them and offering their residents security of tenure, seem in my view to have been very successful. In Dar-Es-Salaam, the biggest and most famous squatter area of Manzese was the first settlement to be included in the squatter upgrading program. All house owners were provided with security of tenure, and services like roads, street lights, and water kiosks. In Iringa town, the Kihesa area was included in this program.

During my first visit in the Manzese and Kihesa areas in 1987, I was able to notice the following new developments:

1. The roads are much better than the former ones.
2. There are now street lights and water kiosks as opposed to none in 1974. In Kihesa there are five water kiosks, and only eight in Manzese, although of late only three are operating in Manzese.
3. Housing construction has been improved enormously. More people are using permanent building materials like burned bricks, tiles, and cement blocks.
4. At least 50% of the housing units have electricity connections. More than 25% of the houses in Kihesa have their own water taps, although due to the low pressure of water, women have to go out to fetch water.
5. In both areas, hotels, guest houses, *vilabu* or *pombe* shops (places where local brew is sold), and bars have increased and their mode of operation has been modernized. For example, most of the *pombe* shops are equipped with sophisticated musical instruments for "disco dancing".

It may be argued here that the assurance of security of tenure and also the government's attitude of accepting and recognizing the squatter settlements as they are have played a great role in the process of improving these settlements. The house owners have been investing the money they get from rent in the improvement of their dwelling units precisely because they have been assured by the government that they are not going to be resettled. This means that the squatters, once accepted (and if they are given time) are capable of improving their dwelling units gradually. Indeed, a recent survey of 400 houses in Manzese showed that 80% of the houses have been completely rebuilt with permanent building materials.[50]

One issue which appears to be problematic to the urban poor as far as the squatter upgrading approach is concerned is the fact that as investments of capital are made in these areas, they continue to increase. For example, provision of serviced roads, street lights, water, and electricity raises the value of the land. This also pushes up the amount of monthly rents demanded by the landlords. Findings from both Manzese and Kihesa confirm this trend.

In regards to the slum clearance approach, there are concrete examples which show that the government is still demolishing some of the squatter areas. Officially, the government abolished the demolition of slums in 1969 because it was realized that the net addition to housing was minimal and the social and economical costs involved were greater.

In practice, the government has continued to demolish and intends to demolish all those settlements which, in the opinion of the urban planners, are "undesirable" and "shameful" to the nation. The worst thing about the present clearance program is the fact that, unlike the former slum clearance which paved way to the construction of new NHC housing units, the present approach of demolishing slums is applied in order to make room for construction of ultra-modern office buildings, factories, and hotels. The slum dwellers whose houses are demolished are very minimally compensated, and, in most cases, they are not provided with new plots.

For example, after having threatened to raze the famous slum area of Kisutu in Dar-Es-Salaam for several years, one morning in 1974 the city council finally invaded the area with bulldozers and caterpillars, flattened and set ablaze the whole Kisutu area. The next morning the government-owned paper reported this as follows:

> As the 93 huts that made Kisutu a world of its own succumbed, the last batch of its residents rushed here and there in uncertainty, gathering the last belongings. Two men were rushed to Muhimbili Hospital after walls or roofs had fallen on them. Eyewitnesses said they were sleeping when the caterpillars began their operations.[51]

It is clearly known that the former residents of Kisutu were not provided with new "modern" accommodations. Some of them were minimally compensated, and the majority got nothing.[52] After demolition, an ultra-modern office building housing "The National Correspondence Institute" has been constructed. Thus, the demolition of Kisutu had paved the way for the construction of this building and not for the construction of low-cost housing. It follows from this, therefore, that the demolition of Kisutu was not in the interest of the Kisutu residents. The urban poor of Kisutu lost their dwelling units, and their whereabouts has remained a mystery.

Another famous squatter settlement of the Buguruni area in Dar-Es-Salaam was also demolished in the early 1970s, and the government handed over the area to the NHC which built residential flats in the area whose rent was 800 Tshs. in the early 1980s, and since 1985 has been raised to 3,872 Tshs. Such a rent, as I have already argued, continues to exclude the majority of urban poor.

In late 1978, the biggest well-known slum settlement of Tambuka-Reli in Dodoma was cleared by bulldozers in order to make room for the construction of office buildings for the new capital city. It is clearly known what has happened to the Tambuka-Reli residents. The government directed that demolition of the area had to be effected only after making sure that the residents had been compensated and allocated with new plots. However, this was not actually the case. Demolition went ahead immediately after compensation but before plot allocation. The Chamwino "B" area which was supposed to house the former Tambuka-Reli residents had not yet been surveyed. As a result, the majority of the Tambuka-Reli residents invaded the Chang`ombe squatter settlement and built their slum-type dwelling units there again. Thus, the death of the Tambuka-Reli slum settlement gave birth to the Chang`ombe slum settlement. Data collected from the Capital Development Authority (CDA) office shows that there was only one house in the Chang`ombe area since 1972, but after the demolition of Tambuka-Reli in 1978, the number of houses rose to 144 in 1979. My findings in 1987 show that 92% of the 750 dwelling units existing in the Chang`ombe area at present had been built after 1978. My findings show also that almost 60% of the squatters living in new squatter settlements of Maili Mbili, Chaduru, and Chinang`ali are former residents of the demolished Tambuka-Reli settlement. One fact which confirms that the government did not take care of the former residents of Tambuka-Reli is the fact that 436 plots which were later surveyed in Area "B" were allocated to non-Tambuka-Reli residents.

In summary, the technocrats tend to see squatter areas as dangerous manifestations of social disease and chaos. They harbored and generated several types of what is considered immoral behavior which made the areas negative elements in Tanzanian urban areas. None of these officers during my interview expressed anything positive about these settlements. It is thus obvious that the squatters are seen as a headache to the town planners. It is evident that what follows from such thinking is the eradication of such settlements.

On the other hand, the opinions of the representatives of the squatter residents was opposed to the opinion of the technocrats. Their views have been summarized below.

1. "People have settled and established themselves here for the past several years. Resettlement will create a lot of disturbance, and given the economic crisis facing the country, and *umaskini wetu tulionao* (our poverty), most of us are not prepared, and in fact cannot afford to start a new life elsewhere."
2. "We can accept resettlement only if the government provides us with ready-made houses. From our experience which we have learnt from other already resettled people confirm that the compensation which they got was not enough to erect even house foundations. We are sure that the same thing will happen to us if we accept compensation. That is why we are against the whole idea of relocation."
3. "We can only accept to be resettled if the government can let us value our buildings so that we are able to determine on our own the amount of money we would like to be paid as compensation."
4. "We are against resettlement because we know that we will be resettled far away from our places of work, a situation which will make us spend the meager income we have on transport. This is something which we are not prepared to accept."
5. "The income earned by most of our people is not enough even to feed them for the whole month. Thus resettlement will mean *mateso makubwa* (great torture) to most of us."
6. "The government should not be ashamed of the existence of slum settlements which are quite close to the residential areas of affluent social groups like Oyster Bay or Msasani. This is a true indicator of the fact that there are rich as well as poor people. This is the reality of Tanzania."

In general, the government and most of its town planning machinery are still in favor of the slum clearance programs. But at the same time, one has to acknowledge that in areas where slums have been cleared, the consequences are not hard to find. They have included

1. high social costs in terms of social disruption and family displacement;
2. generation of social and political opposition among residents of slums (That is why they normally develop a negative attitude toward the state.);
3. displacement of many small enterprises and businesses which had been providing services, employment and income;
4. increasing the burden upon most of the displaced people (like that of transport costs to their places of work and the city center) because they have been resettled in remote, unserviced land areas; and
5. repelling the urban poor rather than attracting them due to the high rent in the areas where low-cost housing has replaced slum houses (Kulaba 1987)

Thus, most of the slum clearance projects have never had a positive impact on the problems of housing, but on the contrary, their principal effect has been to reduce the already existing supply of urban housing. Therefore, rather than solving the problem, the approach of slum clearance has exacerbated it.

Nevertheless, the government has maintained its negative attitude towards slum dwellers. This attitude can be summarized as follows:

> The slum areas constitute communities with pathological characteristics of lower class life. These areas are occupied by poor people of the urban society. They are areas of high social disorganization, unemployment, crime and poor mental health. These communities represent the physical conditions of social chaos. Slums are a menace to the Town Planners, they are an embarrassment to the affluent social groups, and very exciting. To the state they are a headache.[53]

It is obvious that such an attitude leads to creating policies which condone squatters.

Urban Housing, Class, and Status

In Tanzanian urban areas the class divisions can be reflected in the urban residence patterns. The relationship between housing, class, and status reveals directly how the government establishes policies which favor some sections of the urban community.

Although this study does neither, nor does it intend to discuss the class nature of urban areas in Tanzania, but the present government policy of dividing residential areas in urban areas in terms of standards based on income and status, it at least acknowledges the fact that there are divisions of people in terms of either class or status. The best and the worst housing tends to be clustered in enclaves. Luxury housing caters to the privileged sections of the urban population and the spontaneous housing serves the very poor. These extremes are etched into the urban landscape by being visually and geographically separate from what is otherwise a more heterogenous residential pattern. The residential areas of the highly learned elites, highly salaried civil servants, executives of commercial and industrial firms, diplomats and foreign expatriates, are usually located within the city boundaries, and in the case of Dar-Es-Salaam, near the Indian Ocean where there are cool sea breezes. They are clearly isolated from the residential areas of the ordinary people. The Oyster Bay, Msasani, Masaki, and Kinondoni areas in Dar-Es-Salaam are a case in point. Most of the elite housing and luxury flats are publicly or employer-owned, and most of them are provided with all the amenities like running water, electricity, indoor bathing, and kitchen facilities. Other houses have separate servants' quarters and parking spaces and garages. These areas belong to what is commonly known as the *Low-Density Residential Areas*.

The *Medium-Density Residential Areas* constitute all those enclaves of the middle-income people and are distinctive from the above ones in the sense that most of them have been built privately, some by NHC or ROB and are sometimes located right at the central part of the urban area. The Upanga area in Dar-Es-Salaam is the best example representing this residential area. Normally, the area has water and electrical facilities. The areas have been well-planned, and the housing units enjoy the protection of the state.

The *High-Density Residential Areas* are areas which accommodate low-cost, low-income housing. The houses are crowded because of the space provided, and the density of the population is normally high. In some houses, water and electricity is available, and in other houses it is not. Most of the houses are privately built and owned. Most of them are built in surveyed and well-planned plots. Therefore, like the above, they enjoy the protection of the state. Because of the scarcity of building plots in Tanzanian urban areas at present, one sees that this area is being occupied also by the middle-income earners. Our discussion of Sinza and Mikocheni area has already revealed this fact.

The fourth type of residential pattern is *Spontaneous Housing*. While the first three types of residential patterns are officially planned and accepted by the government, this fourth type is deliberate and illegal. This pattern is associated with squatter settlements. The next chapter will describe in detail the characteristics of this kind of housing by discussing the characteristics of the nature of life in squatter areas. In comparison with the above types, it is at the opposite extreme, and usually beyond city boundaries in suburban or peri-urban areas.

It is obvious at this point that the government continues to use these class-laden, so-called technical planning concepts of *high*, *medium*, and *low density* areas. In reality, these planning concepts simply stand for differentiation of residential areas of the *poor*, *middle class*, and *rich* people.

At the same time, the government and most of its parastatal companies provide housing to their employees of higher or senior ranking, such as ministers, principal secretaries, directors, managers and director generals, and officers on short-call emergency duty posts like doctors and teachers.

In order to implement these policies, standing orders for civil servants and directives from the Standing Committee of Parastatal Organization (SCOPO) have been issued in order to divide workers in terms of those who are entitled or not entitled to

1. housing by the employer;
2. official transportation by the employer;
3. free medical care;
4. a housing allowance; and
5. an entertainment allowance.

For example, the colonial/class legacy of such directives and standing orders is summarized well by Section 4 of the 1967 SCOPO Directive Number 2 on housing allowances which states that

The organization's obligation to provide housing and furniture will be confined to senior managerial and executive staff who are either in receipt of a basic salary of not less than 3,000 Tshs. per month, or who are occupying such positions (for example Branch Managers) as may be considering by the Headquarter Management of the organization concerned to confer upon these employees housing eligibility status.

In late 1972, the cabinet decided that all government and parastatal employees occupying public houses would pay a rent on a sliding scale system of 7.5%, 10%, and 12.5% of their income. Originally, as Stren has argued in 1979, it was felt that the upper-income earners, who would pay more rent under the new system, would in effect be subsidizing the lower-income earners who would generally be paying less than before.[54] In practice, this has not been achieved because most of the low-income earners are legally not entitled to be given accommodation by their employers, and even where the employer has several vacant housing units the sliding scale rent system influences the employer to house only those employees of the high income category (even if they are not his employees) in order to get a reasonable amount of money as rent contribution. The minimum wage earners have to depend on the housing market in the private sector where they are always at the mercy of their landlords. The Rent Restriction Act of 1984, which was created by the government in order to regulate and control the landlord-tenant relationship, has a lot of loopholes and has not been able to operate in favor of tenants. Cases of tenants being evicted from houses are numerous and common. The message carried out by the *Sunday News Paper* of November 16, 1986 confirms this argument.

Eviction of Tenants
In recent weeks we have witnessed a number of tenants — especially in Dar-Es-Salaam — being thrown out of their houses in the most cruel and senseless manner.
The unbecoming behavior is particularly common in houses owned by individual landlords who are all out to reap a fortune at the expense of the people's welfare and dignity.
For example, a landlord with an insatiable desire to earn more money through hiked rent would simply order tenants out of his house at short notice, denying them a chance to look for alternative accommodation. . . .
Due to shortage of official conventional housing, more urban dwellers have been forced to seek accommodation in houses owned by private landlords. *The rents here are comparatively too high and are frequently*

hiked at the whims of landlords, completely ignoring the plight of tenants whose income have more or less remained static over the years. Tenants who fail to comply with hiked rents have always found themselves at the mercy of greedy landlords who would exploit the least excuse to punish the "culprits". More often than not the victims are insulted, humiliated and even summarily evicted in the most disgraceful manner.

In brief, it is now clear that the kind of urban housing policies Tanzania has adopted and implemented have not been able to solve the housing problems of the majority urban poor. The urban poor are the least economically advantaged, the least socially involved, and the hardest hit by the housing problem, but paradoxically the least institutionally assisted people in the urban areas.

Housing policies reveal the gap between theory and practice in Tanzania's urban planning. What is the reason for this? The gap is largely attributable to the contradiction within the particular type of dependent development taking place within a neo-colonial situation. By perpetuating and enhancing the inequality through new regulations at the level of housing, and neglecting what the Arusha Declaration promised, the state has created an empirical contradiction (problem of housing) as well as a theoretical one (the essence of socialism). While the state is failing to solve the first contradiction, it has failed to defend and explain why its practice contradicts its ideological position. If the state has failed to assist the poor in housing matters, what have the urban poor themselves done in order to solve this problem? Chapter 4 looks at the socio-economic conditions of life in squatter settlements in Dar-Es-Salaam.

4
Squatter Settlements and the Politics of Urban Poverty in Dar-Es-Salaam: A Case Study of Three Settlements

Introduction

This chapter is best introduced by the following two qualifications. Larissa Lomnitz argued in 1974 that

> A common prejudice found in the sociological literature on poverty consists portraying the urban poor as people bedeviled by a wide range of social pathologies, amounting to a supposed incapacity to respond adequately to social and economic incentives. More social scientists have directed their attention towards the material and cultural deprivation that meets the eye than toward the socio-cultural defense mechanisms which the poor have devised.[1]

Similarly, Marris (1970) has observed that

> The systematic analysis of squatters, shantytowns or slums receives scant attention in general textbooks, but in the world of political and social affairs these 'irregular' residential areas figure prominently. Indeed, a mention of them tends to be in terms of 'problems' which need 'solutions'. Yet, it is not always clear for whom the squatters constitute problems. For urban administrators, for politicians, or even for themselves?[2]

In the previous chapter, I have demonstrated empirically the views and opinions held by most of the planners, bureaucrats and others in Tanzania about these settlements and their residents. In summary, I have argued that most of their views are negative, and as a result of this, all policies emanating from planners of this kind tend to emphasize the elimination of these settlements.

In order to examine the validity of these negative views on squatters, I conducted a field social survey in three squatter settlements in Dar-Es-Salaam city in 1987/88, namely Shimo la Udongo, Kipawa, and Kiwalani. My main interest was first to identify the physical characteristics of these settlements, and second, identify the kind of people living in these areas, their economic activities, and occupational categories and income. Third, I was also interested in observing the kind of social and political organization which existed in these settlements. A total number of 320 household heads (200 men and 120 women) who constituted my random sample were interviewed. Methods used in data collection included formal and informal interviews, a designed questionnaire, and both participant and non-participant observation. Quantitative surveys were also used in order to substantiate some major conclusions. Hence, most of the statistical data which I present in this chapter is used in order to fill out the conceptual model based either on my own observation or from the information which I got via the interviews.

The Research Site

Kipawa is located about seven kilometers away from the city center, and it is between the ending point area of the Pugu Industrial Estate. It is the beginning point area of the Dar-Es-Salaam International Airport on the southwestern part of the city. Kiwalani is located behind the southern part of the Pugu Industrial Estate. Kipawa and Kiwalani are very close to one another. Shimo la Udongo is between four and five kilometers away from the city center. It is situated on the southern part of the city, and it is very close to the harbor. The settlement lies between the famous Kurasini affluent residential area and the Port Access Road.

The following typical characteristics and reasons made me choose these areas for my study.

1. These settlements have grown very fast recently as residential areas of the low-income section of the urban population.

2. Although they are unique as a squatter cum settlements, they serve as good examples of unplanned housing, so-called "illegal" high-density areas in Tanzanian urban areas in general, and particularly in Dar-Es-Salaam.
3. As squatter settlements they display most of the physical and some of the social problems encountered by such communities.
4. Since 1982 the government earmarked the Kipawa settlement for demolition in order to make room for the expansion of the new airport. The Kipawa residents succeeded in resisting this move. At present these residents again, and this time including the Kiwalani residents, have been told to vacate the area in order to provide enough expansion space for the Pugu Industrial Estate. The Shimo la Udongo residents have been told to vacate their area, too, because the government wants to construct some warehouses on the area.
5. Because of these three facts the three settlements are similar though not identical. Their presence is not supported by the government. The residents of this settlements share the same experiences, problems, and uncertainty. Indeed, they do not know what their fate is going to be. The way these people organize themselves and forward their demands to the state reflects the way the urban poor fight within their own environment and resources in order to survive. This is what I call the "Politics of Survival" throughout this study.

Physical Characteristics of Housing

It is difficult to estimate the population of these settlements at one time because they are characterized by a rapid growth and a population influx. Besides that, rate of migration and temporary lodging with relatives and friends (especially if someone is a new to the city) varies a lot. The lack of reliable population statistics presents the difficulties of being able to precisely determine the population density either per area or housing unit. Most of the houses are built without proper planning.

Housing conditions are generally poor. There is inadequate water supply, inadequate provision for washing, hygiene, and provision for sanitation. There is also a high level of overcrowding of houses in relationship to land and within houses. Houses are built very close to one another, leaving virtually no space between the houses, so privacy is non-existent. Some houses are very close to each other to the extent that one's pit latrine may just be two meters away from one's open kitchen and the streets or corridors in between are very narrow.

However, the quality of housing is considerable. Most of the better housing is found along the main road. This is precisely how it is in Kipawa and Shimo la Udongo. Most of the overcrowded houses which are substandard by the criteria of urban building codes are located on the backside of the seemingly good and modern houses, thus giving a misleading impression of the settlement to any person who happens to pass on the main road. The houses which are along the main road are built of cement blocks and are roofed with corrugated iron sheets. Most of these houses usually do not serve as residences; they are shops, hotels, bars, and pubs. A lot of these are owned by economically successful people. That is why they are located strategically.

In contrast to these, the great variety of houses located behind them has a considerably lower quality of construction and maintenance. Although most of them are roofed with corrugated iron sheets, and some with old flattened cooking oil and paraffin tin sheets (madebe), their walls made of mixed sand, mud, sticks, and some mangrove trees portray openly that the investment incurred in such buildings is limited. This shows that the owners of these houses are of low-income status, and therefore the money available for maintenance and improvement is limited. Electricity and water supply services are very poor. Very few houses have official electricity connections. In some houses, power and water is obtained through illegal hook-ups on power lines and main water pipes.[3] There are two main reasons for this. First of all, it is very expensive and takes a long time from the date one applies for water or electricity connections to the date one gets them. Second, one has to pay extra money as a bribe to some officials of the Tanzania Electric Supply Company (TANESCO) and of the National Urban Water Supply Authority (NUWA) in order to get services. Such costs and procedures are indeed beyond the ability of the majority residents in these settlements. The same thing happens with telephone services. Only six houses in Shimo la Udongo and four houses in Kipawa have private telephone connections. What is even worse is that there are no public telephone booths in the area.

The sanitary and service facilities which exist in these areas leaves much to be desired. Most of the residents fetch their water from nearby public kiosks or nearby houses due to the low water pressure at their own houses. Water comes out only at night or early in the morning and as a result long lines of people in water kiosks are often visible. There are no drainage systems and open pit-latrines are the most common toilet facilities available and used. Sharing of these facilities is common among households or neighborhoods. Most of the pit-latrines are used as bathing places and get overfilled within a short period of time. At the same time there are only a few trucks for emptying and one has to become corrupt in order to get his overflowing latrine emptied. This means that overflowing of human waste in the streets and house corridors is common. In some houses it is possible to see water from *karo* (laundry) littering the corridors. Heaps of uncollected garbage exist almost everywhere. At the Shimo la Udongo food market I was told that uncollected garbage may stay there for more than two weeks. In fact, there are no garbage or refuse containers in the area, so flies breed and reproduce themselves in great numbers and are a major health hazard. Access to health services is difficult and poor environmental conditions mean that the people are at higher risk of contracting a variety of infectious diseases. An informant told me that the prevalence of infectious diseases was common. Unfortunately, we did not make a comprehensive medical examination or an in-depth health study in the area, but information collected from many respondents indicate that diseases like malaria, dysentery, whooping cough, tuberculosis, measles, pneumonia, colds, diarrhea and other waterborne diseases are rampant in the area. Due to a lack of playgrounds, children play in an appalling environment, a situation which is indeed a health risk.

Although the settlements are characterized by this appalling environment, the houses never remain empty due to the great demand. Because of the housing problem, housing units in these areas do not seem as bad to the urban poor as one might think. The rents range from 200 to 400 Tshs. per room, and go up to between 600 and 800 Tshs. per month for two or three rooms. As of 1993, such rooms could cost up to between 3,000 and 6,000 Tshs. per month. However, the urban poor can only afford the cheapest possibility. My interview with a tenant in Shimo la Udongo reveals the dilemma faced by the urban poor. I have reproduced a summarized version of this interview below. (Q and A stands for Question and Answer respectively).

Q: How long have you been living in this area?
A: For the past seven years.
Q: So you have been staying in this house for the past seven years?

A: No! Immediately after arriving in this area, I rented a room in a house where the roof was made of *makuti* (coconut tree leaves).
Q: Did you like staying in a *makuti* roofed house?
A: *Hakuna apendaye shida* (none likes hardships). That was the cheapest possibility I managed to get. After all, I was unemployed by then and could not afford to rent a room in a *Nyumba ya Kisasa* (modern house).
Q: What do you mean by a "modern house"?
A: Of course, a house built out of cement blocks, roofed with corrugated iron sheets, provided with water and electricity. In short, like those in Msasani and Oyster Bay.
Q: But you are now working with Usafiri Dar-Es-Salaam Company (UDA). Why don't you rent a room from what you consider to be a modern house?
A: I work there as a messenger. *Mimi ni mtu wa kima cha chini* (I am a minimum paid employee). The rents in these modern houses are very high. Although I am employed, still I cannot afford them. But at least *nimejikwamua sasa* (I have liberated myself). Look, I am now renting a room in a house whose roof is made of corrugated iron sheets.

The analysis emanating from the above interview reveals that it is the economic position of an individual which determines where one lives. In addition to this, any slight improvement in one's accommodation is regarded as a step towards liberating oneself from poverty.

Income, Poverty, and Housing

In order to determine the income potential of the residents in these settlements, I listed the economic activity or occupation of the head of the household. This data has been summarized in Table 4.1. This information must be treated with caution because it is not easy to get an exact figure of income. Most of these people, whether employed or not, operate various income-generating activities in order to supplement their incomes. It is therefore not easy for an outsider to get reliable figures of people's real income.

TABLE 4.1
Occupations of Household Heads in the Three Settlements

Occupation Category	Men Cases	%	Women Cases	%
1. Petty Traders	06	03.0	03	02.5
2. Informal Sector Craftsmen	30	15.0	11	09.2
3. Unskilled laborers (on irregular jobs)	71	35.5	03	02.5
4. Unskilled laborers (on regular jobs)	31	15.5	02	01.7
5. Skilled workers in the formal sector (low income)	10	05.0	07	05.8
6. Skilled workers in the formal sector (middle and high income)	07	03.5	04	03.3
7. Servants	04	02.0	40	33.3
8. Landlords	05	02.5	09	07.5
9. Unemployed	36	18.0	18	15.0
10. Housewives	00	00.0	23	19.2
Total	200	100.0	120	100.0

Source: Research findings 1987/88

It is obvious from Table 4.1 that most of the men are unskilled (51%). This group includes all those who have never acquired any specialized skill formally or informally although they might have gone through the general primary education school system. Quite a lot of them are hired casually, or on a part-time basis in construction sites, as steve-doers or lorry-truck helpers (35.5%). Their income is basically very low, a hand-to-mouth income. My findings show that their salaries never dropped below the official minimum wage which was between 1260 and 1300 Tshs. recently. The informal sector operators are those who have acquired particular skills formally or through apprenticeship. Most of them work independently as brick-layers, masons, plumbers, construction foremen, mechanics, electricians, drivers, carpenters, cobblers, and some as musicians. In most cases these people earn above the minimum income. Like the unskilled laborers their security is low and their survival depends on the vagaries of the market forces.

The data on women's occupations is complicated and tends to be misleading. This is precisely so with the data on unskilled women and those who work as servants. Most of the 40 women who registered themselves as servants are, in fact, unskilled laborers who have been employed as barmaids, domestic servants, or hotel or restaurant waiters. Those who are registered as craftswomen and operated in the informal sector are experts in plaiting women's hair. My research shows that all the eleven skilled women work in the formal sector either as typists or secretaries.

The traders included all those who got their daily income purely from trade activities, such as street vendors and hawkers. None of these have a steady stable income or social security. Their success depends much on the vagaries of the market. The employed also involved themselves in these trade activities in order to supplement their incomes. Most of the women had charcoal, tomato, and dried fish stalls outside their house doors. Others prepared *vitumbua* and *maandazi* (african types of bread), and another group kept on selling the burned mosquito killer insectside through the use of child labor.

The research data also demonstrates that there are only a few people who are employed permanently in the formal sector and receive middle or higher salaries. However, they have the advantage of fixed salaries and the majority of them have minimal pensions and social security.

It is evident from Table 4.1 that the majority of households (245, which is 76.5% excluding employees and landlords) have no job security, no social security, and no fixed income. They exist day by day by chance, and they actually have to live as "urban hunters and gatherers". Some get employed as casual workers, and some on a part-time basis.

The findings reveal also that the majority of these people do not own their own dwellings. 65% of the households indicated that they lived in these areas as tenants and not as landlords.

In order to associate the economic base (or income) of a household and the housing characteristics, I classified the kind of housing in these three settlements in the following four types:

Type A:
Houses built out of cement blocks, roofed with corrugated iron sheets, with cement plastered walls and floors. There is a

presence of water and electricity, refrigerators, and cookers. The houses have private toilet systems and bathrooms, and some have shared systems.

Type B:
Almost the same as Type A, except they do not have electricity. There are shared toilets and bathrooms and a few have single used toilet systems.

Type C:
The same as Type A, but they do not have running water; most of the houses have shared toilets and bathrooms.

Type D:
The houses are small and have no foundation material, the walls are made of mixed mud and sticks, it is roofed by either corrugated iron sheets, flattened cooking oil and kerosene tin sheets or thatched grass (*makuti*). Most of these houses do not meet the official standards.

If we consider that the kind of housing is a reflection of the economic background of an individual, and therefore the standard of living of the person, then the 320 households included in the example can be distributed in the following housing standards. (Table 4.2)

TABLE 4.2
Distribution of Levels of Living

House Type	Number	Percentage
A	19	06.0
B	18	05.6
C	23	07.2
D	260	81.2
Total	320	100.0

Source: Computed by author from research findings

Table 4.2 confirms the argument that the level of living correlates highly with the economic base of the head of the household. Most of those who do not have job security, social security, and fixed income live in the low standard housing of Type D. These are the ones who are usually referred as *wanyonge* (the weak, exploited and oppressed) in Tanzania. Some of them belong to the KCC group (Kima Cha Chini) which includes those who receive the lowest minimum wage. These are the ones who "eat water" and "live from hand to mouth". In summary, they are the poverty-stricken section of the urban population. Most of them live as tenants renting one or two rooms, although they have big families.

Nine household heads classified in Type A housing own their dwelling units. The remaining 10 household heads live as tenants. Three out of these 19 household heads earn their living through landlordism. The rest are permanent employees in the formal sector within the middle- and high-income group. Some of the houses belong to absent landlords. Type A housing displayed complete assimilation to the urban way of life. Although Type D houses are officially regarded as below standard, the atmosphere inside and arrangement of their few belongings and furniture present a different picture. The occupants' belongings are low quality, but the way they arrange them, as well as their communication skills and their future ambitions show that the deep-seated movement of urbanization is within them. However it seems to me that a further improvement of these housing units will solely depend on the improvement (income-wise) of the people who own them as well as those who rent them.

Social and Political Organization

The Social Dimension

Most of the people living in these areas are related in one way or another, or have a more or less common background. Some new urban migrants move in these areas because they have relatives and friends who assist them in the gradual adaptation process of urban life. 70% of the respondents indicated that they had known somebody in the area before they moved in. It is their hosts who initially provide them with accommodation and food. Others assisted them in establishing urban connections and contacts in matters related to employment. It is also the hosts who act as key advisors to the new-comers on the strategies of surviving in urban areas.

In Tanzania, the extended family, villagemateship, and friendly relationships play a significant role in enhancing the adaptation process to urban life. Accommodating a new migrant, assisting him in looking for employment, and establishing important urban contacts is always regarded as a traditional family obligation by the majority urban dwellers. It is this system of relationships which is responsible for the presence of spatial settlements of immigrants with easily definable ethnic clusters, or the same tribal or religious background in Tanzanian urban areas. For example, while Manzese and Mwananyamala are typical Zaramo people and their places are more Islamic with more mosques than churches, the Ubungo Kisiwani, Kimara, and Msewe areas accommodate a mixture of ethnic groups from the countryside, most of whom are Christians. This situation suggests the presence of specific urban settlements with orientations based on people's cultural and ethnic backgrounds.

It is also possible to have settlements accommodating groups of people working in the same area or company, or those who belong to the same occupational categories. The best examples are Mlalakua, Msewe, Ubungo Kisiwani, and Savei as areas accommodating people who work at the University of Dar-Es-Salaam. My findings of the three settlements do not present such specialized human settlements. The areas are mixed culturally and accommodate people of diversified religious backgrounds. The peculiarity of these three areas is evident in the fact that the majority of the residents are low-income earners. Although they are mixed, people usually manage to find some common characteristics of the basis of identification with their immediate neighbors on which interaction can be initiated and friendship developed. A visitor who happens to stay in these areas for a short period of time probably would not be able to identify the heterogeneous nature of the residents. What is the reason for that?

My observations at Kipawa, Kiwalani, and Shimo la Udongo suggest three factors which, in my opinion, hold these people together to the extent that they appear as if they belong to one family. I have summarized these into ideological, social, and political factors. I will start by briefly describing the first two, and the political factor will be described in the next section.

The fact that these people essentially earn the same incomes tends to make the majority of them hold the same ideologies. Most of them are part of the poor section of the urban population. They live quite close to one another and in overcrowded conditions. There is no doubt that they share more or less the same experiences and problems. Sometimes even their attitude towards the state is similar. Because of this, they tend to consider the privileged affluent people to not be a part of their group. In reality, they know where the wealthy live and identify them by their residential areas. In Shimo la Udongo, one respondent described to me the wealthy section of the Dar-Es-Salaam City population in the following way:

> Shimo la Udongo is an area of residence for the poor people. A rich person cannot stay in this area. The rich people have their own places in Oyster Bay, Msasani, Masaki, and Upanga where they live in prestigious houses.

Such feeling is held by the majority residents of the squatter settlements. As a result of that, there tends to be quite a sense of community cooperation among the squatters.

Living in such areas has significant consequences for the image of the residents and their adjustment to the urban environment. One's self-image is determined not only by the way he thinks his peers view him, but also by his standing in the community at large. The physical surroundings of the place a person lives, his home, his neighborhood, and his community determine how he evaluates himself. When an individual lives under crowded conditions of abject poverty and squalor, and when he sees this in contrast to middle class patterns of life such as those in Oyster-Bay and Msasani, this cannot help but influence how he evaluates himself.

The second factor holding these people together may be categorized as social. There is very close interaction among the housemates and neighbors which results from houses being built close to one another. It is not easy to retain one's anonymity while sharing cooking, laundry, and sanitary facilities. The lack of private recreational space in individual living rooms or houses and the use of public services like water kiosks (where women go for water and gossip) simply adds to the close interaction among individuals. The children move freely and mix with other children, thus providing additional channels of interaction and sources of information. The children grow up in mixed residences. Because of this they learn at least to be bicultural and sometimes even bilingual. Since they have to associate with people of varying cultural backgrounds, these children begin an assimilation process that adds another cultural layer to their social or ethnic heritage.[4] One must not forget the role played by the Swahili language, which is the most common language used in the urban areas. Due to this proximity, most residents know the home places and sometimes the occupations of their neighbors. The women who are always at home as housewives sit together in verandas or outside the corridors of their doorways selling small food items. While waiting for their customers they are always busy either knitting, plaiting hair, or gossiping. In general, all these factors help to bridge the differences between the social groups within the settlements. Residents also cooperate in many situations, (such as funerals) or problems at night concerning thieves where one needs to blow a whistle and the neighbors assemble in order to provide assistance.

Some issues like those of marriage or baptism ceremonies are, in most cases, arranged and performed within family lines. There are also local brew bars (*vilabu*) which vary along tribal or ethnic lines. The best example are those for *tembo* brew for the Zaramo and Makonde people, *kindi* and *kimpumu* brew for people coming from the Mbeya region, and *kangara* and *komoni* brews for the majority of Southern Highlanders. The presence of tribal specialties in these local bars and pubs should not be seen as a perpetuation of tribal differences and mentalities among the squatters. Instead, it should be seen in terms of their ability to serve the needs of the diversified cultural backgrounds and tastes within the community.

Apart from church or other religious organizations, there are no other formal organizations existing and operating in these areas. There are very few tribal organizations or associations whose membership includes people living outside the areas. 45 respondents (14%) indicated that they were members of such associations. The associations identified were for the Kagera area (West Lake Region), one for the Pare people, and the other one for the people coming from the Njombe district in the Iringa region. These associations are highly organized in the sense that they have an elected chairman, secretary, and treasurer. The main functions of the organizations are to assist the members morally or materially in matters concerning funerals, weddings, and others. Another function, which is political and developmental in my view, concerns a situation where money is collected and sent back home to assist developmental projects like school or health center construction. This shows how some people living in urban areas are conscious of development taking place in their home areas, and would like to maintain contact with their home areas.

There are also few informal groups or organizations which have emerged as a result of similar converged interests, hobbies, and activities. For example, there are male local drinking groups. These people drink together at regular times and have set up rules, regulations, and dues. A drinking relationship among men is exceedingly important and usually takes precedence over one' marital relationship. From a psychological standpoint, drinking together is considered a bonding relationship which involves absolute mutual trust and the baring of one's soul. From the economic point of view, Lomnitz argued in 1974 that drinking together implies a mechanism of redistribution through drinks which ensures that all members remain economically equal. Finally, the social aspect is expressed by the fact that it reinforces existing social networks and extends the influence of networks in many directions since a drinking circle may contain members of several networks.[5]

Women have also their own groups whereby they perform joint economic activities on a cooperative basis. The most common activity is local beer brewing and selling. In the Shimo la Udongo area I also noticed a local banking system among some women. This money-saving system is locally known as *Mchezo wa kupeana* (the game of giving to each other) or *Upato*. Each has to contribute a fixed amount of money at the end of each month and then the total lump-sum collected is handed over to one member at the end of the month so that she can have reasonable capital to start a meaningful economic project. The money is provided to each member on a rotating basis. My observation reveals that the system operates without problems, and the selection of members is based on a very close and strong understanding among the members. These informal credit schemes are very important and are one type of survival mechanism since they assist the members by providing them with reasonable capital to establishan income-generating project.

Most of the youth tend to put themselves in various interest groups. The most popular youth interest groups are those which are concerned with football. In all of the three settlements the football fans have grouped themselves into two dominant opposing football clubs in Dar-Es-Salaam: the Young Africans (Yanga) and the Simba Sports Club. It is easy to identify which fan belongs to which club by the color of the clothes they wear. While the supporters of Yanga prefer to put on yellow and green colors, the Simba fans are always in red and white. Most of the forms of organization of the majority interest groups are rudimentary in nature and very *ad hoc* in approach. For example, the opposition between the Yanga and Simba groups becomes very pronounced and sensitive on those days when the two teams meet for a football match.

The Political Dimension

The nature of political organization of these areas is another factor which binds the residents together. In discussing the political organizations, the role of the political party, Chama Cha Mapinduzi (CCM), becomes very important. It is precisely because of what CCM does to these people that the residents of these areas tend to have a higher respect and judgement on the party.

There are no other local formal organizations for solving common problems of the squatters in these areas. The only available possibility of political organization at the community level is CCM. Politically, the settlements are organized through CCM's structure. There are several CCM branches, starting with the Ten-Cell Leadership system (*Nyumba Kumi-Kumi*) being lead by a CCM Ten-Cell leader called *Mjumbe wa Nyumba Kumi-Kumi*. The Ten-Cell Yanga-Simba system forms the smallest branch of the CCM organization called *Shina*. The chairman of Shina is both a party and a government representative. He is elected by the party members of the area, and normally there is a CCM flag hanging at his house so that he can be easily identified. From this level the political organization goes to the Ward-Level (*Kata*) where there is a CCM Ward Secretary (*Katibu Kata*) who is an employee of the party but works also as a government representative. The Shimo la Udongo area belongs to the Kurasini Ward, and Kipawa and Kiwalani belong to the Kipawa Ward. What is the implication of this kind of political organization in urban local politics?

Both the *Mjumbe* and the *Katibu Kata* work more effectively as people who have been employed by the party. In practice, this means that CCM seems to be much closer to the people than the government machinery. A normal squatter sees the *Mjumbe* and the *Katibu Kata* as his immediate sympathizers. The two leaders also have their offices in the same area where the squatters live. Most of them live together with the people, where they experience the same problems. The government machinery begins to be felt at the divisional level and finally at the city or town council level. Thus, in reality, it is CCM which is active and deals with the daily problems of the local urban community. There are several cases where the squatters band together under the umbrella of CCM for crucial issues. For example, through CCM the residents of Shimo la Udongo succeeded in requesting that the government install several public water kiosks in the area. At present it is through CCM forums that these residents are petitioning the higher levels of the government against the plans to resettle them. As the Kipawa residents argued against resettlement in 1973, it was CCM which stood behind them and helped them win.

Issues pertaining to defense and security at the urban local level are also more the responsibility of CCM than the of regular police force. The CCM's office and night patrols in these areas are guarded and carried by people's militia soldiers (*Askari wa Mgambo*). Most of the Mgambo soldiers originate from the same area. Becaues the Mgambo people know most of the thieves and culprits and the techniques which they use, security tends to be much easier to maintain. At present, most of the car owners like to park their cars at night around CCM's office because the security is highest there and sometimes it is even safer than at some of the police stations.

Thus, there is no reason why people should not support CCM more than they do the government. Most of the residents confirmed the fact that they look at CCM as the police office and political organization which will rally behind them when they have problems. This political factor, together with the already discussed social and ideological factors, are playing a great role in holding the squatter settlements' community together.

Having seen the social and political organizations of these areas at a community level, what remains at this point is to identify the kind of social networks that exist at family levels. This is the subject to which I now turn.

The Social Networks

Barnes (1954) saw a network as a social field made up of relations between people.[6] He argued that in normal cases these relations were defined by criteria underlying the social field. While Barnes saw a network as essentially unbounded, Meyer (1962) showed how certain types of migrants encapsulate themselves in a bounded network of personal relationships.[7]

In these three settlements in Dar-Es-Salaam, we find networks defined by a criteria of neighborhood, social distance, and family background within which exchanges of goods, services, ideas, and moral togetherness take place. Having already discussed the development and operation of the social relationships which are a result of proximity, I will now concentrate only on those social networks whose basis is a family background.

In Shimo la Udongo, Kipawa, and Kiwalani, all social networks based on family background are made up of both nuclear and extended families. Each of the 320 respondents (heads of defined nuclear families in most cases) indicated that they had either stayed with their relatives immediately after arriving in the city or had been hosts to the new immigrants to the city. 260 respondents (81.2%) indicated that they were still housing some of their relatives who were either students in Dar-Es-Salaam, were looking for employment, or had been employed in the city but had not yet secured their own accommodations.

In the city, unmarried migrants often live with their young brothers, sisters, or cousins, whom they sometimes help out while they try to find a job. 70% of the respondents indicated that they had been able to secure employment and accommodation through the assistance of either friends, relatives, or rural home-mates. All respondents (100%) showed that they have been able to get used to the urban life and have established broader urban contacts through the assistance of friends, home-mates, work-mates and relatives. There is a definite continuous reciprocal exchange of goods, services, and moral support within these networks.

Exchange of material things occurs normally within the nuclear family and to very close extended family members. Exchange of material goods is less frequent outside these family boundaries because most of the families in these settlements do not have enough resources to maintain a general day-by-day exchange with other large family groups. These family networks help to manage, facilitate, and simplify the gradual adaptation to urban life for new immigrants.

Economically, some family networks go to the extent of pooling their resources to help establish a joint economic project like a stall for selling tomatoes, onions, charcoal, and other items. 20 respondents (6.2%) operate such economic activities in collaboration with their family members.

The exchange of goods and materials may take the form of borrowing tools, food items life salt or sugar, or sometimes money. Some of the assistance may be in the form of labor. For example, some may give assistance in cooking when a particular family has a wedding, funeral, or several other ceremonies. In general, the most important objects of exchange in these social networks include:

1. **Information**: Especially in terms of urban survival and how to manage the urban way of life (e.g.,where to find employment and housing easily);
2. **Loans**: In the form of money, food, clothes, and other goods;

3. **Services:** Includes lodging and care of visiting relatives, looking after children for the working mothers, assistance among men in house construction, and others;
4. **Sharing of facilities:** Like toilets or bathrooms, some of which the families might have built jointly;
5. **Moral and material support:** Especially during funerals, wedding ceremonies, and several other occasions; and
6. **Training and Apprenticeship:** This sometimes includes training and establishing a relative as a competitor. For example, a shoemaker (cobbler) may take his newly-arrived relative to assist him or to teach him how to repair shoes. Then he may share earnings with him and eventually assist in making him an independent shoemaker. In Kipawa, seven carpenters told me that they learned their skills through this system, and that at present each of them was working with at least one or two trainees to whom they are related.[8]

Sometimes the relations of exchange may go beyond family ties. For example, a married woman would feel free to ask for financial assistance from a close friend of her husband (*shemeji*), especially if the husband is not around.

In fact, the mode of exchange and the things which are exchanged provide important evidence (in support of our argument) about the way the urban poor struggle to survive. This has been called "Ideology of Assistance" by other sociologists (Lomnitz 1974). This ideology is dominant in urban areas in Tanzania, especially where people are living together under conditions of extreme poverty and overcrowding. It is this ideology which works as reinforcing mechanism of the exchange relationships. A family member may sell his or her labor as a worker or servant on the urban labor market, yet it is the ideology of assistance among relatives or friends and neighbors which ensures his survival during frequent and lengthy periods of joblessness. Through either being assisted or sharing the intermittent resources available from friends or family, the sharing group may successfully survive, whereas individually each of them would certainly fail. Thus, these social networks are sometimes economic structures which maximize security and their success spells survival for the majority section of the urban population.

Maintaining rural contacts and relationships is also important for the urban residents. Findings from Shimo la Udongo, Kipawa, and Kiwalani confirm that such relationships continue to exist. 92% of the respondents indicated that they still maintained contacts with their friends and relatives from their home areas in the countryside. The contacts are maintained with regular visits to their home areas during which they carry along with them some presents like clothes, sugar, and salt for their rural relatives. Some of them assist their relatives financially. 78% of the respondents provide such assistance. Fortunately, the visits are reciprocal in the sense that relatives from the countryside also visit their colleagues in town and get food and accommodation from their hosts in the urban areas. The visitors coming from the rural areas may carry food items with them like bananas, maize, flour, beans, dried vegetables, and others which they think are not easily found in urban areas. Sometimes during food shortages, the urban residents send some to the countryside to assist their relatives in agricultural production, and go to collect part of the produce during the harvesting periods. In practice, this is common among the urban residents who originate from places which are quite close to Dar-Es-Salaam where transport is available, easy, and cheap.

The strength of such exchanges between rural relatives depends very much on the nature of the relationship with those countryside relatives. Thus, such contacts may continue as long as very close relatives of the nuclear or extended family are still either alive or still live there. This is confirmed by one respondent who presented his reasons for having stopped his previous contacts with the rural relatives as follows:

> We have never been to our home village since the past seven years when we attended the funeral of our mother. This is because father married another woman, and we do not get along with our stepmother. Sometimes our father visits us. But our stepmother has never paid us a visit.

Another respondent argued,

> Both of my parents died a long time ago. All my brothers and sisters are no longer living in our home village. Two of my sisters who are married live with their husbands in towns. One of them is in Tanga and the other one in Arusha. My brother lives and works in Mbeya. In fact, I sometimes visit them there, and they also visit us here. Why should I then go to my home village? Whom will I visit? After all, where will I sleep, eat and . . . ?

This means that rural-urban contacts operate best in a situation where there are very strong family ties still existing in the rural areas. Proximity, need, and purpose sometimes determine the mode of operation of these contacts, what transpires in between, and more likely, the frequency of these contacts. These contacts are strong and can be experienced in several urban places in Tanzania. Such contacts, I would argue, help to stabilize most of the urban residents directly or indirectly and are part of the urban-rural dynamics.

At the outset of this chapter, I stated that its objective was to lay bare the facts of life and physical characteristics of squatter settlements in Tanzania. The basic purpose was to challenge the official so-called bureaucratic view on squatters and their settlements.

The empirical evidence derived from an in-depth study of the three settlements has revealed and confirmed the opposite. The settlements reflect the urban conditions of abject poverty and squalor. They are the most disadvantaged in terms of all urban infrastructure and service facilities. From medical care facilities, roads, water, street lights, and other social facilities like community halls, etc. I label these residents the "forgotten (by the state) section of the urban population".

Although the physical environment of these areas is appalling, the squatter community in general is a viable one. It does not display the social pathological characteristics often held by bureaucrats and attributed to them. The ideology of assistance, social dimension, and organization plays an important role in easing the adjustment process towards urban life. The social organization of the squatters may be described as a collection of family, ethnic, and political networks which assemble and disband through a dynamic process. The official community operates under CCM structures. This, together with other factors, plays an important role in keeping the squatters together. Clearly with the present introduction of multi-party politics, there are bound to be changes in the nature of political organization. More studies are required in order to see the extent to which these changes may affect political organization at squatter settlement level.

The physical conditions of these settlements, the problems which they face, and the way they surmount them affects the squatters' image of themselves, how they evaluate themselves, and the image they feel the outside world has of them.

The solutions to the problems of these settlements have to take into consideration this psychological dimension. The demolition of squatter's housing units even with the intention of providing them with better conditions may worsen the psychological stress of the squatters. It may also damage the already existing family relationships, the neighborhood, and the integration which, in fact, allows for self-regulation of behavior within the community. Putting great emphasis on gradual house improvements would seem to me as the best possible solution.

This approach would convey a message to the residents that the government does not judge the worth of people by the conditions in which they are forced to live. Instead of destroying them along with their dwellings, they should understand that they have problems which they need help in solving.

This may help the squatters to be convinced that the outsiders are prepared to assist them. If the social organization already existing in the squatter settlements is utilized, self-help projects whereby the residents help to improve their own conditions could be inaugurated. In case this should happen, the advantages are bound to be more than physical. And the squatters themselves may begin to feel that they are able to control the conditions under which they live, and can influence their fate in society.

5
The Crisis in Urban Civic and Social Service Facilities and Urban Poverty

Introduction

Several facts have now been established concerning the nature of the Tanzanian economy at present and the essence and forms of the urbanization process in the introduction and previous chapters. Two facts are apparent. First, the Tanzanian economy is in crisis. Second, as if the economic problems were not enough, Tanzania, since independence, has been faced with the problem of rapid urban population growth which its urban authorities are unable to cope with. The present nationwide economic crisis, rather than solving this particular problem, has accelerated it. The most pressing questions at present are, "What has actually happened to the urban areas?" and "What has been the impact of this crisis in the provision of civic and other social service facilities in the urban areas?"

This chapter examines the problems that urban residents experience in terms of provision of social services. The argument here is that the civic life of urban areas depends much on the availability of necessary social services like health facilities, education, recreation, and physical urban infrastructure like water, electricity, communication, an efficient urban transport system, sanitation, and drainage. That is why a city almost cannot exist without the presence of these services. The nature of these facilities is examined in urban areas in general, with a lot of concrete examples drawn from the metropolis Dar-Es-Salaam in particular. Although most of the data presented here may only appear descriptive, comparing it to the rate of urban population growth and the necessity of these facilities and services exposes the critical nature of the urban crisis in Tanzania.

Due to the economic crisis, urban areas in Tanzania have not experienced positive development. Most of them are in a state of chaos and decay. Their problems have multiplied geometrically during the last two decades. The majority of the urban population has difficulties in accessing clean water, adequate shelter, and other vital services like hospitals, employment, and efficient urban transportation. One who has ever lived in Dar-Es-Salaam would be familiar with the completely overcrowded and infrequent Usafiri Dar-Es-Salaam (UDA) and "Dalla-Dalla" buses bulging with chickens, bags of *mchicha* (spinach), *mihogo* (cassava), and *mapapai* (pawpaws), and commuters from the suburban areas around Dar-Es-Salaam. One would also be familiar with frequent water cuts which sometimes leave areas dry for more than a week, frequent electricity blackouts, telephones which maintain an erie silence, inadequate parking spaces, overflowing sewage, lack of traffic regulation, hospitals without medicine (but with fly-infested garbage), pick-pocketing, and armed robbery.

This does not mean that Tanzanian cities suffer from a lack of developmental efforts, planning, or management initiatives. As already demonstrated in the previous chapters, luxurious buildings have been built and are being built. Airports have been expanded and multi-story houses are being built, especially in Kariakoo in Dar-Es-Salaam. Sophisticated and very luxurious hotels continue to be built. The Sheraton Hotel conglomerate has also found a home in Tanzania. At the same time, shanty housing which reflects conditions of abject poverty and squalor are also there and are increasing. The number of luxurious air-conditioned saloon cars is going up, yet the number of beggars and disabled people in the streets of Dar-Es-Salaam is increasing as well. Official as well as unofficial "illegal income activities" like corruption, prostitution, hoarding, and black-marketing are competing with each other and have increased very rapidly during the last few years. All these issues and activities which reflect the coexistence of wealth and poverty are just two sides of the same coin.

The Nature of Urban Civic Facilities and Services

I have divided these facilities into two main groups. First are those which provide *social services* like health, education, and recreation centers. Second are those which are part of the *urban physical infrastructure* like electricity, water supply, sanitation and drainage, the urban transportation systems.

The Social Service Facilities

Health

The quest for the provision of a good and adequate health care system in Tanzania has been overdue for a long time. In urban areas the main health problems result primarily from diseases associated with infection. Most of them are water-borne diseases which multiply daily due to poor environmental sanitation. Emphasis still lies on curative hospital services rather than preventive measures. Critical problems associated with the provision of health care in Tanzania at the moment include shortage of health and medical staff, medical equipment, and medicine.

In 1978, there were only 275 dispensaries in all urban areas of Tanzania. Out of these, 81 were owned by government, 21 by voluntary agencies, 89 by public parastatal organizations, and 84 were owned privately.[1] During this period the service ratio was 21,000 people which was much below the official required national standard of one dispensary for every 8,000 people.[2] In 1982, there were only 24 health centers in urban areas. Given the total urban population of approximately 2,957,674 at that time, the service ratio was 123,236 people for one health center which was far below the national standards of one health center for every 50,000 people.[3] During the same period there were 67 hospitals with 11,366 hospital beds.[4]

The number of these facilities has remained constant during urban population growth. These facilities do not provide their services to every urban dweller. They are segregative in the following sense. Those which are owned by the Agha-Khan organization are private and are essentially providing services to Asians, Europeans, and to very few affluent Africans. Those which are owned by public parastatal organizations provide free services but serve only their employees and their families. The unemployed people have to depend solely on public owned health facilities which provide free medical services. But these services are extremely poor and they often lack medicine. In the case of Dar-Es-Salaam, the urban poor have to depend on the services provided by the Muhimbili Medical Center, Mwananyamala, Ilala, Temeke, and Magomeni health centers. Given the present population of Dar-Es-Salaam, these health centers are very inadequate and complaints about their poor services are common.

While the above is the only alternative available to the urban poor, there are government directives and circulars which allow some employees, especially senior ones, to get treatment from the expensive privately-owned hospitals. The poor, the unemployed who are the majority, experience critical health problems in urban areas due to the nature of the environment in which they live. However, they are the ones who have access to poor medical and health care. The affluent, who in general experience less health problems, have access to all types of medical and health care facilities at the government's expense. Others are sometimes sent abroad for treatment.

Apart from the environmental conditions which are appalling in most of the government-owned hospitals, corruption is also rampant. Good treatment depends on technical know-how. The moral code of conduct of most of the doctors has been eroded by inflation and the high cost of living. As a result, corruption has deeply entrenched itself. The situation is worse to the extent that the Director General of the Muhimbili Medical Center in Dar-Es-Salaam, while appealing to the government to review the law governing private medical practice, said on September 21, 1986 that

> One of the side effects of the law was the switching of the doctors into rearing chickens, pigs or excessive drinking during spare time. (Sunday News Paper, 9/21/86).

On October 21, 1987, the government reviewed the price structure of medical treatment rendered by private hospitals. Some of the reviewed charges announced were as follows:

> In-patient (full board) a day, Tshs. 600/- for adults, 300/- for children. Tumors excision-simple tumors - Tshs. 700/-, embryonic origin - 1,700. Treatment of fractures-arm, leg, femur, spinal and pelvic from Tshs. 1,800 to 2,300. Operation of Kidney, ureter bladder and prostate

Tshs. 4,000/- Abdominal operations between Tshs. 800 and 4,000/-, Eye treatment range from Tshs. 500/- to 4,000/- while for the ear and nose are between Tshs. 500 to 2,000/- Fees for specialized laboratory tests range between Tshs. 300 and 1,200/-. (*Daily News Paper*, 10/21/87)

Looking at the above fees in private hospitals, it is obvious that such charges are far beyond the reach of the majority of urban dwellers. Thus, if even the government allows more private health centers to be opened, it will still remain to be seen whether such a move may be of great assistance to the suffering majority. These prices have been reviewed recently and the government has also introduced user charges in public health facilities.

A study on health and infant-feeding practices in Dar-Es-Salaam conducted in 1979 and 1980 found that, when respondents were classified into two groups, there was a correlation between income and mortality rates of children under five. The lowest income group, which included those households earning up to 799 Tanzanian shillings per month, had a mortality rate of 110 per thousand, while those earning 2,000 to 3,199 shillings and those earning 3,200 shillings and over a month had mortality rates of 64 and 13 per thousand respectively. (Kahama, et al: 1972). The 1991/1992 Demographic and Health Survey report shows that the trend has not reversed.

Birth weight is another health and development indicator that must receive attention because it has a major impact on infant mortality and it is also closely linked to the mother's general condition. The occurrence of low weight reflects physical and psychological stress on the mother, which may be caused by a variety of social, economic and health factors, especially malnutrition and unregulated fertility (Bantje, 1980). The Dar-Es-Salaam study cited above showed that the average birth weight did indeed progress with income. 3.06 kilograms was the average weight for the poorest group while 3.26 kilograms was the average weight for the wealthiest. (Kahama, et al:1972).

Education

Although Tanzania has worked vigorously to achieve equality of opportunity in education, certain inequalities can still be observed between urban and rural, men and women, and between different classes. In 1978 there were a total of 383,483 school age children (age 7-13) living in all urban areas of Tanzania out of which 122,436 children or

31.9% were not attending school due to lack of space.[5] The rapid rise of the urban population has not gone hand in hand with an increase in the number of schools. The result of this is overcrowding in classrooms, lack of teachers, shortage of desks, textbooks, exercise books, and other equipment.

For example, while the Ministry of Education recommends a total of 14 streams each with 45 pupils for a primary school, making the minimum size 630 pupils, Mapambano Primary School in Mbeya had an average of 102 pupils per classroom.[6] In Dar-Es-Salaam more than 50% of all primary schools have a total of more than 1,000 pupils each (Dar-Es-Salaam City Council). Information quoted from the Sunday News Paper with the title, "*Shortage of Desks*", reveals the extent of the problem.

> Shortage of desks continue to hit most primary schools in Dar-Es-Salaam, forcing pupils to sit on the floor during the lessons. The city has 136,593 pupils but at the same time a shortage of 50,519 desks. During a visit to primary schools in Kinondoni, Temeke and Ilala districts, the Deputy Minister for Education Ndugu Nalaila Kyula, urged parents to help the Government in providing desks. He said when talking to a committee comprising representatives from Mabatini, Buguruni and Kinondoni primary schools that the Government cannot solve the desk problem single-handedly. (Sunday News Paper, 3/23/86)

In essays which I administered to 7th grade pupils in 16 primary schools in Dar-Es-Salaam, this particular problem of lack of desks was obvious. 422 pupils out of 605 (69.8%) stated that their schools did not have enough desks. Most of them indicated that they have been sitting on the floor for a period of five out of their seven years of primary education. They also mentioned a lack of books, teachers, classrooms, and few opportunities for further education, i.e. secondary school places, as critical problems which confronted them.

Although this is the situation which faces most of the schools in urban areas, there are still schools which cater to the children of the wealthy. Such schools are available in every town. They are well-equipped with good and modern facilities, and in most cases have no problem of shortage of good and qualified teachers. Just to mention a few, such schools include Oyster-Bay, Bunge, Muhimbili, Forodhani University Hill (Mlimani), and International Primary Schools in Dar-Es-Salaam. Information from the Ministry of Education shows that schools of this kind have always been leading in terms of the number of pupils selected for secondary education.

In reality, these schools usually accommodate the children of the affluent social groups. Because of that they are favored by the system in each and every respect. Most of these children face problems neither at school nor at their homes. Thus, the atmosphere both at home and at school is conducive to learning. The parents of these pupils can afford to give their children books and other necessary learning aids. Some have easy access to video tapes and other learning equipment and their parents can afford the cost of extra tuition.

The children of the urban poor do not have these privileges. They are the sons and daughters of the urban hunters and gatherers, and like their parents suffer the maladies of urban crisis and poverty. The children of the poor lack clean water, housing, adequate drainage, well-equipped schools, efficient and cheap transport and have no chance to join private schools because their parents cannot pay tuition. Some of these problems are the main causes of ill health, which in turn reduces the ability to learn, employment, job security, and hence misery is perpetuated.

A study by Puja (1981) on the effects of socio-economic background of Dar-Es-Salaam City 7th grade pupils on their school performance revealed that pupils whose parents or guardians were highly educated tended to score highly in both English and Mathematics, while children whose parents or guardians were at least literate tended to score more highly in Mathematics than in English. Children whose parents or guardians were illiterate tended to receive poor grades in both English and Mathematics. Puja noted also that pupils who received private tutoring after school hours were likely to score higher in both subjects than those who did not. But attending a private institution depended much on the socio-economic position of the parents or guardians (Puja 1981: iv).

Most secondary schools and other institutions of higher learning are urban based but serve the whole national population. Dar-Es-Salaam and Morogoro each have a University. In brief, the urban areas in Tanzania have a monopoly on educational institutions and they are indeed centers of elitism. The concentration of these educational facilities in urban areas is a legacy of colonial policy, and is indicative of the dispatch and design with which the colonialists proceeded to transform the social order in Tanzania as a whole.

There are also private secondary schools. These schools charge high fees which the urban poor can not afford. The officially accepted fees as of 1993 were not below 30,000 Tanzanian shillings for day schools and 40,000 for boarding ones. With such trends it is difficult to imagine the kind of education opportunities the urban poor can manage to afford.

Socio-economic biases at higher levels of education also exist and have been difficult to eradicate completely, partly because of the superior early preparation and higher aspirations that are likely to characterize students from middle-class and upper-class homes. Furthermore, as Kahama, (et al, 1981) has argued, there is some evidence that high-ranking individuals can successfully circumvent the system to assure educational opportunities for their children. It has been estimated that in certain years up to one-third of Form III students were transferred from private into public secondary schools, with public headmasters and mistresses being obliged to make space for these students because of their parents' influence (Kahama, et al 1981: 186-87).

In summary, as far as education facilities in urban areas are concerned, it can be argued that the quality of educational institutions has increased since independence, but has not been consistent with the increase in the urban population. Hence facilities are inadequate. Lack of books, desks, and classrooms, and the rampant problems of overcrowded classes with some underqualified teachers means that the quality of education they offer has definitely declined. This situation raises more questions than it answers. What is the use of having a school without books and teachers? What is important, *quantity* or *quality*?

Recreation

Recreation centers are either non-existent or there are very few in several urban areas. Where they are to be seen, they include movie theaters, social dancing halls, discos, and others. In Dar-Es-Salaam most of these centers are located around the Central Business District and therefore serve very few people indeed. Organized sports and cultural activities are very popular in Tanzania but the problem is that only a few places or areas have been provided by the government in order to facilitate these activities. Football grounds and leisure parks are rare. There are few open spaces in low density areas which can be used for sports activities. In some towns, due to the crisis in urban planning, lack of housing plots, some of these open spaces and some official playgrounds have been invaded by people and have been developed as residential areas against the planning laws and regulations. There are also recreation centers for the affluent groups like the Gymkhana, Railway, Yatch, and Golf clubs in Dar-Es-Salaam. These clubs have entrance fees and therefore cater to a limited section of the urban population. There are no play centers for children in the high density areas or in squatter areas. Children of the urban poor have to play on streets flooded by open sewage, a situation which makes them vulnerable to health risks and car accidents.

A local brew-selling pub in a squatter settlement in Dar-Es-Salaam

Physical Infrastructure

Electricity and Water Supply

Most of the urban areas are served by either hydro or thermal electric power systems. Dar-Es-Salaam, Morogoro, Arusha, Iringa, Dodoma, and Moshi are served by the national grid system which provides 84% of the total power generated.[7] This does not mean that each urban citizen uses this power. With the total urban population of 2,257,921 in 1978, the number of electricity consumers was only 122,710 housing units in 1980, and this increased to only 154,724 in 1984 (26%).[8] In Dar-Es-Salaam alone the number of consumers has increased from 63,584 in 1980 to 74,981 or 18% in 1984 (in terms of housing units).[9] The majority of the urban dwellers still do not have access to electricity. Areas which are affected most are the planned high density residential areas, as well as the unplanned squatter areas which accommodate more than 70% of the urban population. The power tariffs are indeed high and beyond the ability of low income earners.

The wisdom of TANESCO forced them to accept in 1986 the recommendations of the World Bank and the Meta System Company of the U.S.A. which are actually far beyond the true ability of the majority urban dwellers. The tariffs were raised by more than 50%. Most of the people cannot afford paying, and the result is that people shy away from applying for official electricity connections, but still use it through illegal hook-ups.

At the same time, the procedures for one to get private power connection are long, cumbersome, and expensive. Kickbacks and bribes are necessary in order to speed up the bureaucratic process. Information collected from TANESCO headquarters in Dar-Es-Salaam shows that a customer has to fulfill the following conditions in order to get private power connection:

1. A payment of 30 Tanzanian shillings as fee for filling the agreement forms;
2. Payment of a deposit for the materials to be used in connecting the power to one's house, i.e. poles, wires, insulators and transmission lines;
3. One's house must be insured and must be electric power worth;
4. Payment of the cost for building the service line from a nearby transmission line to the site in question; and
5. The electrical wiring in the house has to be inspected by TANESCO officers and approved by them, after which a customer has to fill out forms for meter application.

The price estimated for one pole is 3,000 shillings (1987 prices). The meter deposit is 1,500 shillings and the price for other items depends on the size of the house and the mode of power wiring. These rates have increased tremendously recently. For example, the down payment alone was 35,000 shillings in 1993.

Even after having succeeded in getting the connection, problems persist. For example, there are false meter readings in favor of TANESCO or customers. Due to corruption, the latter is always the case. Due to poor town or city plan design or lack of it, coupled with few TANESCO meter readers who lack official transportation, it has proved impossible for TANESCO to pursue a very precise meter-reading exercise every month. Hence, most of the power bills, especially in Dar-Es-Salaam, are approximated. Other power problems are fluctuation of the power supply and unreliability.

A similar problematic situation concerns the supply of water. Like the other civic facilities, the water supply system in Tanzania only serves a minor section of the urban population well. In Dar-Es-Salaam, water stoppage is the order of the day. The city is being supplied by two main water pipes and sources, namely the "Upper" and "Lower" Ruvu river. The two sources are old and dilapidated and were built at a time when the population for Dar-Es-Salaam was not more than 200,000 people. Since then the population has multiplied at least ten times, and the area of the city has widened ernomously. But the two water sources have remained undeveloped. The pipes are old, full of rust, and burst frequently.

Procedures for application for water connection are cumbersome, long, and costly. These procedures, together with the high water rates, have forced some people to connect their water pipes to the main water pipes illegally. At present, illegal water connections are a critical problem facing NUWA to the extent that NUWA has recently declared a war against such people (*Daily News Paper* /2/13/88).

Other problems include faulty meter readings and old and torn out meters. Corruptive actions described in the discussion of TANESCO are also common in NUWA. Even if everything were alright, the shortage of new water pipes for those who would like to have private water connections is another menacing problem. The message quoted from the Sunday News Paper of July 3, 1988 helps one to understand how critical the shortage of new pipes is in Tanzania.

> More than 105 underground water pipes valued at Tshs. 525,000 were stolen at Changanyikeni near the University of Dar-Es-Salaam this week leaving many parts of Dar-Es-Salaam without water. Subsequently a water pumping machine at Mlandizi broke down leaving even more residents without water. (Sunday News Paper, 3/7/88).

Therefore, due to the scarcity of pipes, thieves are unearthing even pipes already laid underground in order to resell them.

Since independence, the public water supply has increased tremendously in Dar-Es-Salaam. Private water connections have increased from 17,669 customers in 1968 to 57,410 in 1984.[10] Yet one who lives in Dar-Es-Salaam would agree that the proportion of population served has not increased significantly. More than 85% continue to be served by public water kiosks and stand pipes.[11] These facilities are scarce and some do not operate. Combined with low water pressure, this results in long water lines which can be easily spotted out in Dar-Es-Salaam at any time.

This problem of water, as I will demonstrate below, has also lead to poor sanitation of the city of Dar-Es-Salaam.

Sanitation and Drainage

It is at the level of sanitation and drainage that the urban crisis can openly be seen. Most of the urban areas are poorly serviced and organized. Dar-Es-Salaam central sewerage and drainage system was designed and built during colonialism. Very few houses (10%) are connected to this system. Through this system, the waste water and runoff is discharged into the Indian Ocean through the main pipe in the Ocean Road Street, which is an environmental disaster and health hazard.

Of the twenty regional headquarters (towns), only eight have central sewerage which serves less than 10% of the population of each respective town.[12] All the other towns are served by either septic tanks, soak away systems or pit-latrines. In Dar-Es-Salaam only 10% of the population in the low and medium density areas is served by septic tanks and soak away systems. The remaining 80% use pit-latrines and unspecified sanitation systems.[13] Experience shows that the problems associated with these systems are many.

The urban centers with central sewage system treat their sewage in waste stabilization ponds and collection dumping stations. Most of these systems are old and clogged with other waste materials and therefore do not work.

The Dar-Es-Salaam Sewage and Sanitation Master Plan of 1980 revealed that only the central sewage system of Dar-Es-Salaam was functioning. The failure of the other systems has been due to mechanical breakdowns, lack of preventive maintenance, and inadequate supply of spare parts.[14] The result of this has been the discharge of overflowing sewage on the streets creating a very pungent smell and public health risk. A study in Moshi town revealed that the waste stabilization pond located northeast of Pasua has been the source of cholera and other water-borne diseases for residents who are using river Rau water for domestic purposes.

Complaints about lack of sanitation are common in Dar-Es-Salaam. The following quote from *Daily News Paper* shows that the problem is long overdue.

Help to Keep the City Clean
A lot has been said about cleanliness of the city but very little has been done by the City Fathers to keep it clean. It is a common thing to see pieces of paper, bus-tickets, chewing gum wraps and other litter scattered all over especially at bus stands. (*Daily News Paper*, 1/2/87)

Dar-Es-Salaam City has been without public toilet facilities for the past 10 years. There were still no public toilets even at the period when this study was carried out (1987 to 1988). This is confirmed by the following message which appeared in the *Daily News Paper*.

Rehabilitation of City Toilets Starts
The Dar-Es-Salaam City Council (DCC) has started rehabilitating 15 out of 87 public toilets in a bid to keep the city clean, the City Medical Officer Dr. Hamisi Mponezya, has said. The toilets have been out of use for more than a decade now. In an interview, one city resident said that the toilets were closed in 1974. (*Daily News Paper*, 7/1/88).

The equipment which could enhance the cleanliness of urban areas is lacking. This includes cesspit collectors or emptiers, refuse collectors, tractors, harrows, grass cutters, and others.

In 1983 to 1984, Dar-Es-Salaam City produced six million liters of waste water daily. During this period, due to lack of spare parts and breakdowns, Dar-Es-Salaam had only nine cesspit emptiers out of a total of 32 which were operational. Hence, the nine emptiers managed to remove only 480,000 liters (8%) of sewage daily.[15] During the same period, the city produced 900 tons of solid waste and this was growing at 11% per year. However, only ten refuse collectors out of 45 were operational, and these managed to collect only 100 tons per day.[16] The crucial question at this juncture is, what happens to the uncollected waste? The presence of piles of uncollected garbage and the presence of overflowing sewage and waste water in the streets of Dar-Es-Salaam explain the fate of the uncollected waste products. In 1985 and 1986, the city generated 1,200 tons of solid waste daily. Dar-Es-Salaam needed 120 vehicles to remove all this garbage. By then, the city had only 12 vehicles on the road.[17] In order to be able to remove all the waste water, the city needed 150 emptiers during this period.[18] However, until March of 1988, Dar-Es-Salaam had a total of only 20 cesspit emptier trucks operating on zone basis. Specifically, there were ten trucks in Kinondoni District, five in Ilala, four in Temeke and one at the state House.[19] The total number of refuse collector trucks during the same period of time was only 24. 15 operated in Ilala, six in Kinondoni and three in Temeke.[20] The number of these vehicles is indeed far below the required minimum. The city's population has increased, so of course more solid waste as well as sewage water waste have also increased. Lack of sufficient refuse collectors as well as cesspit emptiers means that a lot of garbage is left uncollected, and streets flood with overflowing sewage. If the situation is so bad in affluent areas like Samora Avenue, one can just imagine what the situation looks like in the forgotten, unplanned squatter settlements.

Cesspit emptying done by the City Council is a chargeable service. It costs 1,100 Tanzanian shillings for a commercial premise and 600 shillings for a private residential house.[21] The affluent social groups living in Oyster Bay whose houses are connected to the central sewage system pay nothing. But the poor have to pay in order to let their pit-latrines be emptied by the City Council lorries. The poor pay for this service more than the rich. The logic and rationale behind this is hard to understand. The scarcity of these vehicles means that one has to be corrupt in order to have his overflooding latrine emptied. Hence, in practice, the amount paid for these services ranges between 1,500 Tanzanian shillings to 3,000.[22] The poor cannot afford this amount of money.

The other towns face more or less a similar situation. This is evidenced by the *Daily News Paper* of 1/9/87:

Filth Threatens Shinyanga Town
Residents of Shinyanga town face health problems resulting from filth unless immediate steps are taken to provide the town with enough refuse trucks and cesspit emptiers. The Shinyanga Health Officer, Ndugu Vedastus Mushumbusi said in Dar-Es-Salaam yesterday that there were a lot of garbage in the town. The Town Council has one garbage truck which cannot meet the demand. The vehicle can only collect 25% of the 60 tons of refuse daily...He also said that Shinyanga with a population of 100,000 was also being served with one unreliable cesspit emptier which can only meet 30% of the town requirements. (*Daily News Paper*, 1/9/87)

Tanga Municipality, which required at least 19 refuse collectors, had only four vehicles on the road in 1985 which collected only 25% of the daily accumulated garbage.[23] Mbeya town had only five vehicles which collected 45% of the daily accumulated 120 tons of garbage, and Arusha Municipality had a functional fleet of three such vehicles out of a total requirement of 15 vehicles.[24]

The poor urban sanitation services have had a very adverse impact on the urban conditions in general. All urban dwellers are being affected by this situation but not in the same way. Thus Ntukula (1985) in her study on the problems confronting squatters has argued that:

> Different types of disposing faeces affects differently the transmission of communicable disease. For those who were abandoning the overflooded latrines and made new ones, the rate of transmitting communicable disease was smaller compared to others. The rate of infection is higher for those who emptied their latrines by use of buckets. The findings revealed that 96% of them had infectious disease against only 4% who had none. The highest rate of transmitting disease was for those who continued to use their overflooded latrines.[25]

The communicable diseases identified by Ntukula were dysentry worm infection, typhoid, cholera, diarrhea, malaria and tuberculosis. Thus, although the poor quality of sanitation affects all, it is, however, the majority urban poor who suffer most. Indeed, the diseases which most of them suffer have to be seen within the social context of their class position.

Bank, Postal, and Telephone Services

In most of the urban areas in Tanzania, bank services are far from sufficient. Dar-Es-Salaam has very few bank branches. This is including the Bank of Tanzania (BOT), Tanzania Housing Bank (THB), Cooperative and Rural Development Bank (CRDB) and the Post Savings Bank. The most common bank is the National Bank of Commerce (NBC) in Tanzania. Apart from the fact that banks are few, inefficiency is common and lines and overcrowding are common. The customers are so numerous that NBC does not allow the employers to remit the salaries of the low income earners (minimum wage) through the bank.

The whole city of Dar-Es-Salaam has only one big post office, and few other post office branches. Letters are distributed through the post box rental system. In a situation like in Tanzania where no streets exist and towns are poorly planned and managed, it is not possible to use the common system of most European countries of distributing letters in the letter boxes in respective houses. Most of these post office boxes are allocated to government offices, public institutions, public and private organizations and to very few individuals who happened to have influence and the ability to pay the rental fee. Those who do not have private letter boxes have to use their employer's if they are employed. The unemployed have to use the care of (C/O) system. That is via the addresses of their relatives or friends or the nearest CCM offices. Data collected from the Tanzanian Posts and Telecommunication Company Limited revealed the critical shortage of these letter boxes. The number of applicants for private rental letter boxes has increased from 7,456 in 1977 to 34,528 in 1985, an increase of 363%.

Inflation and high cost of living have eroded the moral code of conduct of some of the post office workers. Pilferage of packets, opened letters, posted money being stolen, and other related problems are common. These complaints are not new in Tanzania.

The telephone service system is in a state of chaos, distrust, and disorder. The more Tanzania tries to modernize the telephone exchange service system the more it is a disaster. Apart from the fact that such services are few and inadequate, their functionality leaves much to be desired. Telephones maintain an erie sound when one dials. Communication interference within the line is also common.

The public telephone booths which are functioning are almost nonexistent in urban areas. In 1978, Dar-Es-Salaam, with a population of 769,445, had only 34 public telephone booths. By 1988 the number of booths was the same with only two functioning.

Urban Transportation System

In Tanzania problems associated with urban transport are multiple and varied. They include

1) Lack of sufficient and adequate transportation facilities like buses and others;
2) Poor road conditions (Most of the roads are worn out and are full of pot-holes.); and
3) Poorly designed, narrow urban roads. There are no adequate car parking places, pedestrian ways, or ways for

cyclists. There is a lack of adequate traffic control equipment like traffic lights, and those which are there operate well only occasionally.

In Tanzania the condition of all urban roads leaves much to be desired. The tarmac roads are very old, and have not received adequate maintenance for decades. The roads are full of potholes. Likewise, the murram and earth roads are not good either. They have potholes and gulleys cutting across them, they are muddy and slippery during the rainy season, and remain almost unpassable.[26] Many open drains for storm water drainage have been blocked by refuse and garbage because urban residents have turned them into dumping grounds for garbage which the urban authorities fail to collect. Information quoted from the *Daily News Paper* provide a clear picture of how the roads look in Dar-Es-Salaam. (The picture has been omitted).

> If you have the nose for money, there is no reason why you should go hungry in Dar-Es-Salaam. Just pray for heavens to open up with a heavy down-pour filling the many pot-holes and depressions on the city`s roads, and suddenly you have a job. Ferrying people across the ponds at a price. These three youths (two at the back and one in the front) earn their living by taking those smart ladies and gentlemen across a water pond at Chang`ombe in Dar-Es-Salaam. The services seem indispensable to those who do not like the bother of removing shoes and socks, walk through the water to the other side, dry their feet and put back the footwear... Why bother? With Tshs. 2/- during low hours and Tshs. 5/- during peak hours you can be home dry. There are two such 'Mikokoteni' (hand carts) each with a six person capacity. (*Daily News Paper*, 12/30/87)

Thus, in Dar-Es-Salaam the jobless youths exploit the bad conditions of the roads in the city by identifying their own strategy of survival.

Bad, narrow roads, lack of parking places, poor or lack of basic traffic control devices, and the presence of mixed traffic roadways have been the main causes of urban road accidents in the main urban areas in Tanzania. If this looks like chaos to a person who is not used to such a mixed traffic system, it is precisely the result of planners favoring automobiles and neglecting people. The Tanzanian urban pedestrians are perhaps the most neglected and ignored by transportation planners to date. The inadequacy of pedestrian paths, bridges, or tunnels at points of intersection between roads has meant that almost half of the accident deaths in Dar-Es-Salaam are pedestrians (Traffic Office DSM). The recent Mbeya Master Plan has revealed that an average of 205 accidents, most of which cause serious injuries and deaths every year.[27] The annual average reported traffic accidents for Dar-Es-Salaam stands at 3,729, of which 155 are fatal.[28] Alcoholism and careless drivers who recite prayers while driving at high speeds through a red traffic light also contribute to these accidents. Corruption also plays a role in worsening these problems. Driving licences are available to anyone who has the ability to bribe. Competence in driving is no longer the determining factor. When careless drivers are apprehended, they manage to find their freedom through bribes and kickbacks.

Usafiri Dar-Es-Salaam (UDA): Dar-Es-Salaam Transport Company

In 1985, UDA owned 98 buses with a capacity of carrying 90 passengers each, 58 articulated Ikarus buses with a capacity of 150 passengers each, and 39 mini buses which could carry 31 passengers each. Thus UDA had a total of 191 buses.[29] During this period, the population of Dar-Es-Salaam was about 1.4 million people.[30] The services provided by UDA have been far from adequate. In March of 1988, UDA had a total fleet of 201 buses of which only 50% were on the road.[31] A quick calculation provided by National Transport Corporation (NTC) indicates that a total of 750 90-seater standard buses is required in order to provide adequate transportation in Dar-Es-Salaam whose population is approximately 2 million people.[32]

Table 5.1
Modes of Urban Passenger Transportation in Dar-Es-Salaam

MODE OF TRANSPORT	1965	1968	1979	1982	1985
Walking on Foot	66.9	67.8	52.0	31.0	26.0
Private Car	02.2	03.5	16.0	07.3	07.0
Public Bus	17.7	20.2	26.0	60.0	66.0
Bicycles or Motorcycles	13.2	08.5	06.0	01.4	01.0
TOTAL	100.0	100.0	100.0	100.0	100.0

Source: Research and Planning - MAWASILIANO. The Rationalization of Urban Passenger Transportation in Dar-Es-Salaam, Ministry of Communications and Transport, United Republic of Tanzania, Dar-Es-Salaam, April 1984.

Although there are other modes of transportation in Dar-Es-Salaam, Table 5.1 shows that public bus transportation accounts for more than 60% of urban passenger transportation in Dar-Es-Salaam.

Constant breakdowns and lack of spare parts due to lack of foreign currency are the major problems which have been confronting UDA for decades. While UDA had 374 buses in 1975, of which 257 were serviceable, in 1980 there were 249 buses of which only 142 were road worthy.[33] Reading from these figures, it becomes clear that the number of buses owned by UDA has been going down progressively while urban population has been increasing. This has led to overcrowded buses.

Overloading and overcrowding in buses is not only a life risk to the passengers on board, but also exacerbates the rate of wear and tear on the vehicles. Overcrowding is also a very conducive atmosphere for pick-pocketing and transmission of infectious diseases. Table 5.2 summmarizes the nature of breakdowns of UDA buses. Viewed carefully, it can be observed that most of the defects or breakdowns are those which are caused mainly either by overloading or bad roads. See, for example, the first five.

Table 5.2
Breakdowns on UDA Buses

Type of Defect	# of Breakdowns	%
Tires	262	20.5
Brake System	175	13.7
Clutch and Gear Box	168	13.2
Engine	138	10.8
Suspension	124	09.7
Electrical System	101	07.9
Steering	048	03.8
Body and Door	063	05.0
Indicators and Pedals	036	02.8
Compressor	036	02.8
Miscellaneous	125	09.8
Total	1276	100.0

Source: UDA statistics 1983: Quoted from Banyikwa, W.F. Nature of Urban Passenger Transport Services in Dar-Es-Salaam, 1986, Appendix 5, page 177

It is the inability of UDA to provide adequate services to the Dar-Es-Salaam population which forced the government to legalize "Dalla-Dalla" buses.

The "Dalla-Dalla" Buses

These are private buses, most of which are of *Mini* and *Chai Maharagwe* type. Dalla-Dalla buses were legalized in 1983 and represent the most informal means of transportation which has existed for decades in Tanzania.

The involvement of these type of buses in Dar-Es-Salaam is not rare. They have been operating illegally for a long time. People used to call them *Thumni-Thumni* between 1970 and 1974. They got this name because of the 50 cent coin commonly known as *Thumni* in Swahili which was the fare they used to charge.[34] Later between 1976 and 1981 they became to be known as *Sanya-Sanya,* a word which implies a process of accumulating money from all sources available (most of them illegal). In this case it meant accumulating money by providing chargeable transportation to urban residents without official permission or pirating an urban transportation service.[35] In 1981, this mode of transportation came to be known as *Dalla-Dalla*. This nickname came from a Tanzanian five shilling coin which resembles the American silver dollar.[36] The buses got this name because they used to charge 5 Tanzanian shillings for fare.

In 1985 there were a total of 218 such buses in Dar-Es-Salaam, and in March 1988 only 138 buses were on the road. At present, their number is considerable. Although the Dalla-Dallas have in a way eased the burden of UDA, still their services are inhuman. They deny students access because the official fare for students is 5 shillings instead of 50 shillings. The Dalla-Dalla crew normally observes no traffic regulations while hurrying and scrambling for passengers. Sometimes they operate without fixed routes. They normally service the roads from which they think they can reap most. Dalla-Dallas are very sensitive to passengers flow and peak hours. As Banyikwa (1986) has argued, they are efficient and frequent during peak hours, and they are unavailable during non-peak hours.[37]

Other Means of Transportation in Dar-Es-Salaam

Other means of transportation in Dar-Es-Salaam include buses belonging to parastatal companies (staff buses), staff cars, motorcycles, taxis, pickups and lorries, and also walking on foot. The staff buses provide services only to those employees of the respective public company. It is class and status which determines the mode of transport one uses. Those who occupy senior, well-paid positions, like General Managers or Directors have publicly-owned saloon cars. The low-paid workers have to depend on either staff buses if any, or overloaded, overcrowded accident-prone UDA and Dalla-Dalla buses. The fact that the problem of transportation is critical in Dar-Es-Salaam can be seen in the rapid increase of the private taxi, *Teksi Bubu*. These are cars owned privately which operate illegally as taxis. It is common to find such cars, pick-ups, lorries, and other types carrying passengers via the already mentioned *Sanya-Sanya* process.

Inadequacy of transportation facilities has far-reaching consequences to both commuters and transport operators. Overcrowding, passenger insecurity, and long walking distances are the problems which the commuters face. The majority of the poor have to walk several kilometers in town, not because they would like to keep their bodies fit, but they walk because they are poor. Inefficient transportation and lack of punctuality at workplaces has had an adverse impact on the economy of the country as a whole.

At the same time, the difficulties of finding a bus, taxi, or any other means of transportation are legend. Long hours of waiting for buses, exorbitant fare changes, students denied transport in Dalla-Dalla buses, unsafe vehicles, and bad roads have intensified the nature of the urban crisis. Urban public transportation is inadequate and inefficient not simply because of the lack of foreign currency, but more due to mismanagement, corruption, poor planning, and organization. These problems, altogether, have taken away all possibilities of amelioration of urban transportation bottlenecks and difficulties. Sometimes UDA cannot even collect the actual revenue from bus fares because some unscrupulous conductors in collusion with their supervisors take the money from the passengers and do not issue tickets.

Urban accidents are numerous. Even though traffic policemen are scattered throughout the urban areas, especially during weekends, accidents occur in front of them. In theory, vehicles and drivers are supposed to undergo rigorous inspections and road tests respectively. On the other hand, vehicles that are not roadworthy account for 50% of total vehicles and operate as if the traffic police are all on leave. In principle, every vehicle has to undergo a thorough inspection before it is registered, but due to corruption vehicle inspection is theoretical rather than practical. Corruption is so widespread that policemen have made their authorities and powers into a commodity to be exchanged for favors and bribes. The Dalla-Dalla buses overload while carrying some uniformed policemen as passengers, and their drivers drive carelessly as if the policemen were not there.

Periodic public campaigns to enforce law and order and stringent actions always have negative impacts on the urban population. Vehicles that are not road-worthy stay off the roads and this increases the suffering of the urban population. In Dar-Es-Salaam, everybody knows what happens to commuters when the traffic police do decide to arrest all defective Dalla-Dalla buses. These not arrested refrain from organizing and find their refuge in backyard garages. The implication of this is common. The vehicles become scarce, the fare goes up, overloading is intensified, again raising the rate which is demanded by the traffic police, and this again pushes up the fare rates.

The Mini Dalla-Dalla buses are an important means of transportation in urban Tanzania.

The *Mikokoteni* carts are another important means of transportation.

As if the transportation problem was not obvious, the Dar-Es-Salaam City Council (DCC) daily wages a war against *mikokoteni* (pulled or pushed hand carts). The DCC regards them as slow-moving vehicles which impede the flow of motor vehicles, cause accidents, and thus deserve to be banned. However, *mikokoteni* are the cheapest means of cargo transportation affordable even by the very poor people in Dar-Es-Salaam. *Mikokoteni* are realistic and practical. They are not impeded by *mashimo* (potholes) in the roads, and can manage to go through very narrow corridor-like streets which can be found in most parts of the city. DCC does not understand the functional necessity of *mikokoteni* in Dar-Es-Salaam. By so doing, DCC is divorcing itself from the reality of the dynamics of the city. Although they are officially prohibited, in reality they still operate, and their number has increased considerably during the past few years. This confirms the presence of an increasing demand for such services. The *mikokoteni* boys operate illegally and pay bribes to the DCC officers and police when apprehended. In brief, this shows how ill-advised policies which do not reflect reality may lay ground for corruption.

Given such a situation, it is indeed hard to imagine the plight faced by the unemployed or low income earners in Dar-Es-Salaam. In every item and issue one has to struggle. It is a struggle to get good housing. It is a struggle to secure employment, to get medicine in a public owned hospital, to deposit money in the bank or to withdraw, to get telephone, electricital, or water connection. It is also a battle to board a bus to and from city center, pay the normal official fare, and come back home safely. Once you are at the city center and you feel like going to the toilet, it is again a hustle. All these problems confirm the critical nature of the urban crisis in Tanzania.

It is important to understand that poor urban facilities are not only a menace to urban residents but have also negative implications to the economy as a whole. If people cannot reach their work places at the right time, if they are always sick and cannot be properly treated, and if they reproduce their labor with difficulties, such people cannot be productive. Added to that is the fact that poor urban infrastructure means that inefficiency and irregular running of the enterprises becomes the rule of the day. This leads to less production output which breeds scarcity, hoarding, and corruption. Government revenues become minimal and hence there is no money for development projects and for financing the social service sector. At the end the country is left with a vicious circle of problems. It is no wonder that the government has recently introduced cost-sharing measures or user charges in education and health, decisions which are affecting the poor a lot.

If this is the reality of nearly all urban areas in Tanzania, and the vast majority of the urban residents lack these facilities and economic security and have no support from organized welfare, how do they survive? The following chapter deals with this issue.

6
Urban Poverty and Survival Politics

Introduction

The nature of the economic crisis as it has been presented here makes it clear why life has become so difficult to the majority people. The official incomes which people get do not correspond with their cost of living.

The impoverishment of the majority wage earners and other people can well be observed in the following data. The prices of almost each item have been shooting up rapidly while the wage increases have been slow. Between 1977 and 1986, the price of food items alone increased by 711.4%. And for a decade now, galloping inflation has been estimated at between 30 and 40% per year. These trends have have several effects. One obvious effect is that the majority of the wage earners have suffered a great erosion in their purchasing power for the last two decades. A 1990 study by Bagachwa and Maliyamkono noted that one day's minimum wage in 1973 could buy 10 kg. of maize or 4.8 kg. of rice. However, in 1985 it could only buy 2 kg. of maize or 1.6 kg. of rice because of the market prices. But since things were bought in black markets it meant that the day's minimum wage could only buy 1.3 kg. of maize or 0.8 kg. of rice. ILO (1982) has argued that the real wage in 1980 was lower than what it was in 1963.[1] Thus the degree or level of poverty has increased, and the income of the majority of the people has not.

Since prices have been going up between 1985 and 1988 at a yearly inflationary rate of more than 30%, there is no reason for one to think that the situation has improved. Worse is the fact that Tanzania has for some years controlled a number of prices, and it is these official prices which are used in calculating the price indexes. However, since the early 1980s, a large part of economic transactions have been and are still taking place outside the official sector at much higher prices. Black-marketing and hoarding characterize the distribution trade sector of essential commodities. And recently, due to SAP policies of liberalization, the government no longer controls the prices of most items. As a result of this, and in order to cope with the situation, moonlighting has become an important source of supplementing household incomes, particularly in the urban areas.

The Reality

Several methods of data collection were applied in order to find out the opinions of the urban dwellers themselves concerning the economic crisis, the urban crisis, what it meant to them, and how they managed to cope with the situation. First, I conducted an interview with a sample of 280 people in 15 wards *(kata)*. 14 wards were in Dar-Es-Salaam and one was in Dodoma. This sample was drawn from specific residential areas (low-, medium-, and high-income) which are typical of other such areas in both cities. Second, I administered a written essay to a total of 605 7th grade pupils from sixteen primary schools. 14 of these schools are in Dar-Es-Salaam and the other two are in Dodoma. The title of the essay was: *Jinsi hali ngumu ya uchumi inavyoathiri hali ya maisha ya Mijini,* which means "The Impact of the Economic Crisis on Urban Life." Pupils were asked to write anything concerning the topic, focusing on how the economic crisis affected their life as pupils at school and their general life at home. They were advised to pinpoint crucial problems which confronted their families and themselves. Last, they were also asked to provide suggestions or recommendations which they would like the government to implement in order to solve their problems. Third, I also conducted an informal survey, interviewing a variety of people operating within the informal sector. The other people whom I interviewed will be mentioned as the discussion of these findings goes on. What follows below is a presentation of the major findings derived from the data collected with the above methods.

TABLE 6.1
Respondents by Type of Residential Area

Type of Residential Area	Percentages
Low Income Area	75
Medium Income Area	17
High Income Area (Area for the well to do)	8
Number of Respondents	280 = 100%

Source: Research findings

As Table 6.1 indicates, the majority of the 280 respondents resided in low-income residential areas and only a quarter of them came from medium- and high-income residential areas.

When these respondents were asked to list the most critical problems they experienced as urban dwellers in Dar-Es-Salaam and Dodoma, they mentioned the following: (Table 6.2)

TABLE 6.2
Critical Problems Experienced by Urban Dwellers

Nature of Problems	Percentages
The cost of living is very high	100
Scarcity of essential food items like rice, sugar, maize, and wheat flour	100
Water problems	100
Electricity problems (lack of and frequent power cuts)	100
Poor medical service	98
Lack of employment opportunities	97
Shortage of housing	93
Lack of efficient urban transportation system	91
Poor telephone services	21
Number of Respondents	280

Source: Research findings

The information presented in the above table is self-explanatory. Cost of living is high, scarcity of essential commodities, water and electricity problems, poor medical services, and a lack of employment opportunities and housing seem to be the main crucial problems which the urban poor in Tanzania face at the present. Thus, they all consider the existence of the run-down civic facilities to be an acknowledged fact. As the survey proved, the national consumer price index is useless because of the skyrocketing cost of living and the extremely low incomes. Even during the oral discussion, the majority of the respondents showed that problems one and two were very serious and critical. They argued that essential commodities were extremely hard to find. Once found, they were being sold at double or three times their official prices. The respondents identified hoarding, black-marketing, and *ndugunization* (nepotism) as factors which hindered normal and rational distribution of essential commodities. These problems have eroded the codes of conduct of various state organs whose role is, for example, to enforce the application of official prices. Some of the respondents argued that the *Tume ya Bei* (National Price Commission) was there to announce theoretical prices, but did not make sure that the prices are applied. Hence, by raising the official prices now and then, the commission was in reality helping to push up the black-market prices. These respondents provided a list of items with their official prices as well as the black-market ones. None of these items can be seen displayed openly on store shelves. One has to go through the *mlango wa nyuma* (back door), or has to *kuzungumza vizuri* (talk well), which in practice means corrupting, bribing, and buying the items at hiked black-market prices.

Most of the respondents argued that it was the prices of essential commodities which posed problems in coping with the urban life. This argument is not new. Mapunda (1985), in his article in the *Sunday News Paper* argued that

> The Government's decision to form a salaries review commission (*Sunday News*, 10/20/85) is good and warmly welcomed. But the news has been received by the public with joy on the one hand and fear on the other. Experience has taught us that salary increase to civil servants and parastatal organization in our country is no longer as much a source of joy as it was expected to be. It only stimulates our already spirting headaches. In fact, our major problem on the salary issue is not the thinness of our present minimum wage 810 Tshs. but the everlasting chain of deductions (taxes, levies) and untold high prices of commodities. If the prices were reasonable and well controlled by

the government, and unnecessary deductions were either reduced or abolished, the present minimum salaries would be at least of some value to the earners. But if the system remains as it is now, increase in salaries will be doing nothing less than adding burdens to the would-be payees.[2]

It is a fact that the present wages are far below the cost of living in urban areas. This is also confirmed by the response of the 280 respondents. When asked them to approximate the monthly income that a family of five would need in order to survive in urban areas their response was the following: (Table 6.3)

TABLE 6.3
Estimated Monthly Basic Necessary Income (BNI) for a Family of Five Members in Urban Areas in Tanzanian Shillings (Tshs.) in 1988

Monthly BNI in Tsh.	% of Respondents
5,000 to 7,000	28
7,001 to 9,000	66
9,001 to 11,000	6
over 11,000	–
Number of Respondents	280

Source: Research findings

Two thirds of the respondents indicated that they needed a monthly BNI of between 7,001 Tshs. and 9,000 Tshs. in order to survive. More than a quarter were for a BNI of between 5,000 Tshs. and 7,000 Tshs., and only 6% needed a BNI of between 9,001 Tshs. and 11,000 Tshs.

The data in Table 6.3 shows that there is a wide gap between the official incomes which people receive and the BNI which they need in order to survive. How is this gap bridged? In order to understand how these people supplemented their incomes, I asked them to list their sources of extra income. A wide range of income-generating activities was listed. An analysis of these activities was done and a summary of them is presented in Table 6.4.

TABLE 6.4
Sources of Extra Income

Income-generating activities	Percentages
Informal sector economic activity like petty trading, hawking, and street vendoring	87
Small-scale urban farming activities, mchicha, onion, and tomato gardening, especially along the Msimbazi, Mabibo, and Mtoni basins.	85
Poultry keeping	17
Dairy cattle keeping	10
Others	07
Number of Respondents	280

Source: Research findings

It is clear from the table that more than four-fifths (87%) of the respondents supplement their incomes through informal petty trading activities. Many also involve themselves in the production of some of their food items. Thus, small-scale urban farming activities are not far behind. Gardens and other small farming plots full of *mchicha* (spinach), onions and tomatoes can be seen along the Msimbazi and Mabibo basins in Dar-Es-Salaam and Mkalama Valley in Dodoma. In Dodoma, some middle- and high-income classes have joined the vineyard cash-crop production. Some people operate small poultry and dairy cattle projects. This type of urban farming requires expensive initial capital investments, and the business itself is difficult to handle for a normal poor person who does not have influence and contacts which can enable him to secure the very scarce chicken feed and other necessities. A few respondents indicated other methods of supplementing their incomes. They did not mention them openly probably because of their illegality or immorality. However, deeper informal discussions with some respondents revealed such methods of "corruption", which they referred to as *kuuza wajibu,* which literally means selling one's official responsibility by accepting bribes or kickbacks in order to provide official services to customers. A section on corruption will deal with this issue in detail.

Most of the women stated that they have been forced to change some of their living habits because of the economic crisis. Some complained that they have changed their eating habits. The amount of meat and spices eaten per meal has been reduced tremendously. Boiled beans and *mchicha* have turned out to be a common sauce menu for the majority. Others argued that they now buy just one pair of *kitenge* or *kanga* per year as opposed to in former times when they used to buy each new pattern of this women's attire. They argued that they now depended on *mitumba* (imported second-hand clothes), without which some could reach the point of going naked. Women also showed a greater concern for the deterioration of services in government-owned hospitals and dispensaries in general, and the poor conditions of the maternity care facilities in particular.

There is a very close association between the information collected from the adult urban citizens from the 15 wards and that from the primary school pupils. The response of the pupils revealed two sets of problems. The first set concerns only those critical problems which they face as pupils or members of the school community. The second set represents those problems which they face as members of urban families and urban community in general. For the first set, the pupils cited lack of books, desks (sitting on the floor in classrooms) too few teachers, and urban transportation problems. For the second set they identified the high cost of living, water problems, lack of or unreliable electric power, poor transportation, poor roads, and lack of telephone facilities in town.

There is no doubt that there is a similarity between the problems cited by adults and their recommendations to the government and the views expressed by the pupils. This confirms that the urban crisis is an acknowledged fact at present.

However, the crisis has not affected all people in the same way. Since independence, household official income has more than tripled, but the cost of living has gone up over ten times more than the income. The range of available consumer goods has expanded many times, but, of course, not parallel with the demand.

A substantial number of low-, middle- and upper-income class households have emerged whose life and consumption pattern have changed. Some have gone from good to bad but others have actually moved toward an improved standard of living. Although the standard of life for the majority urban people is better than rural life, social disparities among various groups have sharpened. These disparities are most visible along class lines. Yet there are intra-class differences that distinguish between the educated and the uneducated, the influentials and the ordinary, and between those with possibilities of black-market earning and those who have no such means and have to survive by hunting and gathering and eating from the garbage. All these are products of the contradictory politics of development that have characterized Tanzania since independence. This point requires elaboration.

Given the gap between theory and practice (policy and implementation), class inequality has widened rather than diminishing. Given the present economic crisis, one's position in the social system determines the kind of strategies one adopts in order to survive in an urban system. In order to understand the kind of income-generating activities which people undertake in order to survive, a discussion of the activities in the informal sector is necessary. But before embarking on such discussion, a brief identification of the present social classes in urban areas and their pattern of consumption may place the analysis of the informal sector activities in its proper theoretical perspective.

Urban Social Classes and Their Consumption Patterns

Tanzania's urban population can roughly be divided into five social classes of distinct consumption patterns. I shall describe these classes here mainly in terms of their consumption behavior. But this has to be seen as a product of the position these classes occupy in the urban social system and production.

At the bottom are the unemployed, domestic servants, hawkers, street vendors and those whose earning and survival depend on luck and the vagaries of the urban system. In most cases, their survival is sporadic and very uncertain. Most of them operate in the informal sector as employees and not as masters or owners. They live under very poor conditions without adequate food and shelter. In Dar-Es-Salaam they can easily be seen scattered around the streets selling juice, water, nuts, chewing gum, ornaments, women's rings and different types of fruits. Some work as parking boys, quick-service cheap prostitutes (for women) and others as casual cargo loaders and off-loaders in bus stations with buses destined for the up-country (*vibaka*). Many of them come from Manzese, Tandika, Mabibo, Keko, Buguruni, Temeke, and other squatter settlements. Sometimes they survive on mutual help of their friends or relatives and put on very cheap imported second hand clothes (*mitumba*). Their security is uncertain. Their feet are their major means of urban transportation and local brew like *Chibuku, Kangara, Kimpumu, Uraka, Tembo*, (and to some an illicit drink called *Gongo*) are their common drinks. For the youths belonging to this class, looking for employment is a matter of *kufa na kupona* (life or death). While girls may resort to prostitution, boys scramble for odd jobs.

The second group of consumers consists of the very low level of the middle class. These include the unskilled and semi-skilled employed minimum wage earners. Some may be janitors, messengers, clerks, or small craftsmen. With the present crisis, their consumption pattern and behavior is more like to resemble that of the first group. The only difference is that these are officially employed. In reality, they cannot afford to buy new clothes or eat well and live luxuriously. Most of them have changed even their drinking behavior. The majority have switched away from the so-called modern bottled beer to locally made beer brands which are cheap. Like the first group, most of them live in the squatter areas as tenants. My research findings reveal that most of these people have also joined the activities of the informal sector and use often the labor of their children or relatives in order to supplement their incomes. One respondent belonging to this group stated as follows:

> The ones who do not have the capital and ability to operate small economic projects live by borrowing and shuffling debts, and through other legal or illegal methods. There are wide horizontal differences and disparities between this group and the first one depending upon specific jobs and economic activities one is engaged in, and urban network affiliations and contacts. Those with some contacts with people with influence are sometimes faring better than those who lack such contacts. Those minimum pay recipients who have obtained an official living quarter are much better off than their colleagues who do not have this privilege. The ability to corrupt may also lead to differences in the levels of living.

The third group is that which comprises the middle-income earners. Most of them are employed in the formal sector as teachers, lecturers, doctors, or administrators. These are all those whose income range is between twice the official minimum pay and the lowest level of the high- income earners. These people have officially stipulated social benefits and job security and some have access to official transportation. Some have official cars with drivers. Due to their official position, most of them have several fringe benefits like official housing, free medical treatment, and higher night allowance rates. Their consumption pattern varies, but it is far better than the first two groups. The majority of them prefer drinking bottled beer from the West.

The fourth conspicuous class of consumers consists of all the most senior officials from government, party, and parastatal organizations and other upper echelons of the formal sector. Senior civil servants like principal secretaries, directors, very senior military officers, director generals, general managers, some politicians and some professors in institutes of higher learning like the University belong to this group. One can see that, for them, things like food, clothes, and housing have been plentiful. Since independence they have acquired new needs. These people are not hidden. One can identify them by the nature of their residential areas or number plates of the official cars they use. Those working in government offices use cars whose registration number begins with letters "ST" meaning *Serikali ya Tanzania* (Government of Tanzania). Those working in parastatal organizations drive cars with registration numbers starting with "SU", standing for *Shirika la Umma* (Public Corporation) . Senior political party leaders are driven in cars with "CCM" (*Chama Cha Mapinduzi*) registration numbers. Diplomats and others who work in international organizations use cars with special numbers.This means that by looking at the registration numbers of cars driven, one can easily identify who is who in the urban system.

Closely related to this group (especially in terms of consumption patterns) are the very rich private individuals, contractors, industrialists, merchants, and other commercial bourgeoisie. Most of the Asians, Arabs, and Semi-Arabs with business contacts abroad belong to this group. The majority own luxurious cars and villas. The politics of trade liberalization have helped them a lot. Again, like their counterparts above, this group of people has acquired new needs since independence. Trips abroad are common. Most of them own luxurious houses which are fitted with satellite dishes, television and video sets, and cars. These people are always not far behind the West in adopting new products. Imitative Westernism is the hallmark of the majority of this class, and the glitter of their lifestyles stands in sharp contrast to the abysmal living conditions of the masses.

Some of the members of group four above collaborate very closely with this group. The former wield power and authority while the domain of the later is in the economy. Corruptive senior government and public officials align themselves with these entrepreneurs by receiving bribes and kickbacks.

The consumption pattern of these affluent classes has had a very negative impact on the majority. Given a limited production capacity, overconsumption by few segments of the urban population is bound to put other people at a disadvantage in the following way. The availability of public-owned luxury cars which are fueled and repaired at the expense of the government, free treatment in private hospitals at home and abroad, and the creation of duplicates of parastatals (some of which just deal with distribution) has meant that the government has to spend a lot of money in its recurrent expenditures. The financial crisis which the government experiences is indeed a product of this legacy.

These self-serving patterns of consumption influence the kind of economic projects supported by the government. Projects which assist the rich tend to be supported more by the state either financially or through legislation.

The emergence of small but economically dominant groups of conspicuous consumers characterize and shape the mode of urban dynamics in Tanzania. Formal sector activities tend to dominate and, in some cases, ruin the activities in the informal sector. As a result of this, social disparities are widened and enable the process of class polarization to take its course.

So what do the majority urban poor do in order to survive in such an urban system? Most of the urban poor have joined the informal sector where they are forced to operate under very difficult conditions. A survey of 200 informal sector operators in Dar-Es-Salaam presents, in a nutshell, the kind of informal sector income-generating activities these poor people operate, the kind of problems they experience, and how they surmount them.

The Informal Sector and the Urban Poor

There is enough evidence that the majority of the urban poor in Tanzania derive their incomes from informal activities through the sale of informal products or wages (ILO 1982). This sector produces a wide range of basic goods and services for consumption by the majority urban population. Hence, Bagachwa argues that the development of this sector may be a pre-requisite to combating the urban problems arising from unemployment, inequality and poverty.[3]

Bagachwa (1983) in his study of "Structure and Policy Problems of the Informal Manufacturing Sector in Tanzania" conducted a survey covering 71 informal production and repair establishments of basic needs activities employing an average of less than 10 persons in Dar-Es-Salaam.[4] The survey covered only the established units with some fixed capital investment, a premise, and a significant degree of value added.[5] Areas covered included Kariakoo, Gerezani, Manzese, Tandika, and Kinondoni. Table 6.5 below summarizes the major activity group and their coverage.[6]

TABLE 6.5
Employment in the Informal Sector by Activity Category

Category	Number of Establishment	Regular Workers	Casual Workers	Total Workers	Average Total Workers	% of Total Workers
Wood	21	86	28	114	5.4	35.4
Tailoring	18	82	10	92	5.0	28.5
Leather	14	40	08	48	3.4	14.9
Metal Works	13	43	05	48	3.6	14.9
Food	05	09	11	20	4.0	06.3
Total	71	260	62	322	4.5	100

Source: The basic survey therefore excluded non-established informal units such as street vendors, hawkers, and domestic servants with no fixed capital and the distributive trade sector which lack significant value added in the total product. This was done simply to reduce the problem of nonavailability and noncomparability of data.
The table has been quoted from ILO, *op.cit.*, page 342. The same table appears in Bagachwa, M.S.D. *op.cit.*, page 6.

According to the survey, the establishments employed a total of 322 persons. Four-fifths (81%) were regular employees, while almost one-fifth (19%) were employed on casual terms.[7] Bagachwa noted that individual ownership was dominant (70%), and private partnership (usually of two individuals) constituted the major form of ownership.[8] Informal artisans did not prefer to work on cooperative arrangements because of the fear of being registered and hence subjected to income tax, sales tax, and price control.[9] The workers used mainly hand tools and manual labor, a fact which shows that most of these informal activities are less demanding in terms of operational and management skills, and most of the skills could easily be acquired locally. The monthly wages for the regular employees ranged from 480 Tshs. to 980 Tshs. Bagachwa saw that the mean monthly pay for regular laborers was 538 Tshs. The official minimum wage during the period of this survey was 600 Tshs.[10] Since wages were the principle source of income (at least during those days), Bagachwa argued that the majority of the employees in this sector were within the poor, low-income category.[11]

Bagachwa's study dealt mainly with informal sector activities which had permanent fixed premises and which needed some form of fixed capital investment. My 1987/88 field survey of the informal sector concentrated on those activities which had no fixed premises such as hawking, street vendoring, car washing, peddling, illegal dealing of foreign currency, prostitution, and others.

Any new visitor in Dar-Es-Salaam may be surprised by the presence of a vast market which is distributed all over the city, i.e., behind bus stations, along both the main and small streets, by crossroads, and outside famous formal institutions like post offices, churches, and mosques. Hawkers and street vendors selling different types of items (like cigarettes, stationeries, chewing gum, and food items) ply these areas in search of potential customers. The *mishikaki-nyama choma* (roasted meat) boys are plentiful and are strategically located with their meat stalls and burning charcoal stoves roasting meat and frying eggs, potatoes, and cassava chips ready to sell to urban residents. These petty trade activities have developed rapidly recently without technical prescription or foreign assistance. They continue to grow and flourish progressively despite various legal obstacles. What Rosselt (1987) has argued for Peru is equally valid to Tanzania: that the poor there are relying not on government paternalism and planning, but rather on their own wits, energy and ambition in order to survive and prosper.[12]

In order to understand the mode of operation of these activities in Dar-Es-Salaam, particularly in terms of income, ownership and the problems encountered, a survey was administered to 200 hawkers, peddlers and street vendors. One half of the respondents operated in the Manzese area in the Kinondoni District, while the remaining half operated in the Tandika area in the Temeke District. Those interviewed dealt with petty trade activities in the items summarized in Table 6.6 below.

TABLE 6.6
Hawkers, Peddlers and Street Vendors by Activity, Gender and Percentage

Group Activity	Respondents	Males	Females	% of Total
Food Items (mobile)	78	65 (32.2%)	13 (6.5%)	39
Food Items (immobile)	67	44 (22%)	23 (11.5%)	33.5
Drinks (mobile)	29	24 (12%)	05 (2.5%)	14.5
Drinks (immobile)	14	06 (3%)	08 (4%)	7
Others	12	09 (4.5%)	03 (1.5%)	6
Total	200	148 (74%)	52 (26%)	100

Source: Research findings
NB: Mobile food items include all those items which can be sold while the seller is moving from one corner of the city to the other, such as chewing gum, nuts, water, juice, bread, and ice. Immobile food items and drinks refer to all those items which, for technical reasons, the seller has to stick to one selling point at a time, such as roasting meat, frying eggs or cassava, and the selling of cold bottled drinks like Cola-Cola, Fanta, Sprite, Mirinda and Pepsi.

Table 6.6 is self-explanatory. Almost three quarters of the respondents were engaged in petty trading of raw and cooked food items (group activity 1 and 2). The majority of the petty traders were youths (boys and girls 15 to 24 years old, and most of them had undergone primary school education and some were still attending schools. Most of the boys tend to be mobile in their operations and specialize in various items, while the selling of most cooked items like fried chicken, *vitumbua*, *maandazi*, or dried and smoked fish (mostly immobile trade) tend to be the pre-occupation of women. This reflects the Tanzanian traditional family culture of the dominance of women in home economics and kitchen work. Most of the hawkers and street vendors were males (74%). Women comprised just almost a quarter. There are two special cultural reasons for this. First and foremost, most Tanzanian parents are more willing to allow their male children to walk freely in the streets than the female children. This is due to the fear that their daughters might fall prey to men who might seduce them, an event which might result in pregnancies out of wedlock. Second, girls have to spend most of their time with their mothers, helping them with kitchen work. It is girls who cook for their fathers and the rest of the family in the absence of their mothers. It is girls who also take care of their young brothers and sisters. That is why, even in a situation where they are engaged in petty trading activities in streets, they do not operate far away from their areas of residence. Sometimes they are forced (by their parents) to operate only in particular strategic points of the city where they can easily be traced and monitored by their parents, guardians, or relatives.

The majority of the respondents (93%) stated that the business did not belong to them, but to their parents or relatives or guardians with whom they stayed. The majority did not have a permanent income, but got non-monetary benefits like free food, accommodation, or money for transportation, clothing and security from the people whom they assisted in the business. In a way this means that most of these petty trading activities are family-based with heavy use of unpaid and, more likely, family labor. Regular wage employment is uncommon in the informal business of petty trading. Sometimes the sellers do sell a commodity at a higher price than that agreed by the owner and pocket the difference. Petty traders in Dar-Es-Salaam and other urban areas in Tanzania work from early in the morning until sunset. Certain items like cooked food take a lot of time to prepare. Whether it is the male youths or male adults hawking in the streets with cooked food items, such businesses belong to and are usually dominated by women. Only 13 out the 200 respondents owned their own business. All of them were adults, and 12 of them sold jewelry, women's rings (*Pete, vibanio na Urembo*), empty bottles (for recycling), cigarettes, and traditional medicines (herbs).

The question of income earned from these activities was hardly thoroughly answered. Most of the mobile hawkers stated an income of between 100 and 150 Tshs. per day, which means a monthly gross income of between 3,000 and 4,500 Tshs. As a whole, the majority of the respondents said that they would rather operate in such economic activities and receive minimum wage rather than by being employed officially. Considering the fact that the majority of these petty traders did not own businesses, such opinions show that these activities pay even non-owners better than minimum wage. It is the income earned from these activities that assists both the business owners and the actual petty traders themselves to survive in urban areas.

Street vendors in Dar-Es-Salaam selling bread to bus passengers at the Manzese-Msufini bus stop

My findings reveal that in a situation of crisis, informal sector activities do not remain the domain of the unemployed urban poor alone. The majority of the employed section of the urban population tend to join these activities in order to supplement their official incomes. They do that by investing part of their wages in these economic activities. More than four-fifths of the petty traders I interviewed stated that the owners of the business were employees in the formal sector. This means that many employed persons have become street hawkers and vendors (through family labor) as a temporary measure to poverty. The conventional argument that informal sector activities are purely a domain of the unemployed urban poor is no longer valid in the case of Tanzania. What does this mean to the real urban poor? Generally, it means that they have to compete with those who have an assured official income. To most of them, such a situation has meant total marginalization and impoverization. It is no wonder that the majority of them operate in this sector on behalf of their masters. This is a result of the situation of helplessness rather than an alternative.

Hawkers and street vendors do not invest all the money they get in expanding their business because it may not be enough even to keep them surviving or because of various other constraints. Expansion of their activities may require more paid labor and fixed premises. Operating such a business in a permanent location may cause them to fall prey to the government arm (regulations). Licences may be required. Health regulations have to be fulfilled or they will end up violating the by-laws that govern such activities and thus be subject to penalization. It is also difficult to evade taxation if one operates in a fixed premise. That is why most of the petty traders prefer to operate small manageable projects which allow mobility. By being mobile, the hawkers and vendors carry along with them their commodities and easily evade the police, health officers, and tax officers. This means that unlicenced or illegal traders

Newspaper hawkers at Salender Bridge in Dar-Es-Salaam

carefully balance the trade-offs between the scale of operation and their ability to evade arrests and minimize losses in fines and confiscations.[13] It is easier to run with fewer articles which are small rather than many big, heavy articles. Hence, some operators retain a small-scale operation for strategic reasons rather than as a result of insufficient capital accumulation.[14]

Newspaper hawkers at Salender Bridge in Dar-Es-Salaam

The information reported by the *Daily News Paper* confirms my argument about the rational behavior of hawkers and street vendors.

Dar Council Bans Sale of Foodstuffs in Streets
Dar-Es-Salaam City Council has banned with immediate effect the sale of foodstuffs in the streets to curb the spread of contagious diseases such as dysentry and cholera. The City Medical Officer, Dr. E.E. Moshi,

issued the directive yesterday saying that the health situation in the city was deplorable and a health hazard. He said it was necessary to take stern measures now because thousands of the people were illegally selling their foods in dirty places such as alleys with oozing sewage water.

Empowered by the Disease Prevention Act, Section 96, the Medical Officer has banned forthwith the sale of the following foods at unlicenced places: vegetables, tomatoes, cabbages, onions, cassava, potatoes, coconuts, madafu, roast meat, and green maize. Other banned foods are dried and fried fish, juice, bread, buns, and ripe bananas. Food stalls which sell homemade food but were unhealthy should also stop forthwith. (*Daily News*, 6/4/86).

The preoccupation of young boys and girls in the activities of the urban informal sector necessitates a discussion of its own. For this reason, the section below looks at the fate of street boys and girls.

The Street Boys and Girls

The present economic crisis has also had adverse impact on the children. As I have already demonstrated, it is the children of the urban poor who suffer most. Cases of children running from their parents or roaming aimlessly in streets of Dar-Es-Salaam are alarming at the present. Ntukula's 1985 findings show that the crime cases involving children and youths, as well as their numbers in remand homes has gone up during the past few years.[15] Most of the children born in the slum squatter areas, some of them from broken families or without known fathers, experience a difficult life at a tender age. Their lives are an example of the survival of the fittest. Their mothers, struggling for survival, leave the children alone, letting them take care of themselves. The information quoted below confirms the widespread nature of such cases.

> *Arrested*
> Two girls from Tuliani town were recently brought before the Tuliani Primary Court Magistrate, Mr. Mkita, to answer charges of running away from their infant babies in order to go to Dar-Es-Salaam to practice prostitution. Confirming the charge, the prosecuter urged that the two collaborated together to run away from their babies. These plans were revealed by their elder sister who reported the matter to the police. (*Mfanyakazi Paper*, 8/14/87; Translated from Swahili by the author).

The officially-owned *Daily News Paper* of May 16, 1989 reported the following fate of nine children in Dar-Es-Salaam:

> Nine Lost Children Look for Their Parents
> Nine children were brought to the *Daily News Paper* offices yesterday morning by officials of the Kurasini Children's Home in Dar-Es-Salaam who said they were looking for their parents. They were picked up from different parts of the city.
> Since then, efforts to reunite these children with their parents have been futile. This shows the present common behavior of some parents abandoning their children precisely because they cannot take care of them.

Some children find life in their families difficult, so they move into the streets as beggars. Some become scavengers for food at hotels and even more so in the cafeterias at institutions of higher learning in big cities like Dar-Es-Salaam. Between 60 to 100 children can daily be seen in the cafeteria at the university scavenging food remains during lunch and supper times. Other children enter into illicit activities of black-marketing various items like cigarettes. In these they are just hired and used by people with urban connections and influence to get huge amounts of cigarettes through official channels. Others enter into the business of pick-pocketing, and others end up as "parking boys" who earn their living through odd jobs. In the effort to escape their misery, they start smoking *widi*, *majani* and *misokoto* (bhang and marijuana). As Ishumi (1984) has argued, others sniff petrol in order to get high and withstand the scorn of the passers by. Some of them "smoke" glue to shut out feelings of poverty, loneliness, and hunger.

Young girls are forced into prostitution at a very tender age. They become aware that one of the means of making quick money and keeping themselves going is through prostitution. In their struggle for survival, the girls go to bed with men who are as old as their fathers, apparently closing their eyes to those haunting moments. Within a short time, some become pregnant and bear children and the vicious cycle of poverty continues.

Most of such youths are truants. They can easily be spotted out on what Ishumi (op.cit.) has called, "jobless corners."[16] Girls loiter outside famous hotels and guest-houses, providing a smile whenever their eyes meet those of the men. They frequent famous discos at night in search of entertainment and money through commercialized sex.

The majority of these youths (especially boys) are homeless. An interview with a few scavengers at the University of Dar-Es-Salaam revealed that it is the hardships at home, marital problems of their parents, and poverty which has lead these youths to experience such situations. The boys loiter in the streets, feed on crumbs, and sleep on the pavement for years. A street boy called Nyasi Marino, while being interviewed by the staff writer of the officially owned *Sunday News* paper responded as follows:

> I decided to leave my home because my parents could not take care of me.... We are seven.[17]

Nyasi told the reporter that a better life to him meant eating well and dressing well and having a good place to sleep. (ibid.). He complained to the reporter about what an ordeal it is for street boys to get food:

> Mama, sometimes you do not feel like eating the left overs. They are spoilt and have a pungent smell. You wait for the next day hoping to get something better . . . but crumbs is the stuff we (street boys) cannot do without.[18]

There are hundreds of such boys in Dar-Es-Salaam and lately they have formed their own solidarity gangs. The boys range from 10 to 18 years old. The most common solidarity gangs are the *Jalala Kuu* (the group to which Nyasi belongs), the *Posta* group, and the *Kariakoo* group. It is the circumstances which force such boys to form these strong bonds that scare off outsiders. The principle is that when you attack one of them, then you have declared a war against the whole group.[19]

The majority of them indulge in illegal business like cinema-ticket racketeering in order to earn some money for food. Others earn their living through *utapeli*, trickstering, and cheating. Nyasi admitted to the reporter that stealing was part of the activities which he and his group took part in.

> We have to do some of these odd jobs to get some money. Moreover, stealing people's property is part of the game and frankly speaking we do this because the circumstances turn us wild.[20]

Ishumi has neatly described the way that pick-pocketing and watch-snatching takes place:

First, when people are waiting for an UDA bus, pick-pockets, usually, in an invisible chain pretend to be doing just that too. Meanwhile, they try to spot and pinpoint would-be bus riders who possibly have large amounts of money, at least a bulging wallet in their pockets, or a fat pouch or briefcase in the hand. When the targets have been established and confirmed, the thieves track them when they are about to board the bus. In pairs of threes, the thieves specialize in tasks. The stronger rushes to the door in order to block the doorway and create artificial pressure from people scrambling, kicking, hitting, elbowing without entering. While this is taking place, the weaker of the accomplices draws closer and begins methodically to push from behind in order to fuel the commotion and to avail himself of the leverage to search into pockets and bags or even to snatch whatever valuables.[21]

This is how some of these boys survive. If worse comes to worst, some of these join the sector of commercialized sex and become sexual partners of some men. Other youths earn their living by engaging in clean activities like washing cars or fetching water in return for food or clothing. In Dar-Es-Salaam, others spend their day at the fish market in Kivukoni scraping fish scales. Others collect valuable items from garbage or elsewhere for recycling or reselling.

In general, the plight of the street children is hard to imagine. Because most of the street children hover on the periphery of other people's lives, most of the people in urban areas tend to look at them in an insubstantial way. They are thus given bad names like *wadokozi* or *wachomoaji* (pick-pocketers) or *wahuni* (hooligans). But the street children themselves are more down to earth. They normally label themselves as *watemi, magangwe*, (which means turf care-free people who are used to problems) and some call themselves as *Born-Town* or *Born-Here-Here*, indicating that they were born in the city and are a product of the urban areas themselves. Young street boys, for example, get a lot of problems from older street boys. Sometimes the older hardcore street boys force the young boys to join them in their criminal activities. Sometimes they share with them what they have collected during the day in exchange of favors of security and protection. Otherwise they end up being beaten and molested by the groups of older boys. They face several hardships but cannot report them to the police because, according to the law, they are also considered criminals ("Idle and disorderly persons"). The problems these children confront in the urban areas and how they surmount them shows in concrete terms that to survive on the streets one needs exceptional fortitude, a creative mind, and an astute knowledge of human nature. Contrary to the conventional belief, these children are not necessarily the dropouts of society, nor are the streets where they live and operate "schools of crime". Hence, the belief that street children are (or will inevitably become) criminals is more of a popular belief than a reality.

Living or Surviving from Begging

The number of beggars in the urban areas in general and in Dar-Es-Salaam in particular has increased tremendously. It is difficult to estimate the number of beggars in this big city at any one time, and it is difficult to get reliable information from them concerning their homes, family backgrounds, income, and other information because they refrain from being interviewed in fear of being assembled, criminalized and finally

Beggars resting on Nkrumah Avenue in Dar-Es-Salaam before resuming their begging.

Begging is carried out by both children and adults in urban Tanzania.

repatriated. Most of the beggars in Dar-Es-Salaam are disabled persons. Some are blind, crippled, or suffering from leprosy, and others are mentally handicapped. The majority of them have no homes, and most of them sleep on the street pavement, cohabitate there (in the case of married couples), and feed their babies there. This shows that the official policy and system of taking care of people with such problems is either lacking or is problematic.

Although the government has built some camps which accommodate disabled people, most of these camps are a disaster. Disabled people prefer to beg on the streets of urban areas rather than staying in such camps. A recent report about the Nunge disabled camp in Kigamboni near Dar-Es-Salaam provides an example of the poor conditions which are typical of most of these camps:

Poor living conditions in rehabilitation centers for the disabled have been cited as the main cause forcing disabled people in Tanzania to resort to begging in urban areas. A survey conducted by *Shihata* at Nunge disabled Rehabilitation Center, the biggest center in the country, revealed that disabled people were fleeing the centers due to pathetic living conditions. The Chairman of the Economic and Planning Committee of Nunge, Ndugu Rasho Kirapa, complained to *Shihata* that life in the camp was 'deplorable' and that the disabled residents had to run to the streets to beg. 'Life here is unfit for human habitation', said Ndugu Kirapa...Food rations have been slashed, and while earlier they were getting tea every morning, they have now forgotten it. 'We only drink porridge without sugar or with salt,' Ndugu Kirapa said. For lunch, the main meal was *ugali* with beans and *dagaa,* most often without cooking oil or even salt. More than one third of the disabled at the camp had no beds and beddings. Some of them had big wounds which they claimed were caused by sleeping on the floor. Some are almost walking naked, and some complained that they were being forced to put on whatever came by, even women's clothes for men. The disabled people at Nunge are being paid 210 Tshs. every three months to buy for themselves small things like cigarettes. The amount, they said, was very small". (*Daily News Paper,* 1/4/89)

Beggars in urban Tanzania

Ishumi (op.cit.) has argued that some are genuinely destitute people with no assistance or base in their homegrounds who have been driven to town in search of public mercy in order to survive.[22] Others are liars, playing destitute during the day, and retiring from it late in the evening or at night.[23] Once spotted and discovered, they change locations in fear of public notice, apprehension, and possible police action.[24] Both the genuine destitutes and those who pretend either walk from one corner of the street to the other, or sit in very strategic areas in order to beg. Begging is illegal, and attempts by the state to surround, arrest, and repatriate the beggars to their rural home areas have been futile. The next chapter discusses the fallacy of these policies in depth.

Problems Encountered by Informal Sector Operators

Reading through this description of informal sector activities and their mode of operation, one might think that there are more advantages involved than problems. In reality, there are risks and constant harassment from the government precisely because, according to law, most of these activities are operated illegally. Following procedures that have already been set means that one has to apply for a licence. This requires a permanent location, payment of tax, and governemnt involvement in setting prices. The procedures involved in achieving these are long and expensive. On the other hand, there are also disadvantages to operating a business outside the country's legal framework. One has to operate in the business with a psychological pressure of uncertainty. One has to work with several eyes in order to see where the authorities might appear. My findings reveal that most of the hawkers, street vendors, and other informal sector operators have to walk with some money in their pockets so they will be ready to bribe the authorities to look the other way. The exact amount of money paid varies from one corrupt official to another. Bribing one officer does not save one from being harassed by another officer. Some unfortunate individuals end up paying out all their daily income in bribes to different officials. The money paid as bribes buys them nothing beyond the freedom to try to earn a living.[25]

Although President Mwinyi recently issued a directive which warns the officials to stop harassing vendors (see below), in practice, such a directive has not eased the hardships which such operators confront before the city council officers.

President Ali Hassan Mwinyi has directed that with immediate effect stern action be taken against any policeman, or militia of the Dar-Es-Salaam City Council found or seen harassing petty traders whether licenced or not. The President has further directed that any of the policemen or militia found throwing away the traders'wares or destroying them should be apprehended by public and taken to relevant law enforcement organizations for necessary action against them...He said the traders were actually engaged in legal activities, trying to struggle against harsh economic conditions facing everybody. He said people must be free to conduct business anywhere until the City Council sets aside special areas in commercial areas where the people would carry out their sales. (*Sunday News Paper*, 3/5/89)

This was the second time for President Mwinyi to issue such an order on the question of petty traders. The issue of harassing petty traders was also discussed recently in the Regional Commissioner's meeting which took place in Dodoma (ibid.). However, the problem continues to reappear precisely because what the President said was a mere statement which does not repeal the City Council bylaws and health regulations which govern its operation. It has to be clear that it is these coercive, unrealistic bylaws which direct the negative attitude of the city fathers toward the informal sector operators. As long as such laws continue to exist, the harassment of these urban poor people will continue. For example, after wishing for a long time to round up all street vendors and hawkers on the famous "Congo Street" in the Kariakoo area, the Dar-Es-salaam City Council finally implemented its decision in early August of 1993.The City Council called out the Field Force Unit of the police which, in turn, rounded up the vendors, beat them, and confiscated their property, all under the pretext of "Putting the City Clean". The vendors reacted violently by beating the police, looting the nearby shops, and vandalizing both public and private property like cars and other things. This situation caused a small war and differences between the City Council and Central Government over the issue became apparent. While the Central Government saw vendoring and hawking as a survival tactic of the poor on the one hand, the City Council held a very negative attitude toward vendors and hawkers on the other. The City Council's view is summarized well in the words of the City Director Mr.Mukhandi who argued that,

> The City Council will continue discharging its duties including ensuring that the city environment is clean and hygienically safe. Most of these vendors are criminals operating illegally and this can be proved if they are rounded up. (*Daily News Paper*, 9/7/93)

Besides the problems associated with harassments, some petty traders complain about the scarcity of customers. Not every day is a good day for petty traders. Traders who deal with perishable articles like food or fruits regret the bad days when customers are few; their food rots. If the demand goes down, it is the petty traders who lose, and if the police, tax, and health officers come and confiscate the items or demand a bribe, it is again the petty traders who lose.

While some people within the urban system eat well, informal sector operators work hard for many hours for little money. The street boys sleep on the street pavement. They are never sure where their next meal will come from and often risk their lives by scavenging. They also have to run away from the police now and then. The street girls experience bodily humiliation at a tender age. They are sexually exploited, abused, and misused. They surrender their bodies to men in exchange for money, drinks, clothes, food, and accommodation in a good hotel or house. Like the prostitutes, they sleep with men whom they do not know. Some are beaten, raped by several men, unpaid for the services they have provided, and vulnerable to sexually transmitted diseases.

The garbage pickers are not free from problems either. They toil for long hours in a hazardous and polluting atmosphere. As they sell the items they have collected, they are subjected to police, tax, and health officers' harassments. The beggars likewise have to spend most of their time dodging the City Council authorities in fear of repatriation. All these problems confirm the fact that it is not easy to operate in the informal sector.

The Sector of Illicit Activities

Between the formal and informal sector there is a scope of illicit activities which needs to be highlighted. As I have already argued, the formal and informal sectors should not be seen as separate economic sectors but instead as a continuum, related to one another, their relations symbiotic rather than contradictory and antagonistic. The same view should be held of the economic sector of illicit activities. It is not a separate sector, but operates in tandem with the other two sectors. As

Quadeer (1982) has argued, many of these are covert activities of legitimate businesses, such as bribery, black-marketing, tax evasion, and organized and unorganized crime. These covert operations have become structured and regular, but most of them are still frequently ad-hoc acts. Some people have turned into millionaires because of their involvement in such activities. These illicit activities include full- or part-time smuggling, prostitution, corruption, stealing, armed robbery (in broad daylight), fraud, and organized crime. The government is also aware of such activities to the extent that it launched a campaign in 1983 against economic saboteurs (*wahujumu*) and established special tribunals which dealt with such cases related to acts of economic sabotage. The so-called "crack-down" on economic saboteurs was an effort by the government and party to stop black-marketing activities and to seize hoarded commodities and illegal foreign currency dealers. All culprits were brought before these special tribunals and got severe punishments. Since 1984, the government has enacted a law titled "The Economic and Organized Crime Control Act" which is aimed at curbing all those acts, organized and unorganized, which are aimed at sabotaging the economy. In a way, the presence of this law confirms that the operations of illicit activities have become an intolerable situation. My intention to discuss the activities of the sector of illicit activities separately does not mean that the sector is independent, but rather aims at describing how this economic circuit operates. Since corruption and prostitution are currently rampant in Tanzania, I will discuss each of them below.

Corruption

In the context of this study, corruption refers to the use of public resources for private gain. It involves, but is not limited to, monetary benefits and material rewards obtained by public officials and civil servants for private use during the performance of their public duties.[26] Corruption takes place in a public organization when an official or civil servant breaks the rules to advance his personal interests at the expense of the public interest he has been entrusted to guard and promote.[27]

In Tanzania, corruption comes in a myriad of forms. It includes favors in the processing of government applications such as building plot applications. It also involves making false declarations on documents with intentions to defraud the government, providing false information in cases brought before the courts, impersonation, offering and accepting kickbacks, and bribery.

Corruption has become the way of life in Tanzania at present, and its negative effects are not hard to see. Corruption has eroded away the reliability of the administrative and market institutions. In reality, it means that in a situation where corruption is dominant, public policies and laws enforcing individual rights, collective rights, and freedom cannot be implemented. It is therefore not so much a question of whether the government and the party have formulated good policies and plans which they need in order to develop Tanzania, but rather whether the two institutions have the kind of bureaucracy and servants they deserve and need. With a corruptive bureaucracy, rules, regulations, and established procedures are no longer effective. Influence, peddling, and kickbacks become the norms which govern and direct the way the bureaucracy operates. All these conditions create uncertainty and distinct social priorities.[28] Black-marketing deprives the poor of scarce commodities and allocates them to the affluent groups. Bribery and kickbacks benefit those who wield power and authority and cause a lot of suffering to the community at large.

Prostitution

In order to set this discussion in its proper context, it is necessary to first discuss the position of women in the informal sector. I must make it clear that I am discussing the involvement of women in illicit activities in the informal sector in order to identify the activities of women coherently and accurately. This inclusion does not mean that all the activities performed by women are illicit.

Very little data exist concerning women's employment and self-employment in the informal sector. Besides the activities which I have mentioned above, it tends to involve food processing, home beer brewing, and petty trade activities, most of which deal with cooked food items. Others, especially young girls, earn their living by being employed as domestic servants. In this culture it is the women's responsibility to provide for the whole family's clothing, medicine, and other expenses. Husbands are obliged to provide basic food and housing for both women and children.[29] Turritin (1987) has argued that economic autonomy is important to women because it contributes to their social power. Through this, married women struggle to become economically independent from their husbands.[30] However, up until now, increased marketing activities have not been able to enhance women's social power.[31] This is precisely because of the beliefs about specific activities and responsibilities of men and women, coupled with demands made by men and children on women's labor. The restrictions on women's mobility has shifted the advantage to men.[32]

In Dar-Es-Salaam, women have engaged themselves in petty-trading for a long time. Some of them sell their wares in big markets like Kariakoo, Tandika, Tandale, and Magomeni. Others place stalls or tables in front of their houses and some sell cold drinks like Fanta, Coca-Cola and Sprite directly from their homes. Others illegally sell imported women's clothing on the black market, e.g., kanga, vitenge, and bikinis. Some black-market scarce items like sugar, soap, and rice. During periods when manufactured goods are in short supply, rich women buy up essential goods from shops and store them to create a shortage so that prices go up. This situation enables such women to make several times the normal profit. Those who deal in selling food items, from snacks to full meals, sell them in very strategic areas like construction sites where they are eaten under shades of trees or out in the open. Such shanty hotels, which are commonly known in Dar-Es-Salaam as *magenge,* are many. Women who sell the food items in these *magenges* are usually called *Mama Nitilie.*

Given the present economic crisis and the high cost of living, more women have joined the entertainment industry. "The Entertainment Industry", a phrase coined by Ross in 1973, consists of the provision of alcoholic drinks and commercialized sex.[33] Several men frequent areas like Manzese, Mwananyamala, Manzese Uzuri, Buguruni, Temeke, and Tandika-Mwisho in the evening, during their days off, or on weekends in order to get cheap beer and companionship. In Manzese, people buy beer as well as sexual pleasure.

Successful women employ barmaids and house servants who assist them in the selling business. Some women who do not own their own beer brewing and selling business work as barmaids in legal and illegal bars and pubs. Barmaids work long hours for minimal pay. Their survival depends on the number of and the kind of *watejas* (customers) they have. It is the *watejas* who buy beer from them and thus play a vital role in terms of the amount of bottles they sell. Some of these *watejas* are also barmaids' partners in commercial sex. It is on the basis of this that one can argue that almost all barmaids in Tanzania are, in fact, prostitutes. They work as barmaids not because of the pay, but rather because it is in these beer-selling centers where there is a potential market for commercial sex. Working as a barmaid puts one in a strategic position where she is exposed to several male customers. It is, in fact, through commercial sex that most of the barmaids supplement their incomes and manage to survive in urban areas. This is the essence of commercial sex. The relationship between a man and a woman is purely expressed in monetary terms. Nelson (1979) has argued that women recognize and value sexual attraction, affection, and companionship, although most of them would assess the relative merits of their men based on their generosity with money.[34]

Professional prostitution has also increased tremendously in Tanzania. Dar-Es-Salaam's prostitutes can be divided into the following six main groups:

1. **The *Danguro* (Brothel) Prostitutes**
   These are full-time prostitutes who own or rent brothels in cheap residential areas. They are the most popular. These prostitutes are relatively cheap and serve customers of all types provided they are able to pay. They are normally available from six in the evening to late into the night. Because of this they go to bed very late and wake up late the next day.

2. **The Street-Loitering Prostitutes**
   These are mobile prostitutes that may be full-time or part-time. Sometimes they ply the streets in search of customers during the day, but usually this takes place at night. Some of them position themselves at certain vantage points on the street and one can easily spot them around Ohio street and Samora Avenue in Dar-Es-Salaam. Their charges are relatively moderate and they are more interested in a quick relationship. Those prostitutes who frequent the expensive tourist hotels are always interested in foreign customers and demand to be paid in foreign currency. These are generally expensive.

3. **The Prostitutes Stationed in Guest Houses**
   Most of these have their own homes, but they usually rent rooms in hotels or guest houses and operate from there. Depending on the hotels in which they stay, some of these are sophisticated women who go with clients of very high status. They always dress well and appear attractive enough to appeal to reputable men. They are also mobile and normally move into areas where important events are taking place. These are expensive, considering that the amount

of money they charge for a brief encounter exceeds the daily rent of their rooms.

4. **The Hard-Core Prostitutes**
   These are the old veterans of prostitution. Some have been able to accumulate profits through their prostitution and currently own either brothels (with rooms for other prostitutes to rent out) or private beer pubs *(stoo bubu)*. They also employ girls who serve customers drinks and provide sexual pleasure. I label these girls, most of whom are young and new in the profession, "prostitution trainees" or "dependent prostitutes."

5. **The Barmaids**
   Most of these provide services in bars and other beer drinking pubs.

6. **The "After Office Hours" Prostitutes**
   Usually these are employees in the formal sector which flood the commercial sector industry after office hours in order to supplement their meager incomes.

Prostitutes have their own social networks. They do not operate independently but have agents and other people who assist them in identifying new areas which are potential markets for prostitution. Prostitutes are also well-organized. Most of them operate in groups and in specifically defined zones. They also assist each other in locating areas for potential customers, as well as in issues regarding security and protection. They also share information about where one can get assistance in problems such as treatment of STDs, abortion, and birth control. The zoning system assists them in safeguarding the appeal of the older prostitutes and presents difficulties to the new, seemingly beautiful young prostitutes.

Working as a prostitute in Tanzania is not an easy exercise. Prostitution is considered to be both an immoral and an illegal means of earning income under Section 176 of the Penal Code of the Tanzanian Laws. Prostitutes can also be sued under the Human Resources Deployment (Nguvu-Kazi) Act of 1983.

Making prostitution illegal has far-reaching implications. First and foremost, it forces the business to operate secretly. Second, (and related to the first point), since prostitutes operate secretly, the business is neither controlled nor monitored. Hence, prostitutes in Tanzania (unlike their counterparts in Western European countries) are not medically checked because the government acts as though they are not there. With such a situation, the presence and spread of venereal diseases like *Ukimwi* (AIDS) cannot be monitored or controlled.

Poverty is scandalous. These women prostitute their bodies not because they are addicted to sex and would like to sleep with several men per night, but because, like other human beings, they need shelter, food, and clothing. These basic human necessities are not provided freely. One has to struggle in order to get them. Thus, to some women, prostitution remains the plausible alternative. It is poverty which forces people to practice commercialized sex. For some women, absence of viable employment opportunities in the formal sector has long been a route to commercialized sex. In Tanzania, increasing economic differentiation has produced major income disparities between classes and genders. At the same time, the current structural adjustment programs are arguably exacerbating this. Without wider action against poverty and gender inequality, these forms of commercialized sex are likely to continue to flourish or increase.

If prostitution is regarded by those women who practice it as a solution to their situation of poverty (or a survival tactic), the most crucial question is: To whom are prostitutes a problem? Women who commercialize their bodies take that advantage precisely because there is a high demand for it. Most male customers decide to pay for sexual pleasures because that is the cheapest way one can satisfy his sexual desires. A general discussion with some women prostitutes in Dar-Es-Salaam during my field work stated that most of their customers were either unmarried men or married men that weren't living with their wives in the city. This statement has to be handled with caution. It does not mean that married men living together with their wives do not buy sexual pleasure. There are others who have sexual relationships with prostitutes.

One bachelor boy told me his reasons for having commercialized sex. He also explained why he was not interested in establishing normal friendly relationships with girls, and why he did not want to marry.

> I like prostitutes because they are cheap and relationship with them is purely defined. Decent permanent ordinary girlfriends are nowadays very expensive. If you have one, you have to maintain her all the time (supplying her with material goods) or else she will abandon you and look for other men. I am a minimum wage worker recipient. The wage I get is not enough even for my personal essential needs. How can I pay a house rent for my girlfriend? Where will I get the money to buy her a new *kitenge* or *kanga*. Most of the girls have at present

developed the so-called modern consumerism behavior. They like visiting cinema halls every weekend, and outings in modern good hotels is their way of life. Personally I cannot afford that. On the other side, prostitutes are different. What they want is money in exchange of a bed-ride. The majority of them have fixed payment rates. Unlike the ordinary girl friends, most of the prostitutes are not jealous if they see you with another woman. What they are interested in you for is your money. So I am better off paying 100 Tshs. per month to a prostitute rather than having an ordinary girlfriend, spend more and experience several problems. I do not want to marry because of my poverty. I can neither maintain a girlfriend nor a housewife.

The opinion presented above has got some truth in it. Studies on prostitution elsewhere in Africa, e.g., Nelson's 1979 study in Nairobi, have also shown that prostitutes are cheaper than normal or ordinary girlfriends in the Third World. In Dar-Es-Salaam, the majority cheap prostitutes (*danguro*) operate in squatter areas. Most of their customers are the urban poor, and those who receive a very low wage. These people buy sexual pleasure not because they have a lot of money to waste, but because they are poor. One can conclude from the above analysis that most of the prostitutes are poor women and they prostitute their bodies for the same reason. Likewise, the majority of their customers are also poor people, and they buy sex because their situation of poverty forces them to do that. Prostitution becomes the easiest and the cheapest means of satisfying their sexual desires.

Operating as a prostitute is difficult, dangerous, and a life-risking activity. Women who entertain a large number of strange customers run the risk of being beaten, robbed by unscrupulous, drunken, bhang-smoking, or drug addicted customers.[35] Some end up with unwanted pregnancies, diseases, and several other problems. Sometimes they are harassed by city council authorities, threatened by repatriation, and others spend a lot of money bribing the authorities in order to force them to turn their backs and act like the prostitutes are not there.

In concluding this chapter one can argue that there is some truth to the idiom, *Tanzania ni Nchi ya Bongo*, or, "one has to use his brain in order to survive in Tanzania."

High cost of living, unrealistic incomes, inflation, and the like have eroded away the moral codes and ethics of the society. These economic circuits have given birth to another economic circuit where corruption and other illicit activities provide a means of survival to some urban dwellers. It is an acknowledged fact in most urban areas in the Third

World countries that a lot of people survive from the activities of the informal sector. Tanzania is no different. Some people have turned out to be millionaires through black-marketing and corruptive tendencies while others are purely surviving from illicit activities. The economic circuit of illicit activities is now popular and dominant. This is confirmed by the fact at least everybody knows that the number of those who survive through legal and clean business is negligible. It is this kind of development which, in my opinion, justifies my use of the concept for purely analytical purposes.

In both the illicit and other legal informal sectors activities, it is the urban poor who experience difficulties. The hawkers and street vendors have to offer bribes in order to encourage the authorities to look the other way. The support which they get from the state as urban poor is unknown.

If people have reacted to the situation of urban poverty and economic crisis in the way described above, how has the state reacted? Is the state in a holiday? Does it support them? What kind of state policies have been introduced in order to fight the situation of urban poverty? Can these policies manage to solve the essence of the problems? Chapter 7 looks at these questions in brief.

7
The State and the Urban Poor

Introduction

Having seen the strategies of survival which the majority urban residents in general and the poor in particular adopt in order to confront the difficult urban way of life, several questions remained unanswered. If the poor have had the initiative to identify methods of survival, what has the state been doing? How has it reacted regarding the situation of urban poverty? What kind of policies has it implemented in order to confront these problems? What have they achieved?

The State's Attitude Toward the Urban Poor

The chapters discussing housing and squatter settlements have shown in concrete terms the negative opinions held by most bureaucrats and policymakers regarding slum squatter settlements. Likewise, the chapter on survival tactics has also shown how most of the activities carried out by the unemployed and the other urban poor are illegalized and criminalized.

All these problems have happened, and continue to happen, because the state views the urban poverty in terms of poverty itself, not in terms of the general social relations dominant in Tanzania in general and in the urban areas in particular. Hence, the urban poor are seen as responsible for their situation. They are seen as a social cancer which has penetrated the Tanzanian towns and cities.

Section 176 of the Penal Code deals with what the law terms "Idle and Disorderly Persons". This section has been in the Penal Code since Independence.[1]

The section identifies seven categories of persons who are defined and deemed by law to be "idle and disorderly persons". Among these are prostitutes, beggars, gamblers, pimps, and others who fall into related groups.[2]

The seven categories are:

1. Every common prostitute behaving in a disorderly or indecent manner in any public place or loitering or soliciting in any public place for the purpose of prostitution;
2. Every person wandering or placing himself in any public places to beg or to gather alms, or encouraging or forcing any child or children to do so;
3. Every person playing at any games of chance for money or money's worth in any public place;
4. Every person wandering abroad and endeavoring to obtain or gather alms by exposure of wounds or deformation;
5. Every person who publicly conducts himself in a manner likely to cause a breach of the place;
6. Every person who, without lawful excuse, publicly does any indecent act; and
7. Every person who in any public place solicits for immoral purposes.

The code states that anyone convicted of being an "idle and disorderly person" is liable for a fine not to exceed five hundred Tanzanian Shillings or imprisonment for a period not to exceed three months or to both such fine and imprisonment.[3]

Section 177(1) states that anyone who is convicted twice of the above offence under section 176 is deemed to be "a rogue and a vagabond" and is liable on the first offence to an imprisonment of three months (without the option of a fine) and on a subsequent offence to an imprisonment of one year.[4]

The Written Law (Miscellaneous Amendments) (No. 2) Act of 1983, among other things, amends the Penal Code (Chapter 16 of the Laws) section 176 by adding two more categories to the already existing seven categories of idle and disorderly persons. They are:

8. Any able bodied person who is not engaged in any productive work and has no visible means of subsistence;
9. Any person lawfully employed who is, without any lawful excuse, found engaging in personal entertainment at a time when he is supposed to be at work.[5]

To whom does the eighth category refer? Basically, these are people who are unemployed and actively yet unsuccessfully seeking work. According to this law, they are criminals and therefore subject to either a fine of 500 Tshs. or three months in prison or both. This also includes workers who have been labelled as unneeded and thrown out on the streets by no fault of their own.[6] Thus, as I have already argued, there is no attempt to see the unemployed as victims of the social and economic system as a whole.

The Legal Aid Committee of the Faculty of Law at the University of Dar-Es-Salaam has argued that, under this law, the unemployed are being punished twice. First, they are punished by being deprived of the employment through which they would earn their living and second, by being made criminally liable for that state of unemployment.[7]

The committee argues further that:

> Politically, it is adding insult to injury to lump a section of the working class together with gamblers and pimps. Legally, it is a grave folly and an act of desperation to believe that social and economic problems like unemployment can be solved by criminalizing them. This is besides the insurmountable problems of enforcing such a law and giving a fair and just interpretation of such terms as 'productive work', and 'visible means of subsistence'.[8] (Emphasis added.)

The ninth category refers to any employed person who leaves his work or place of work for reasons unconnected with his duties. By doing so, such a person is committing an offence.[9] The practical implications of this code to the urban poor will become clear in our discussion of the *Nguvu-Kazi* Act of 1903. But it is now becoming clear that the state's view on the urban poor has, since independence, been negative.

The post-colonial state inherited this kind of conception from its predecessor, the colonial state. Since the 1940s, official colonial state reports began to register concern over the perceptible drift of Africans from up-country to the towns in numbers which bore no relation to the degree of industrial and commercial opportunity offered by the towns.

Thus, a group of urban unemployed was created for the first time in major Tanzanian townships.[10] In Dar-Es-Salaam, a total of 20,000 unemployed was estimated in 1957, of whom only 8,000 were registered.[11] Even though, as Armstrong (1987) has argued, the control over rural-urban migration by the colonial state in Tanganyika was markedly less strict and authoritarian than in most neighboring colonies such as Kenya, the Rhodesias, and the Belgian Congo. In these places they have laws to discourage Africans from settling in towns and provide elaborate systems of registering new arrivals using photographs and finger prints.[12]

In 1944, the colonial state enacted a law called "Townships (Removal of Undesirable Persons) Ordinance Chapter 104 of the Laws." This law empowered the administrative officer currently in charge of a district to remove undesirable persons in the area under his jurisdiction by way of a "removal order".

The ordinance stated that the removal order could be used in any of the following circumstances:

1. If the person has been sentenced to a term of imprisonment (other than in default of payment of fine or compensation) for an offence against a person or involving property, or for an offence against the Native Liquors Ordinance or the Intoxicating Liquors Ordinance; or
2. If the person has no regular employment or other reputable means of livelihood.[13]

The law gave police officers the power to arrest any person whose name was on a removal order. They did not need a warrant and could hold that person in custody for up to one month. A person found guilty of any offence mentioned in this ordinance was liable for a fine of up to two hundred shillings or to imprisonment for up to three months, or both.[14]

This ordinance defined a "destitute person" as any person without employment and unable to show that he has visible and sufficient means of subsistence.

These statutes were later inherited by the post-colonial state and gave the state the necessary legal powers to remove the destitute and the unemployed from the cities and towns.

With the presence of these ordinances, it meant that the colonial state in Tanganyika had also started exercising some control over the process of urbanization.

In 1955, proposals were made that would require every resident to carry a passport or an identity card and this prompted the majority of Africans to rise in revolt.[15] In 1983, Yeager arugued that such proposals were made precisely because of the emergence of hooliganism in which unemployment was believed to be a contributing factor.[16] The police rounded up and repatriated a lot of unemployed people out of Dar-Es-Salaam. Suggestions were also made to force people who intended to migrate to Dar-Es-Salaam to pay for a pass which would allow them to migrate and present themselves before the Liwali's court.[17] Other methods of restricting people from migrating to Dar-Es-Salaam included radio broadcasts advising people against doing so becasue of the presence of unemployment.[18] Some provisions of the Colonial Labor Utilization Ordinance (Chapter 243) of 1947 also restricted and discarded the presence of the unemployed persons in urban areas. Hence, all policies emanating from this legislation always focused on repatriation.

The policy of repatriation was also inherited by the post-colonial state. Commenting on repatriation a decade ago, President Nyerere observed the following:

> . . . it has been announced more times than it is easy to count that every able-bodied person in Tanzania must work. . . . Then on every occasion, there is a great 'drive' to road up the unemployed in towns and repatriate them. For a week or so the criminals and idle parasites hide in their houses while responsible workers and peasants on legitimate business are harassed. . . . Then the whole campaign dies away until it is realized that the problem of criminals in towns and of people not doing a hard day's work is still with us and the process repeated.[19]

Confirming Nyerere's observation, the official *Daily News Paper* paper carried the following report on Dar-Es-Salaam on March 11, 1978.[20]

> Beggars are back in Dar-Es-Salaam once again, scarcely three years after they were rounded up in a major sweep in September 1975. According to a survey conducted by the *Daily News Paper* in the past two weeks, the beggars spend nights on pavements of houses belonging to wealthy Asian shopkeepers. Social Welfare authorities have charged that the businessmen use the beggars as watchmen. . . . Meanwhile it has been learned in the cause of investigations by this newspaper that over one hundred beggars assemble at an open space along Mrima Street in Kisutu area every night after begging sessions during the day. . . . An on-the-spot investigation March 9th showed that about 60 to 70 beggars, some of them preparing the day's 'meal', had already assembled at that area to spend the night. More were expected to join the 'congregation'.

As Ishumi (1984) has commented, the March 15, 1978 edition of the newspaper of the CCM political party, *Uhuru*, was even more vocal on the matter. Deploying the resurgence of the beggars in the city, the editorial went further in criticizing the government for not having found a permanent solution to the problem.

> ... The problem of beggars is not a recent one; it is an old problem. Whenever it seemed to go beyond proportions, the 'medicine' that has been applied is to round up the victims and to repatriate them to their homes (in the rural areas). ... This method of street-capturing repatriation relieves the town only for a short while; it is a piecemeal, short-lived solution, for the beggars soon re-appear. We need a more permanent step.[21]
>
> Although the Central Committee of the Party had called on the government to look into this problem in 1975, and although those concerned promised to give a solution soon (including legislating against alms-giving), nothing has as yet been done and we really wonder why.
>
> In a country that has declared a socialist policy, it is shameful and indeed inexplicable to find its citizens roaming about in streets begging and turning garbage bins over in search of food. (*Uhuru*, March 15, 1978. Translated from original Swahili by Ishumi 1984: 26)

As if these experiences and criticisms were not enough, the late Prime Minister Ndugu Sokoine, in his budget speech to the Parliament in 1983, directed that:

> All residents in Dar-Es-Salaam and the other towns in mainland Tanzania who have no work from which to earn a living *must return to the villages where they came from or must be given farms outside of Dar-Es-Salaam region*, so that an able-bodied person works to feed himself and if possible provide the surplus to the nation. Even those with shops, factories, and those rendering services should be given licences on the condition that they have registered themselves for land allocation so as to produce their own food and alleviate the problem of food shortage in the country. Equally, workers' families living in towns should grow their own food.[22] (Emphasis added)

In his speech, the Prime Minister estimated that at least 40% of the Dar-Es-Salaam city residents were jobless, and that they took a greater share of the national "pie".[23]

President Nyerere's speech on the Saba Saba day (7/7/83) gave more weight to the Prime Minister's speech. In this speech, Nyerere gave a notice to the loiterers and other unemployed persons in Dar-Es-Salaam to return to their respective regions and engage in agricultural production before the government started acting on them.[24] Later in his speech to the Regional Commissioners and Regional Development Directors (RDDS) on September 25, 1983, Nyerere equated the loiterers to economic saboteurs and racketeers when the nation had declared a war on them.[25]

It is on the basis of such views that the state came up with the *Nguvu-Kazi* Act. However, the content, objectives, and mode of implementation are exact replicas of the previous colonial and post-colonial strategies of solving the urban unemployment problem. It involves repatriation and restriction of excess rural-urban exodus. In order to situate the analysis of the *Nguvu-Kazi* Act in its proper historical perspective, a discussion of the nature of urban poverty policies between independence and the *Nguvu-Kazi* period (1961-1983) is necessary. The section below presents a brief critical evaluation of such policies.

The State's Policies on Urban Poverty (1961-1993)

The "Back to the Land" policy (or "repatriation") has characterized all post-independence policies which have been implemented to solve the urban problem. Several methods have been used in order to achieve this goal. They include political campaigns like *Kila mtu afanye kazi* ("every able-bodied person should work"), legislations, radio broadcasts, settlement schemes, and ad-hoc round-up operations.

The 1961 independence did not alleviate the colonial draconian methods of confronting urban poverty, and, in a way, it intensified the previous colonial efforts.[26] Police round-ups continued and in 1964 the police officer in charge of the repatriation program in Dar-Es-Salaam was reported to have dealt with more than 15,000 cases over the previous eight years.[27]

A nationwide campaign against the urban poor and those intending to migrate to Dar-Es-Salaam took place in March of 1964 with radio broadcasts carrying messages such as these:

> Those of you who may be thinking of leaving your *shambas* (farms), stay where you are unless you have guarantee of assured employment in the towns.[28]

As Armstrong (1987) has argued, the town-dwelling unemployed were urged to return to their homes, plant their crops, attend their livestock, and become worthy citizens of Tanganyika.[29] All the unemployed in urban areas were asked to register themselves voluntarily so that the government could know the number of the people unemployed before it prepared plans to offer them work.[30] Positive measures included the establishment in 1964 of a committee to examine job creation. Settlement schemes, especially near Dar-Es-Salaam, were already in operation. A 3,000-acre scheme to settle 200 unemployed on farm allotments had already been opened by the regional commissioner.[31] Many of the first recruits into the newly created National Service Program in 1964 were unemployed youth.[32] Other unemployed people were at the same time advised to seek employment in sisal plantations (work widely known to be hard, unpleasant, and poorly paid) while waiting for better well-paid jobs.[33] Nevertheless, these campaigns did not help, and at the end of the day the state returned to its coercive approach after realizing that the rate of unemployment continued to rise unabated. Forced repatriation become the agenda.

As of October 10, 1964 it was declared an offence for unemployed persons to reside in Dar-Es-Salaam. Under this order, all unemployed people were required to report to the nearest police stations.[34] The police flooded the streets demanding identification cards from suspects, and those found unemployed without their cards were deported to their home areas.

Other measures involved the driving away of beggars and destitutes, and strict regulations were introduced to the process of issuing licences for some informal sector activities like petty trading, hawking, shoe cleaning, knife sharpening, etc.[35] The operation continued, although with less momentum. The youth wing of the ruling party (the Tanu Youth League, or TYL) later joined the operation by assisting the police force in the rounding up of all those who were considered to be unemployed. Beggars were moved to alms houses and idlers were packed off to their home districts. (*Tanzania Weekly News* 3/31/67, Armstrong 1987: 16).

Both the campaigns and the repatriation operation did not last long, and in the years following that, the *Tanzania Weekly* of 8/31/67 reported a comeback of beggars in the streets of Dar-Es-Salaam and the presence of long lines of unemployed people at the labor office.

After realizing that the situation was again out of hand, the state announced another campaign in 1967. All urban residents were supposed to possess identification cards.[36] The same procedures were used again, starting with voluntary registration of the unemployed. The government advised them to leave the city on their own accord. Later the police started rounding up people by force, this time assisted by special police constables. The state argued that the aim of the operation was to wipe out hard-core criminals. Strict controls on the issuing of licences on petty business resurfaced. For example, water selling businesses in Dar-Es-Salaam were declared illegal and all water sellers were marked for repatriation. Such a blunder caused what Armstrong (1987) has termed the "Battle of Water Sellers" because of the outcry from the public. This stemmed from the fact that 100,000 people in Dar-Es-Salaam lacked a nearby water source and relied heavily on their services. Due to this outcry, the Minister of Labor intervened and announced a formal reprieve for the water sellers (Armstrong 1987: 16). Again, an unemployment committee was established in Dar-Es-Salaam. Villages near urban areas were targeted for resettlement programs. Round-ups were haphazardly implemented, leading to the suffering of innocent individuals; most of the unemployed went into hiding.

Further campaigns were again revised in 1969 and 1970. In April of 1970, the police rounded up criminals and several unemployed persons in Dar-Es-Salaam and Tanga. People who looked suspicious were stopped and questioned about their residences and places of work, and those failing to satisfy the police were arrested. (*Tanganyika Standard* 5/1/70, Armstrong 1987: 17).

The press criticized the whole operation, comparing it to the colonial laws of the past, drawing attention to the role of the unemployed as the "scapegoats of society" and expressing the feeling that this task was not being performed as expeditiously as it might be.[37] Indeed, as usual, the unemployment problem remained in spite of the campaigns and the forced repatriation. To some leaders it became clear that a permanent solution existed outside the urban areas. This is confirmed by one statement in one of Nyerere's speeches where he stressed that:

> The control of rural outflow would depend largely on the village leadership making rural areas more relevant to youthful aspirations.[38]

In 1969, the Social Welfare Division of the Ministry of Health had already started conducting educational programs in the rural areas designed to dissuade people from moving to urban centers (Armstrong 1987: 17).

In 1975, the ruling party issued a directive aimed at fighting the problem of unemployment via the umbrella of the operation known as *kila mtu afanye kazi*. Earlier on in 1976, Nyerere had already declared a

"War on Loiterers" (*Vita dhidi a Wazurulaji*) (*Daily News Paper*, 6/26/76). Thus, "Operation *kila mtu afanye kazi*" was a follow-up policy of the previously declared war. The highlights of this war labelled the unemployed as "loiterers" (*wazurulaji*), "lazy" (*wavivu*), "drunkards" (*walevi*), and "exploiters" (*wanyonyaji*). They were also regarded as *maadui wa siasa ya ujamaa na kujitegemea* (enemies of the policy of socialism and self-reliance).[39] The argument raised against them was that it would be for the good of the nation and also there was no need of having unemployed persons at a time when Tanzania had plenty of free land to work on (*Daily News Paper* 6/26/76).

The usual procedure of carrying out such operations reappeared, from the voluntary registration to the forced round-ups. Plans to resettle the unemployed were made, and several other positive and good promises were made by both the government and political leaders. A pilot project to resettle 18,000 jobless residents in Dar-Es-Salaam into more than 30 new villages was initiated.[40] It was during this period that new and very famous villages like Kibugumo, Tegeta, Mwana-Dilatu, and Geza-Ulole suddenly emerged in the outskirts of Dar-Es-Salaam city. It has been estimated that the government spent more than 11 million Tanzanian shillings to resettle the unemployed between 1976 and 1977.[41]

This time it was the people's militia force (*Askari wa Mgambo*) who assisted the police operations. The round-ups are known to have been harsh and poorly planned and implemented, thus causing a lot of suffering for innocent urban dwellers. The creation of the Kibugumo and Geza-Ulole villages and others became sensational and were the talk of the city. Government-owned jazz bands composed and played dance music which praised the whole operation and the creation of the resettlement villages. The following song played by a jazz band owned by Urafiki Textile, The Urafiki Jazz Band, dominated and became the most popular song on Radio Tanzania.

> *Baba na mama, shangazi na mjomba mji hautufai, twendeni Geza-Ulole. Biashara ya kahawa, maji na samaki sisi haitufai, twendeni Kibugumo. Kibugumo na Kimbiji, Tegeta na Mwana-Dilatu hayo ndiyo makazi mapya ya mwana-wa-kimapinduzi. Geza-Ulole baba; Geza-Ulole mama; Geza-Ulole baba; Geza-Ulole twende sote.* . . .

Translated, this means,

> Dear father, mother, aunt, and uncle. The city is not good for us, let us go and join Geza-Ulole village. The business of selling coffee, water, and fish is not good for us, let us go and join Kibugumo village. This

village, and others like Kimbiji, Tegeta, and Mwana-Dilatu are new residential areas of a revolutionary individual. Let us go and join them. . . .

Critics of this operation have argued that the resettlement strategy proved administratively cumbersome. They said that it lacked cooperation among the officials involved, and it experienced financial difficulties and a shortage of building materials, facts which point to a lack of plans, preparations, and well-conceived policies.[42] Armstrong (ibid) has noted that within a few days after the exercise had begun, the population of some villages dropped to negligible levels. The majority of the unemployed dispatched in these villages returned to Dar-Es-Salaam, indicating a total failure of the 1976 operation. At present, the names of these villages belong to the museum of antiquities. People read about them, but none talks about them.

It is against this background that the *Nguvu-Kazi* Act of 1983 can be understood. One vital question at this point is: What have been the common characteristics of these pre-*Nguvu-Kazi* policies and strategies? What can one learn from them?

First and foremost is the fact that all the post-independence policies and strategies aimed at combating urban poverty are a replica of the colonial methodology. They differ in form, but they are actually similar in content and essence. Second, and in fact related to the first point, is the continuation of the view that the urban poor are responsible for their own situation. The post-independence politics have not been in a position to provide a radical viewpoint quite different from the colonial one. The outcome of this has been the implementation of policies and solutions which treat the symptoms rather than the root cause. Third is the lack of learning from previous mistakes and experiences within the *modus vivendi* of the political system in Tanzania. This is confirmed by the reappearance of similar mistakes in each campaign, strategy, and policy. In all the programs we have seen that a lack of preparation and haphazard implementation have been typical characteristics. Fourth, there is a gap of years between operations, and each one has always started out with great fanfare and then lost its momentum. Why is this so? It could be explained by a lack of seriousness among politicians. The other reason is precisely that policy planning and implementation in Tanzania has always been carried out on a random basis, and has not been seriously considered as an ongoing process of the transformation of the overall socioeconomic system. Most of the policies are a result of state responsiveness to political pressure. This happens more often with the policies which focus on urban issues.

Mlay (1979) argues that these urban control programs have always proved temporary, half-hearted, unpopular, and inefficient.[43] Commenting on the relationship between these urban control campaigns and strategies, Armstrong argues that

> Urban control measures are often accompanied by, or coincide with, local drives against crimes, vagrancy or for city cleanliness and civic pride, or nationally instituted initiatives aimed at raising productivity and reducing corruption and inefficiency. Campaigns, it should be stressed, are often only a well-publicized offensive in a continuous war against the many related urban-based evils which form their target. Thus, regular, if not very thorough, steps to detain not only petty criminals but also unemployed appear to form part of the urban police force's normal duties.[44]

Quoting the study of IL0 (1978), Armstrong argues further concerning the impact of various bureaucratic restrictions on informal sector trade activities, licencing, and urban dwellings. Such restrictions, he argues, assist in maintaining continued pressure on the urban poor.

An interval of about seven years elapsed since the year of the last hot operation from 1976 to 1983 when the government passed another law titled "The Human Resources Deployment (*Nguvu-Kazi*) Act of 1983" which again necessitated the use of harsh operations against the unemployed. What is the content of this act? Does it reflect a difference and thus a sense of learning from the previous operations? What are its tenets? What has been its impact on the urban poor? Has it achieved its objectives? The section which follows explores these issues in detail.

The Human Resources Deployment (Nguvu-Kazi) Act of 1983

The Act

The *Nguvu-Kazi* Act was passed by the Parliament in April and assented by the President in May of 1983. The Act emplowered the Minister of Labor and Social Welfare to put the law into effect on October 15, 1983. The Prime Minister directed the Dar-Es-Salaam city region to start implementing the act before other regions.

The act is divided into six main parts. Parts I and II deal with the establishment of the Human Resources Deployment scheme and its central administration. In these parts, Part II in particular, it is stated that it is the responsibility of the local government authority to make arrangements to ensure that every resident within its area of jurisdiction engages in productive or other lawful employment. It will also be responsible for formulating properly organized employment-generating projects in fields like agriculture, poultry farming, animal husbandry, fisheries, day care centers, and small- and large-scale commercial enterprises.[45] The local governments are also required to

1. make arrangements which will ensure that the undertaking in these projects occupy the residents all year round [Part II(2)(b)];
2. give guidance and assistance to the agricultural and other sectors on the proper combination of hard work and skill in carrying out their daily functions [Part II(2)(c)]; and
3. make arrangements for the proper allocation and use of skilled and high level manpower and to secure the enforcement of their terms of employment in the best economic interest of the nation [Part II(2)(d)].

Part II, Section 8 of the act establishes a national committee known as the "National Human Resources Deployment Advisory Committee". Its role is to advise the Minister on matters related to the full deployment of human resources, especially

1. formulating and coordinating economically viable employment-generating schemes suitable for urban and rural areas;
2. making recommendations to the appropriate authorities regarding matters of employment; and
3. researching ways to use the available human resources more productively in government commercial, industrial, and agricultural sectors.[46]

Part III of the act establishes the "Local Authority Human Resources Committees" whose functions (apart from other directives) are to receive, evaluate, and carry out the policy and plans laid out by the Minister for the purpose of this act. (Part III, Section 12).

Part IV, Sections 13 and 14 (which in this case is very important) deal with the registration of people. This part requires the local government authority to

1. Establish and maintain a register to be known as "Employer's Register";
2. Maintain a register of all residents who are capable of working, including the name of the resident, his address, age, marital status, number of dependents, parents' address, his level of education, skills, present employment, nationality, his original or adopted domicile, and the name of the owner of his residence;
3. Establish and maintain a register of non-skilled, skilled, and high-level manpower who are employed inside and outside Tanzania; the embassy offices have to maintain a register of all Tanzanian manpower living in their areas of jurisdiction; and
4. Establish a system to regulate the issuing of identification cards to people.

Part V (equally important in respect to this study) deals with the transfer, training, and rehabilitation of the unemployed persons.[47] This part empowers the Minister to provide a smooth, coordinated transfer and subsequent employment of the unemployed residents. [Section 17(i)]. In making these arrangements, the Minister should also register residents who have retired from public service, residents who still depend on their parents or relatives for their livelihood, law-abiding adult residents who have no known source of income, housewives, and non-citizens.[48]

Under Part V of this act, the Minister is entrusted with providing training facilities suited to the residents' age, experience, and qualifications under the provision of rehabilitation courses.[49]

Part VI of this act provides some "Miscellaneous Provisions", and Section 29 repeals the "Colonial Labor Utilization Ordinance of 1974, Chapter 243 of the Tanzanian Laws." The second schedule of the act (pages 106-107) provides the National Human Resources Deployment (Interim) Scheme where a full list of economic activities (that could possibly be considered "legal") have been outlined and the local government authorities are advised to carry out any of these activities in the furtherance of the provisions of this act.

Background Ideas to the Act

Besides the failure of the previous urban control campaigns, the economic crisis seems to have been behind the enactment of this act. It seems that the state believes that one of the reasons behind the present economic crisis is the fact that a lot of people are not doing productive work, and this is revealed by the low productivity in all sectors of the economy.[50] Such beliefs can be noted from President Nyerere's speech in Mtwara on the July 7, 1982 in which he called upon those people in towns keeping idle dependants to send them home so that they could engage in agricultural work.[51] Three months later, the CCM National Executive Committee instructed the government to enact a law that would ensure that any able-bodied person would work.[52] At about the same time, the Ministry of Labor (*Uimarishaji wa huduma za Ajira za Taifa Nchini*) in Tanzania served as a basis for cabinet discussion on the issue.[53]

In February of 1983, the late Prime Minister Ndugu Sokoine made the issue of *Nguvu-Kazi* one of the key aspects of his eight-point program (Miti 1983). He argued that the government would struggle against poverty through agricultural undertakings by ensuring that every one, (except children, the aged, and disabled, as stated in the Arusha Declaration) was engaged in productive work.[54]

> Every Tanzanian who had the ability to work must meet his/her needs and ensure that he/she contributed surplus to the nation.... He further reiterated that the CCM government will pass a law that ensures that the party order that everybody must work is effectively improved.[55]
> (*Daily News Paper*, 2/28/83)

It is against this background that the *Nguvu-Kazi* Act was enacted and passed in the Parliament in 1983. At this juncture one may wonder if the enactment of this act was necessary and whether or not its content was a new phenomena.

The colonial Master and Native Servant's Ordinance of 1923 provided law provisions to control and regulate the African migration inflow to towns. The ordinance also had provisions regarding the deployment of human resources.[56] Earlier on in 1913, pass laws were introduced by the colonial government requiring every adult that was 18 years old and living in the territory of Tanganyika to have a special card which specified his or her engagement locality. In a way, this situation forced some Africans to engage in some economic activities.[57] The Master and Native Servant's Ordinance, which came into force in

1924, was enacted in order to enforce the above pass law. An employee who left his master without lawful excuse and without intentions to return was punished by either a fine (not to exceed 507 Tshs.) or three months imprisonment.[58]

The Master and Native Servant's Ordinance was replaced in 1957 by the Employment Ordinance (Chapter 366 of the laws). This law aimed at safeguarding employment contracts and providing work as long as the contract of employment existed. But in 1947, prior to the enactment of this ordinance, the colonial state passed a law called the "Labor Utilization Ordinance" (Chapter 243 of the laws) with the intention of creating "Labor Utilization Boards" whose function was to facilitate the utilization of available resources of native labor.[59]

As I have shown previously, compulsory measures to deploy the urban labor force were again taken between 1976 and 1978 involving the creation of several villages around the outskirts of Dar-Es-Salaam. So, what does this mean in terms of the *Nguvu-Kazi* Act? In brief, it means that its content as well as its objectives are not a new phenomenon. The act is a replica of the colonial as well as the post-colonial measures of dealing with the problems associated with urban poverty. One may wonder what the impact of the implementation of this act has been on both urban and rural areas? Did the implementation of this act benefit from past experiences? An attempt to answer these questions is the subject matter of the section below.

The *Nguvu-Kazi* Act in Practice

In the Parliament the Prime Minister urged that the Dar-Es-Salaam region had to start preparation for the implementation of the law by July 15, 1983; Otherwise, the act would become effective nationwide in October of 1983. According to the Prime Minister, Dar-Es-Salaam was important because it was estimated in 1983 that 40% of the city residents were unemployed.[60]

The Minister of Labor and Social Welfare also stressed in his budget speech in 1983 the immediate registration of loiterers and employed people inside and outside the country.[61] The registration exercise was to be conducted by ward officers in urban areas and CCM branches in the rural areas. The Minister also stressed that the responsibility for preparation and supervision of the implementation process was to fall in the hands of local authorities, but directed the regional and area commissioners to shoulder the responsibility in the meantime.[62] The Minister directed that land should be set aside for distribution to the repatriated people from urban areas, though those repatriated would be free to decide whether to go back to their home villages or elsewhere in the country.[63] Finally, he insisted in the clearing of the loiterers and disabled people from towns and emphasized the necessity of each person carrying an identification card to avoid repatriation.[64]

It was clearly noted from the beginning that most of the authorities concerned with the implementation of this act emphasized on repatriation. The Dar-Es-Salaam Regional Commissioner, while addressing party and government leaders of the Kinondoni District, announced that all residents not engaged in productive work and hailing from other parts of the country would be repatriated.[65] Unemployed indigenous residents would be provided with work in the Goba, Mabwe-Pande, Msogola, and Mantu villages around the outskirts of Dar-Es-Salaam.[66] Nyerere's speech on the July 7, 1983 also stressed repatriation.[67]

With emphasis on repatriation, the whole *Nguvu-Kazi* program ecame to be understood as a measure aimed at clearing the "idlers and disorderly" persons from the urban areas.

Seminars on the issue were organized for leaders and other people who would be involved in the implementation of the act. The ministry responsible for the act emphasized further the necessity of carrying out seminars at all levels before the law came into operation.[68]

As Miti (1983) has noted, the National Executive Committee (NEC) of the party had directed that the implementation of *Nguvu-Kazi* should take place in stages, starting first with the jobless, then those employed in petty shops, and last with those employed in factories and offices.[69]

It was noted at a seminar on *Nguvu-Kazi* attended by Regional and Area Commissioners that the government had already allocated 40 million Tshs. (two million for each region) for the implementation of the act. At the end of the seminar, the participants produced the following resolutions.[70]

1. The focus will be on production in order to reduce the current economic difficulties. Every sector of production should make proper plans to enhance the habit of working for a living.
2. Agriculture should be given priority in the efforts to make the country self-reliant in food production. It should be regarded as a permanent "life and death" program.
3. There should be a general mobilization of the people and means must be found to involve every able-bodied person in work. . . . It should be deemed as an act of liberation and not punishment.

4. Leaders should work hand-in-hand in order to accomplish the task successfully.
5. The National Human Resources Act should be integrated into the National Development Program.
6. There should be no leniency granted to loiterers. They should be dealt with mercilessly and must join the program. Local government authorities should make by-laws in this regard. (*Daily News Paper*, 9/27/83) (Emphasis added.)

Miti (ibid) has also noted the following major points emerging from the national interpretation and the project program procedure of the *Nguvu-Kazi*.

> In the first place *Nguvu-Kazi* is turned into an "operation", a full scale campaign. Campaigns and operations have become permanent features in Tanzania and their mechanisms and effects are well known. This new "operation" had two prongs, that are not quite opposed. *The first prong is that of cleaning the towns of the unemployed as a means of easing town problems.* The second prong is to deploy all the available manpower into agricultural production. . . . *It is not concerned with how those repatriated will be utilized or problems that they are likely to cause in the villages.* [71](Emphasis added)

The Dar-Es-Salaam City region started implementing the act in July of 1983. As usual, a call was made to all the unemployed persons to register voluntarily.[72]

Once again *Nguvu-Kazi* was welcomed as the "most ambitious government project of the past three years" (*Daily News Paper*, 12/15/83). The campaign followed hard on the heels of another dramatic operation to clamp down on economic sabotage, black-marketing, smuggling, and corruption, and was occasionally referred to as a direct follow-up. (*Daily News Paper*, 9/16/83, Armstrong 1987: 7). On the one hand, stricter enforcement of law and order and tightening discipline was stressed by clearing "bad elements" and, in particular, fighting racketeering in which the jobless were often believed to be used as middlemen (*Daily News Paper*, 10/26/83, Armstrong 1987: 7). Quotations from the Bible and Koran and exhortations to socialist and nationalist sentiments emphasized the moral necessity of work and castigated "the vagabonds, rogues, and loiterer", and the sins, not only of crime, but also of laziness, parasitism, and negligence. On the other hand, other statements stressed the campaign's economic goals by citing the strain which the urban jobless placed on the economy and outlining the positive role they could play in enhancing economic production, particularly during the forthcoming season.[73]

The *Daily News Paper* of October 5, 1983 reported that 21,772 jobless people had been registered voluntarily in Dar-Es-Salaam, 13,571 in the Kagera region, mainly in Bukoba town. It was also noted that 16,182 of those registered in Dar-Es-Salaam had indicated their willingness to join villages in Dar-Es-Salaam. 6,500 acres of land had been secured in the villages surrounding Dar-Es-Salaam and 42,000 acres in villages away from the city and there were also 12,503 employees who had registered themselves for farming plots.[74] At the same time, the Dar-Es-Salaam regional government issued a directive categorizing the nature of legal and illegal petty business activities. (See Table 7.1)

On October 4, 1983, the Dar-Es-Salaam Regional Commissioner announced that all those registered jobless people would start leaving for their home regions by Friday, October 14, 1983.[75] He also expressed hope that those whose jobs were declared illegal would be winding up their business so that they could leave the city. (Miti, 1983).

According to the Regional Commissioner, the next stage in the implementation of *Nguvu-Kazi* would be to focus on the jobless who did not volunteer to register themselves. On October 7, 1983, the Regional Commissioner, while speaking to representatives of government, private and public firms, called upon the employers to ensure that all their employees had identification cards by the middle of the month, and ordered that by October 15th everybody should not walk in the streets of Dar-Es-Salaam without his card (ibid.). Furthermore, nobody would be allowed into the city without proper documents identifying him as a worker or allowing him to come in (ibid.).

The police round-ups and nets started on October 17, 1983 when 5,724 people were rounded up. 1,738 of these were in the Temeke District, of which only 295 were detained for further screening. (See Table 7.2)

This indiscriminate sweep by the police and militia lead to an outcry from the public and was criticized for its harshness and harassment. Housewives, domestic servants (buying essentials in shops markets), and some workers with identification cards were arrested and detained in screening centers. Strict restrictions were again imposed in the licensing of various informal trades to prevent the real jobless from escaping the net by this route (*Daily News Paper*, 11/4/83, Armstrong, 1987: 11). Threats of demolishing business kiosks used by unlicensed operators were instituted. Inconsistencies also arose in the implementation of the laws. For example, while the business of shoe shining was declared illegal in Dar-Es-Salaam, this trade was approved and supported by the government as gainful employment in Morogoro only 200 km away (*Sunday News*, 12/15/83).

TABLE 7.1
Legal and Illegal Businesses in 1983

Legal	Legal, But Must Be Licensed	Illegal
Garages	Hair dressers	Shoe shining
Bars and stores	Selling fruits and vegetables (only licensed green grocers)	Selling newspapers (except licensed agents)
Chicken farming	Selling charcoal (only licensed dealers)	Selling "vitumba", "maandazi", and roasted cassava in the street
Employment on casual terms ("vibarua")	Hairstylists	Selling soup and "Makongoro" (against health laws)
Shop owners	Tailoring, carpentry, smithing, repairing of radios, watches, shoes, and electrical goods, selling fire wood, and music recording	Selling local brew and Konyagi (against the law and all small vending stalls)

Source: Miti, K. "Issues Raised by *Nguvu-Kazi* and its Implementation in Dar-Es-Salaam" (mimeo), University of Dar-Es-Salaam 1983, page 8.

The round up was again repeated on October 27 and 28, and by November the sweeps had become almost a daily exercise. Having the identification card did not save one from police harassment, and the police as well as the militia force were already advised not to entertain arguments raised by those who had been detained because that was the task of the scrutinizing panels set up at the district headquarter level.[76]

The final stage of the operation involved repatriating those who had been scrutinized to be offenders. As Armstrong has noted, the numbers of those actually repatriated seem to have been very low indeed. By the end of December in 1983, only 1,500 people from Dar-Es-Salaam had been sent to the rural areas, and the press was already reporting rumors that many were filtering back to the city.[77]

TABLE 7.2
Detention of the Unemployed in Dar-Es-Salaam Campaigns:
Two Sample Days

Monday, October 17, 1983				
District	Kinondoni	Temeke	Ilala	Total
Detained	2000	1738	198	5724
Found to be jobless	194	295	400	889*

Wednesday, November 11, 1983				
District	Kinondoni	Temeke	Ilala	Total
Detained	302	600	654	1724
Found to be jobless	50	98	169	317

Source: *Daily News Paper* October 19-22, 1983 and *Daily News Paper* November 13-14, 1983

* People in this category were apparently those failing to convince the social security panels of their gainful employment and were to be repatriated to their home districts. However later reports indicated that of this 889, a further 330 were released after convincing the authorities they were married women, domestic servants or pursued other gainful occupations.

Analysis

Like the other campaigns and strategies, the implementation of the *Nguvu-Kazi* Act did not take advantage of learning from the abundance of problems that dominated and characterized the previous campaigns. The implementation of this act shows the poor planning of the whole system. The operation adopted similar mistakes from the past as it ignored several appeals and warnings to avoid past mistakes. Learning from past mistakes seems to have been beyond the wisdom of the policy formulators and implementors. The attitude of the implementing authorities is clearly expressed by the Dar-Es-Salaam Regional Commissioner who used to always argue that "*We shall learn as we go along.*"[78] However, as Miti (op.cit.) has argued, "in politics, learning by doing is always a synonym for costly errors and that it is often a painful and on occasion a disruptive process".[79] Under *Nguvu-Kazi* it was not a question of learning as the operation continued, but rather a question of learning from and avoiding the mistakes committed in similar operations of the past.

The outcome of learning as we go along limited the effectiveness of the program and the officials concerned publically admitted "uncoordinated and sometimes haphazard administration", and decried the different interpretations of the act from one area to another. (*Daily News Paper*, 4/22/85).[80]

Armstrong (1987) argues that both the act and the launching of the campaign appear to have been carried out before the authorities were adequately prepared or even before they were familiar with its intentions (page 12). The police round-ups were not aided by the widespread circulation of identification cards, either forged or no longer legitimate (*Daily News Paper* 11/4/83).[81] It was also reported that some criminals and unemployed people found refuge outside the urban areas in the height of the crackdown and this lead to sudden and often unwelcome influxes of newcomers in the villages close to Dar-Es-Salaam. (*Daily News Paper*, 11/22/83, Armstrong 1987: 12). Actual figures of actual jobless netted seem to have been very low. The high proportion of innocent detainees as well as the harsh and occasionally brutal treatment received at the hands of the police caused alienation, insecurity, and disruption.[82] The program was also characterized by high corruption by government officials, rendering the whole exercise useless.[83]

One major weakness of the *Nguvu-Kazi* operation is its perception of the broader issue of unemployment in Tanzania. Because land is abundant, the government and party leaders can't seem to understand why the unemployment exists. They argue that anybody who is unemployed in the urban areas could be gainfully employed in the agricultural sector.[84] It is on the basis of this false assumption that the urban unemployed are given several insulting names like loiterers, exploiters, and lazy. Rural-based agricultural production is seen as the solution to urban problems, but nobody bothers to critically examine the essence of rampant poverty and underemployment that has characterized this sector since the era of colonialism.

As I have argued elsewhere, agricultural production is still subsistence-based. The methods and tools of production dominant in this sector are still archaic. Because of this, cash-crop production is minimal and less profitable.[85] Rural exploitation, impoverization, and pauperization is typical and the use of peasant labor may be almost impossible under these conditions. It is these contradictions which are behind the rampant rural-urban exodus. This is a point based on the reality which both the policymakers and implementors have not yet come to grasp.

The rural-urban exodus continues unabated, and due to the general economic stagnation and the nature of the urban economy itself, the urban employment situation fails to absorb all the immigrants. Their need to survive forces these immigrants to engage in various dubious economic activities. Most of them resort to doing odd jobs which characterize the informal sector. By imposing strict regulations in licensing informal petty business in urban areas, the *Nguvu-Kazi* exercise has been exacerbating the very problem it aimed to solve. A recent survey of 124 jobless people in Dar-Es-Salaam revealed that 21% of the people depended on relatives, 3% on friends, and 76% on operating in informal sector activities.[86] Although this data was drawn from a very small sample, the widespread and rapid development of the informal sector activities in Dar-Es-Salaam shows the involvement of the unemployed in this sector. By forcing the unemployed to become peasants, the act hurts the very beneficiaries of the deployment program, and it denies the fact that life in the rural areas has become unbearable to many. By so doing, the act has been treating the symptoms rather than the cause of the so-called urban cancer.

During colonialism it was the peasant economy which was supposed to reproduce the labor of the urban worker's family. Towns were places for only single male African workers, while their families were to remain in the rural areas. *Nguvu-Kazi* urges urban dwellers to send their jobless dependants to the rural areas.[87] The sociology of the African extended family networks and the kind of interdependent relationships which exist within these networks is not considered. Will resorting to the draconian colonial strategy succeed?

The experience of the last five years has shown concretely that the whole exercise has ended up being a total failure. It has now become clear that the ideas which blame the unemployed for the present economic crisis are false and misleading. If *Nguvu-Kazi* was prescribed as a solution to the economic crisis that Tanzania is facing, it is clear now that its implementation and further existence cannot alleviate the crisis.

It is true that many of the urban jobless hail from the rural areas. It is also true that labor is needed in the rural areas, but it is not true that low productivity in the agricultural sector is a result of rural-urban migration, nor does it guarantee that repatriation (back to the rural land policy) will raise rural productivity. Ignoring these facts lead the highly educated members of Parliament to pass the *Nguvu-Kazi* Act in 1983.

Taking into consideration all the pitfalls that characterize both the interpretation as well as the implementation of *Nguvu-Kazi*, there is no doubt that the aim of the act was reducing the urban population and not economic rehabilitation. If the latter was the case, then plans would have been made to make sure that those repatriated would not face similar problems which forced them to migrate to the urban areas in the first place (Bisanda 1984). What *Nguvu-Kazi* attempted and still attempts to do is to simply transfer urban-based problems to the rural areas. Is this possible?

One might also wonder what issues *Nguvu-Kazi* should be focusing on. The program should have started by either directing or deploying the jobless in different productive activities, assisting them both morally and materially. If performed well, these activities could generate income to benefit both the producer and the nation at large. Projects which assist someone in becoming self-reliant (regardless of whether they are urban- or rural-based) could form a positive point of departure. Practically, this could be implemented by promoting rural and urban economies and employment opportunities through the promotion of small-scale industrial operations. The present initiatives of the Small Scale Industrial Development Organization (SIDO) that concentrate on the urban-based light consumer goods industries (e.g., those producing baby toys, household utensils, electric hot plates, and bulbs) are insufficient. SIDO should also invest in and produce agricultural inputs which could revolutionize the productivity of the rural sector, as well as diverse activities in other industrial sectors. Such a strategy implies that small-scale, labor-intensive industrial investments have to be given a higher priority than large-scale, capital-intensive ones whenever possible.

Nguvu-Kazi is supposed to recognize and assist the operations of the informal sector activities. In addition to that, there is an urgent need to implement a nationwide structural transformation of the existing economic system. A new industrial strategy is urgently needed, one that would create linkages between the various sectors of the economy, providing not only employment opportunities but also aiding in the process of transforming the rural sector .

In conclusion, it is clear throughout this chapter that the state has always understood and continues to understand the causes of urban poverty in terms of the poor themselves. Poverty is not seen as a reflection of the organization of the entire socioeconomic and political system. Because of this, the solutions instituted by the state to solve urban poverty end up treating the phenomenal forms rather than the essential relations behind the problem. In most cases it is these politics which have exacerbated the very problems they aimed to solve. The question then is *Where do we go from here*? This is the subject matter of the last chapter.

8
Conclusion: How Tanzania Should Proceed From Here

In this concluding chapter I provide a very brief summary of all important arguments which have been advanced in this work. I also present some suggestions which could assist Tanzania in confronting, with possible success, its problems of economic crisis, urbanization, and urban poverty.

National planning in Tanzania has been dominated mainly by economists, almost to the total exclusion of other social scientists. They have not been in a position to provide practical solutions to urban poverty. They have not provided for employment, have generally regarded investment in official urban housing as largely unproductive, and have not seriously attempted investments in labor-intensive industries.

Furthermore, even within these limitations in national planning, planning and implementation in Tanzania are sometimes made less effective because of the politics involved. One reason for this is that there are no effective mechanisms to assure that public firms are run productively and economically and are accountable to the people. In a situation like this, there is much irregularity in the rate at which the senior governmental staff is replaced, and in the long run this has had a very negative impact on planning and implementation. For example, since 1978, the total number of ministries and their composition has been changed more than twice. Some ministries have been abolished, others merged, and some newly created. Even so, the number of Ministers has either remained the same or increased.

What many regard to be "paper planning" is also dominant in Tanzania. It normally has long-term developmental plans such as five-year or one-year plans. In reality, most of these plans are inactive. Most of the projects implemented are identified, financed, implemented, and supervised by the agencies that donate aid. These donors have influential power because they wield economic power. Most of the towns have master plans, but these have remained simply static land-use exercises, often influenced to a great degree by the urban planning experience of the more developed nations of the West. As a result, most of the urban plans are conceptually rigid and antiseptic and beyond Tanzania's financial ability. Such plans enhance the maintenance of the cycle of dependence.

Residential segregation based on income continues, accompanied by the unequal distribution of necessary civic urban facilities. I have shown through concrete policies and projects throughout this work how this happens in practice and who suffers.

The special standards that have been designed by the state for urban housing are mainly elitist and divorced from the social and economic realities of the country and its inhabitants. They tend to see development and modernity in terms of what is happening in the West and thus remain imitative, indifferent to actual local experience and therefore they lack the local supply of resources. As a result, they keep on reinforcing dependence and underdevelopment. After all, most of the standards propagated by the state are irrelevant to local culture. The worst thing is that these standards encourage social stratification and thus aid the present situation of inequality. This is not to say that standards are totally nonsensical, but that they must evolve from people's real needs.[1] The building standards which continue to dominate in Tanzania do not reflect the voice and needs of the urban poor but rather the wills of those who wield political and economic power. The ostentatious luxury residential housing areas and environment in Oyster Bay, Masaki, Msasani, and Mbezi Beach in Dar-Es-Salaam stand in sharp contrast to the conditions of poverty and squalor in Tandika, Buguruni, Manzese Uzuri, and Mwananyamala. A review of these standards and security policies of tenure may have a positive impact on the urban poor, especially in terms of housing.

The adoption of these inappropriate planning laws has had unfortunate repercussions. For example, restrictive regulations inhibit new residential construction, they increase the cost of building and if strictly enforced, prevent those with limited resources from constructing new homes.[2]

Turner and others have argued that the solution to housing problems in the Third World lies in the efforts of the slum dwellers themselves.

They have argued that squatters are capable of organizing themselves in order to improve their housing conditions.[3] However, if housing conditions are to be improved through self-help, certain conditions have to be met. Hardiman and Midgley (1982) consider certain conditions to be significant. One of the most important conditions is security of tenure. The other is dweller control. If self-help housing policies are to be effective, people must not only participate in decision-making but they must have full control over their own housing. They should have the freedom to decide what type of house to build and the right to modify their dwellings to suit their changing needs, circumstances, and preferences. People derive satisfaction from their own efforts even if these are considered imperfect by others.[4]

These conditions are equally applicable to Tanzania if it wants to improve the conditions of its urban housing through self-help initiatives. People will be willing to invest their money, time, and effort in improving their houses only if they are sure that they have a permanent stake in their dwellings. Most of the squatters are unwilling to improve their settlements because of the uncertainty of their future. Squatting, rather than being seen as an urban cancer, should be seen as a solution to the problem of housing. In order to confront the problem of housing, policies which increase the supply of official housing or facilitate access to better housing conditions and lead to a more equitable distribution of housing resources ought to be implemented. These might have positive effects on the conditions of life of the majority urban poor.

As I have argued throughout this study, health is another area in which those who suffer most are the urban poor. Information from the Ministry of Health indicates that malaria has become Tanzania's most deadly disease. Diseases transmitted by human feces are widespread. Breakouts of epidemics like typhoid, diarrhea, and cholera are typical and many people lose their lives. Since 1976, Tanzania has been fighting a losing battle against cholera. The conditions under which the poor live play a vital role in determining their health, more than the mere presence of hospitals, health centers, and dispensaries, most which have a shortage of medicine and other equipment. It should be clearly noted that people die from malaria and cholera not because of Tanzania's lack of foreign trade, but because of the lack of proper organization, planning and management. The outbreak of malaria, cholera, and other similar diseases can be explained by the strong theoretical orientation of the politicians. Their solution lies in practical education about the environment, cleanliness, and sanitation. High population density in residential areas, a common situation in the slum squatter settlements, facilitates communicable diseases, as well as a poor water supply and lack of proper drainage systems and garbage disposal facilities. Slogans like *Mtu Ni Afya* ("Health is necessary for a human being") are useless if they are not accompanied by serious and practical policies aimed at achieving them.

Another important sector which merits attention is transportation. It is a major generator of employment and plays a vital role in the distribution of essential goods and services. No economy can flourish without the presence of an efficient transportation network. Herbert (1979) argues that, in order to directly assist the urban poor, the purposes of urban transportation projects should be the following:

1. To provide jobs;
2. To provide access to jobs;
3. To facilitate the distribution of essential commodities used by the poor and help keep the prices of those commodities as low as possible;
4. To facilitate access to essential urban services;
5. To facilitate social interaction;
6. To increase the equipment available to the poor in the transportation sector itself;
7. To increase the assets of the poor through the impact of transportation on poverty values and on the productivity of equipment used by low-income entrepreneurs; and
8. To increase the supply of land suitable for settlement by the poor.[5]

The importance of an efficient transportation system to any country's economy should be equated with the role played by blood veins and capillaries to the heart of a human being.

As far as urban areas are concerned, the state should consider investing in transportation projects which have a potential impact on the urban poor. Such projects would include the construction of pedestrians pathways and bicycle paths and encourage the use of other traditional cheap means of transportation like the human pulled-pushed carts (*mikokoteni*). More traffic control devices and regulations that provide free and safe movement of pedestrians have to be built. The benefits of walking include the absence of capital costs for vehicles, absence of any foreign exchange requirements, and the need for minimal infrastructure.⁶ Parking places and education in traffic regulations have to be provided for both pedestrians and drivers. The latter can easily be achieved via seminars or by including these lessons in the educational curriculum of various institutions.

Concerning the problem of unemployment, the following facts ought to be taken into consideration. Given the present economic crisis and the rural urban exodus, it is likely that the problem of unemployment is here to stay for a considerable amount of time. It is clear that the urban economy will not be in a position to provide employment to all new urban immigrants. *What should the state then do?* The state has to promote economic activities in the urban informal sector. The promotion and assistance of these activities can be achieved by freeing the operators from taxation, licensing them, and by not forcing them to operate in fixed premises. They should be allowed to operate wherever they feel that it would be profitable for their businesses. The role of the state should be to educate the operators in how to maintain hygiene and cleanliness in their businesses. Social workers and health officers can perform this task. The city council also has to make sure that the facilities for garbage disposal are available everywhere. Policing hawkers and street vendors intensifies the problem rather than solving it. No one is interested in spending his whole life picking valuables from the garbage for resale, and nor is there anyone who would like to operate in an unlawful business, facing uncertainties in life and spending most of his time and money dodging and bribing the authorities. It is poverty which forces people to operate in such activities. Beggars, rather than being labelled as criminals, should be seen as belonging to the most needy in the community and least able to help themselves. Priority should be given to services designed to help them.⁷ Rather than dumping them somewhere in a camp in order to control them or repatriating them, they should be trained in productive activities like tailoring, cobbling, or carpentry. Once trained, they should be assisted in establishing businesses so that they can become self-reliant. The extended family and the local community should be used more effectively in the provision of services which assist people of this kind. Similarly, street children should not be sent to remand homes. The latter are worse and assist in destroying them rather than helping them morally and materially.

Prostitutes, like beggars, are victims of the socioeconomic and political system. They practice commercial sex because that is the only way they can survive the hardships of urban life. Appealing to morals and labelling them as criminals is indeed neglecting to see the dynamics of society in urban areas. Morals are not an endowment from heaven but are products of the material society. They can be scientifically and historically explained, and thus they have their material foundation in society. Prostitution is a class issue and not a moral one. No one is born as a prostitute, nor are people born as thieves or bandits. It is the conditions in society which shape them. Condemning them, and creating coercive laws which criminalize them treats the symptoms rather than the cause.

Mbah (1979) argues that prostitutes act as a safety valve for the society and any rapid elimination of prostitutes will be met with an increase in clandestine immodesty. Prostitution is a source of income for both men and women. Some women maintain their families and educate their children with the income accrued from commercial sex. Prostitution serves the purpose of relieving stress, strains, or frustration from married as well as unmarried men in periods of sexual desire. To the majority of unmarried low-income urban men, prostitution provides them the cheapest means of satisfying their physical sexual desires. Legalizing and controlling it, while advising people about safer sex and the risks involved, might bear positive results.

All types of solutions and strategies which I have suggested above form part of what one would call "intra-urban" policies. These are micro policies, most of which can be implemented as short-term solutions. Long-term solutions lie in policy approaches which deal with the problem of rapid urban growth. These are policies which seek to deal with this problem by controlling urban growth and preventing the concentration of the urban population and reducing the rate of rural-urban migration. Such policies require a combination of urban planning, broader regional structure plans, and policy measures which focus on the problems of urbanization in their wider context.[8] Urban planning has to be part of the overall national development plan.

The dichotomy between urban and rural development is in many respects a dangerously misleading one.[9] Through such a dichotomy, urban and rural development are often seen as competitive and, in some cases, rural development has been seen as a solution to problems associated with urban growth.[10] As Herbert (1979) has argued, urban and rural development should be seen as complementary and mutually reinforcing. Mao's slogan that *"We must be good at learning"* must direct the Tanzanian philosophy of development. Mao's China provides the best example of development alternatives from which Tanzania can learn. Mao's strategy of development, summarized by his slogan "*Walking on two legs*", emphasized balanced development between *industry* and *agriculture* or between *urban* and *rural* areas. This approach was further strengthened by another slogan, *"Agriculture is the foundation and industry the leading factor"*. These slogans were not rhetorical, but were effectively put into practice and guided the Chinese mode of development. The outcome of this was the rapid improvement of rural life which redressed the gap between rural and urban areas. Electricity became available to the rural areas and this boosted the dominant policy of spreading light industries to the countryside. This boosted the rural economy, provided rural employment to almost every rural citizen, and improved the standard of living by reducing the magnitude of rural poverty.

Most Tanzanians depend on subsistence farming in the rural sector. At least 85% of the total population live in this sector. The poverty which we see in urban areas is an extention of the poverty dominant in rural areas. People move to urban areas in search of the better way of life. People are running away from the hardships of rural life. Appealing to peasants to produce more food for the foreign market than for themselves and to keep on investing much of their surplus in the urban areas amounts to *"Draining the pond in order to catch the fish"*. This calls for a comprehensive policy on urbanization and rural development.

If agriculture can be made more productive, bringing about sustained economic development in rural areas, and if people have adequate access to social services and other amenities, they will have little desire to migrate to the cities.[11] The best urbanization control is to raise the levels of living in the countryside so that they equal those enjoyed by urban dwellers.[12] Peasants should have the freedom to produce the crops they want to, ones they think would be useful for their lives. Peasants are not ignorant of their desires, and forcing them to produce cash crops (which they do not consume) at the expense of food crops creates more disasters. Likewise, through their cooperatives, peasants should be allowed to determine the prices of their products and where to sell them. State controlled cooperatives are exploitative and are a catalyst of rural poverty.

Provision of education and the building of schools equipped with facilities greatly assists the process of rural development. Every village now has a primary school, and this is a good starting point. But in reality most of these schools lack the necessary books, teachers and classrooms. The curricula they use is irrelevant to their local situation. Tanzania is very wide and has several different ecologies, climates, geographies, and natural resources. Thus, the present system of having a uniform curriculum for the whole nation (at least at primary school level) ignores the reality. Why should a nomadic Masai child from a cattle-keeping area learn how to cultivate wheat, rice, or bananas instead of how to best take care of his cattle and the environment? The point here is that basic primary education has to be relevant to the local situation and has to reflect the realities of rural life. It means nothing to teach somebody about wool production in New Zealand when he does not know the best way to produce his main staple food. Policies on education should focus on the kind of education which assists rural people to master and manage their environment for the betterment of their lives. Such education may assist in redressing rural-urban migration.

Hardiman (1982) argues that social planners should not be employed only to take responsibility for sectoral planning within the national planning organization, but should collaborate with economic and physical planners in the formulation of national and regional projects.[13] They should advise on the likely impact of physical and economic projects in terms of human welfare and should seek also to identify social factors which may impede their implementations.[14]

I have shown throughout this work that the informal sector activities have expanded very rapidly not only without government support, but despite frequent government harassment. A study of nine cities from across the globe done by ILO indicates that the informal sector caters specifically to the needs of the urban poor.[15] In the case of Tanzania, the sector supports not only the urban poor, but also the middle class and people of other income categories. There is a need to support this sector precisely because the urban labor force is increasing due to rural-urban migration and the birth rate. As these processes continue to happen, more women, as is the case now, will be forced to join the labor market in order to compensate for the declining income of their husbands.[16]

Sanyal (1988) argues that in pursuing strategies to tackle the problems of urban poverty, one has to be guided by at least three principles. First, one must acknowledge that poverty is not only a function of disposable income. It is also a state of relative lack of access to such other resources as useful information, social networks, adequate time and space, and above all, political participation in the decision-making process that affects the lives of the poor. Second, poverty-oriented strategies must be directly focussed on the poor. Indirect approaches that rely on the proper functioning of the microeconomy may not benefit the poor, whether following the New International Economic Order (NIEO), or the IMF models. Third, though an active role of the government is a prerequisite for tackling poverty, it often hurts the poorest of the poor by formalizing an informal process.[17]

Policies aimed at solving urban poverty can only succeed if they are part of an overall socioeconomic development plan. In addition, development planning must be democratic, integrated, well-coordinated, and initiated from below. In reality, people must participate in shaping the destiny of their own lives.

Tanzania has undergone three ideological political swings since independence. From post-colonial pre-Arusha Declaration politics to post-Arusha Declaration populist socialism (characterized by nationalizations and villagization) to the present phase dominated by economic crisis, IMF and World Bank politics, and the politics of liberalization. In all these phases, the conditions of life of the majority have not improved.

Since independence, urban areas have undergone growth and notable transformation in their sizes, materials, technology, and institutions, but due to the problems cited above they continue to be ravaged by poverty, inequality and mismanagement. Housing shortages have continued unabated despite the presence of publicly-owned housing cooperatives, housing banks and other institutions. Urban transportation has progressively become unreliable, costly, and risky. All of these are indicators of an urban crisis.

The HABITAT Declaration states that the development of a city or any urban area should lead to the rapid and continuous improvement in the quality of life for all people, beginning with the satisfaction of the basic needs of food, shelter, clean water, employment, health, education, training, and social security. All of this should be done without any discrimination to race, sex, language, religion, ideology, or social origin in a frame of freedom, dignity, and social justice.[18] The HABITAT Declaration is a statement of goals for human settlement development, but it also mirrors current thinking about the development in general. Three notions underline this statement. The first is that development is a process and not a product or state; second, benefits of development must be available to all, or at least there should not be any institutional barriers to improvement in the quality of life of any section of population; and third, development has to encompass physical, institutional, economic, and social improvement, and not be merely a matter of capital works.[19]

Tanzania must redefine development. Development must be seen in terms of social progress, increased health, and the welfare of all people.

Endnotes

Chapter 1

1. Brain, A. *The Political Economy of Urbanization in Tanzania,* Unpublished Ph. D. Thesis, University of British Columbia, 1979, page 12.
2. Coulson, A. *Tanzania: A Political Economy,* Clarendon Press, 1982, page 35.
3. Sabot, R.H. *Economic Development and Urban Migration: Tanzania 1900-1971,* Clarendon Press, 1979.
4. Coulson, A. *op.cit.*, page 35 quoted from Redmond, P. *A Political History of the Songea Ngoni from the Mid-19th Century to the Rise of TANU,* Unpublished Ph.D. Thesis, University of London, 1972, pages 186-187.
5. Brain, A. *op.cit.*, page 41.
6. Coulson, A. *op.cit.*, page 37.
7. *ibid.*
8. Iliffe, J. *Agricultural Change in Modern Tanzania,* East African Publishing House, 1971, pages 12-18.
9. Brain, A. *op.cit.*, page 44.
10. _____, page 45.
11. _____, page 47.
12. Coulson, A. *op.cit.*, page 43.
13. _____, page 43.
14. See also the analysis of this table in *ibid.*
15. _____, page 53.
16. _____, page 55, quoted from 1956 Annual Report of the Department of Agriculture, page 1.
17. Collinson, M. *Farm Management Survey Reports Nos. 1-4,* Western Research Center, Ukiruguru Tanzania, 1963, page 30.
18. Saylor, G. *Variation in Sukumaland Cotton Yields and Extension Service,* Economic Research Bureau Paper No. 70.5, University of Dar-Es-Salaam, 1970, page 27. See also in Coulson, A. *op.cit.*, page 54.
19. Coulson, A. *op.cit.*, page 54, quoted from Kjaerby, F. *The Problem Livestock Department and Villagization among the Barbaig in Hanang District,* Research Report No. 40, Bureau of Resource Assessment and Land Use Planning (BRALUP), University of Dar-Es-Salaam, 1980, pages 16-19.
20. Coulson, A. *op.cit.*, page 54.
21. _____, page 54, quoted from Parkipuny, L. "Some Crucial Aspects of the Maasai Predicament", in Coulson, A. (ed.) *African Socialism in Practice,* Spokesman, 1979, pages 136-157.
22. _____, page 58, quoted from Awiti, A. "Ismani and the Rise of Capitalism", in Cliffe, L. (et al), 1975, page 51-78.
23. *ibid.*, quoted from Raikes, P. "Differentiation and Progressive Farmer Policies". Paper presented to the East African Agriculture Economics Society, June 1972, page 20.

24. The Secretary of State for the Colonies, quoted by the Governor of Tanganyika in 1975.
25. Coulson, A. *op.cit.*, page 74.
26. Honey, M. "Asian Industrial Activities in Tanganyika", in *Tanzania Notes and Records,* 1975, page 55-59, quoted also in Coulson, A. *op.cit.*, page 74.
27. Coulson, A. *op.cit.*, pages 78-79.
28. Berg, E.J. "The Development of a Labor Force in Sub-Saharan Africa", in *Economic Development and Cultural Change, 13 (4),* July 1965, Mason, P. "The Birth of a Dilemma", London, Oxford University Press, 1958.
29. Brain, A. *op.cit.*, page 271.
30. _____, page 17.
31. _____, page 18.
32. _____, page 276.
33. Iliffe, J. *A Modern History of Tanganyika,* Cambridge University Press, 1979, page 385.
34. *ibid.*
35. *ibid.*
36. _____, page 386.
37. *ibid.*
38. *ibid.*
39. *ibid.*
40. _____, page 387.
41. _____, page 388.
42. _____, page 389.
43. *ibid.*
44. Temu, A.J. "The Rise and Triumph of Nationalism", in Kimambo, I. and Temu, A.J. (eds.) *A History of Tanzania,* page 203. See also in Brain, R. *op.cit.*, page 18.

Chapter 2

1. Banyikwa, W.F. "Salient Characteristics of Urbanization in Tanzania", in *Journal of the Geographical Association of Tanzania,* No. 24, June 1985, page 87.
2. *Second Five Year Development Plan,* 1969-1974, page 18.
3. Mlay, W.F.I. "Rural to Urban Migration and Rural Development", in *Tanzania Notes and Records No. 81 and 82,* 1977, page 1.
4. _____, *Recent Rural-Urban Migration in Tanzania with Reference to Movements into Arusha and Moshi Towns,* Unpublished Ph.D. Thesis, London University, 1974.
5. Green, R. "Tanzania's Political Economy: Goals, Strategies and Results", in Mwansasu, B. and Pratt, C. *Towards Socialism in Tanzania,* Tanzania Publishing House, Dar-Es-Salaam, page 19-45.
6. Mlay, W.F.I. *op.cit.*, 1977, page 3.

7. Ministry of National Education.
8. Mlay, W.F.I. *op.cit.*, 1977, page 3.
9. Sabot, R.H. *Economic Development and Urban Migration in Tanzania 1900-1971,* Clarendon Press, 1979.
10. Mlay, W.F.I. *op.cit.*, 1977, page 4.
11. Stren, R.E. "Urban Policy", in Barkan, J.D. and Okumu, J.J. (ed.) *Politics and Public Policy in Kenya and Tanzania,* Heineman Educational Books, Nairobi, Kenya 1979, page 189.
12. *ibid.*
13. _____, page 190.
14. *ibid.*
15. Armstrong, A. *Urban Control Campaigns in the Third World: The Case of Tanzania,* Occasional Paper Series No. 19, University of Glasgow, January, 1987, page 30.
16. Hayuma, A.M. *Urban and Rural Planning in Tanzania,* Seminar Paper on Living in the Cities, Goethe Institute, Dar-Es-Salaam, July 12-18, 1987.
17. Yeager, R. "Demography and Development Policy in Tanzania", in *Journal of Development Areas 16(4),* pages 589-610.
18. *Second Five Year Development Plan,* 1969-1974, page 176.
19. *ibid.*
20. Gambishi, B.N.J. *Industrialization and Urban Development in Tanzania 1969-1981. A Case Study of Arusha and Morogoro Towns,* Unpublished M.A. Thesis, University of Dar-Es-Saam, May 1983, page 3.
21. National Population Census 1967.
22. Gambishi, B.N.J. *op.cit.*, page 37.
23. *ibid.*
24. This data and information has been extracted from the National Population Census Report of 1967 and 1978.
25. Ministry of Manpower Development, *Annual Manpower Report to the President, 1983,* page 16.
26. Stren, R.E. *op.cit.*, page 192.
27. *Daily News Paper,* October 2, 1973.
28. *ibid.*
29. Gibbon, P. *Background Report on Development in Dodoma Capital District and Design for Future Research,* Department of Sociology, University of Dar-Es-Salaam, 1980. page 32.
30. Capital Development Authority (CDA) pamphlet, Government Printer, 1973.
31. *ibid.*
32. Doherty, J. *Ideology and Town Planning in Tanzania,* (mimeo), University of Dar-Es-Salaam, 1975, page 4.
33. *ibid.*
34. *ibid.*, page 5.

Chapter 3

1. Kulaba, S.M. *"Urban Growth and Management of Urban Reform in Tanzania"*, A research project report jointly financed by the International Development Research Center, Ottawa, Canada and the United Republic of Tanzania. (Second Report) Center for Housing Studies, Ardhi Institute Dar-Es-Salaam, 1985, page 53.
2. Most of these factors have been quoted from Kulaba, S.M. (*op.cit.*) page 54.
3. Ministry of Lands, Housing, and Urban Development: *The National Housing Development Policy, 1982.*
4. *ibid.*
5. *ibid.*
6. Kulaba, S.M. *op.cit.*, page 66.
7. Stren, R.E. "Urban Policy", in Okumu, J.J. *Politics and Public Policy in Kenya and Tanzania,* Heineman Educational Books (HEB), Nairobi, 1979, page 196.
8. International Labor Office (ILO), *Basic Needs in Danger, A Basic Needs Orientated Development Strategy for Tanzania,* Jobs and Skills Program for African, Addis Ababa, 1982, page 125.
9. Stren, R.E. *op.cit.*, page 196.
10. *ibid.*
11. *Sunday News Paper,* November 18, 1987.
12. *Sunday News Paper,* November 25, 1984.
13. Stren, R.E. *op.cit.*, page 197.
14. Egero and Henin (ed), "Analysis of the 1967 Population Census", quoted in Chachage, S.L.C. *The Housing Problem and the Policy of Socialism in Dar-Es-Salaam.* Unpublished, B.A. Degree Dissertation, University of Dar-Es-Salaam, 1982, page 28.
15. The analysis of this table has been derived from the study of ILO, *op.cit.*, page 122.
16. The Development Plan for Tanganyika, Government Printers, Dar-Es-Salaam 1962, page 92.
17. *Parliamentary Act No. 45 of 1962, The National Housing Corporation of Tanganyika,* Government Printer, Dar-Es-Salaam, July 1962.
18. Kulaba, S.M. *Housing, Socialism and National Development in Tanzania, A Policy Framework,* Occasional Paper, Center for Housing Studies, Ardhi Institute, 1981, page 20.
19. *ibid.*, page 21.
20. Heuer, P. (et al), *Urbanization and Housing in Tanzania,* Technical University of Berlin, 1979, page 135.
21. Chachage, S.L.C. *op.cit.*, page 36.
22. *ibid.*, page 37.
23. Tanzania: *Second Five Year Plan for Social and Economic Development Vol. 1.* Government Printer, Dar-Es-Salaam 1969, pages 1 and 7.
24. Economic Commission to the Cabinet: *Report No. 7 of 1970.*

25. *Daily News Paper*, February 25, 1985.
26. Kulaba, S.M. *Housing, Socialism and National Development in Tanzania, A Political Framework,* Occasional Paper, CHS. Ardhi Institute, 1981.
27. Tanzania Housing Bank: *Annual Report and Accounts,* Dar-Es-Salaam, 1977, page 58, quoted also in Chachage, S.L.C. *op.cit.,* page 40.
28. *ibid.,* quoted also in Chachage, S.L.C. *op.cit.,* page 41.
29. Kulaba, S.M. *op.cit.* (No. 30 above), page 26.
30. ILO, *op.cit.,* page 127.
31. Mgullu, F.P. *Housing: A Study of National Sites and Services Schemes,* Unpublished LL.M. Thesis, University of Dar-Es-Salaam, 1978.
32. Schmetzer, H. *Housing in Dar-Es-Salaam, A Case Study,* Unpublished Conference Paper, March, 1980, page 15.
33. *ibid.*
34. Brain, A.R. *The Political Economy of Urbanization in Tanzania,* Unpublished Ph.D. Thesis, University of British Columbia, 1970, page 354.
35. ILO, *op.cit.,* page 127.
36. *ibid.*
37. *ibid.*
38. *ibid.*
39. THB, *Masharti ya Kupata Mkopo,* 1985.
40. Chachage, S.L.C. *op.cit.*
41. Kisege, H.S. *The Impact of Capital Development on Housing In Dodoma Town.* Unpublished Diploma in Land Management and Evaluation, Ardhi Institute, Dar-Es-Salaam, 1979, page 19.
42. Data collected from the Dar-Es-Salaam City Council.
43. Kulaba, S.M. "Managing Rapid Urban Growth through Sites and Services and Squatter Upgrading in Tanzania, Lessons and Experiences", in Crooke, P. (ed.), *Management of Sites and Services and Squatter Upgrading Housing Areas,* CHS. Tanzania, Occasional Paper, May 1985, page 36.
44. ILO, *op.cit.,*page 128.
45. Zakaria, M.L. *The Politics of Housing in Tanzania, A Case Study of Sinza Area in Dar-Es-Salaam,* Unpublished B.A. Degree Dissertation, University of Dar-Es-Salaam, 1982.
46. Kulaba, S.M. *op.cit.* in Crooke, P. (ed), *op.cit.,* page 39.
47. See also in *ibid.* above.
48. *ibid.,* page 40.
49. ___, page 39.
50. ___, page 39.
51. Brain, A.R. *op.cit.,* page 339. I also witnessed the demolition of Kisutu slum settlement with my own eyes.
52. Dar-Es-Salaam City Council.
53. Perlman, J.E. in her study of the *"Myth of Marginality", Urban Poverty and Politics in Rio de Janeiro,* University of California Press, 1976 observed more or less a similar government attitude towards slums.
54. Stren, R.E. *op.cit.,* page 191.

Chapter 4

1. Lomnitz, L. "The Social and Economic Organization of a Mexican Shantytown", in Cornelius, W.A. and Trueblood, F.D. (ed.) *Latin American Urban Research Vol.4. Anthropological Perspectives on Latin American Urbanization,* Sage Publications, 1974, page 135.
2. Marris, P. "African City Life", in *Nkanga Editions No. 1,* Institute of Social Research, University of Makerere, Kampala, Uganda.
3. Information collected from *TANESCO* and *NUWA* indicate the problem of illegal power hook-ups and illegal water connections as chronic nowadays.
4. Barnes, S.T. "Public and Private Housing in Urban West Africa: The Social Implications", in Morrison, M.K.C. and Gutkind, P.C.W. (ed.) *Housing the Urban Poor in Africa,* Maxwell School of Citizenship and Public Affairs, Syracuse University, 1982, page 16.
5. Lomnitz, L. *op.cit.* page 151.
6. Barnes, J.A. "Class Committees in a Norwegian Island Parish", *Human Relations 7,* 1954, pages 39-58.
7. Mayer, P. "Migrancy and the Study of Africans in Towns", *American Anthropologist 64,* quoted in Lomnitz, L. *op.cit.* page 147.
8. Lomnitz, L. *op.cit.* observed more or less similar forms of exchange relationships. Some of the summary of the forms of exchange relations have been adopted from her.

Chapter 5

1. Ministry of Lands, Housing and Urban Development, *National Urban Development Policy,* (Unpublished Document), 1986, page 20.
2. *ibid.*
3. *ibid.*
4. *ibid.*
5. *ibid.*, page 22.
6. *ibid.*
7. *ibid.*, page 25.
8. Bureau of Statistics: *Statistical Abstracts,* 1984, page 146.
9. *ibid.*
10. Bureau of Statistics: *Op.cit.*, page 147.
11. *ibid.*
12. Ministry of Lands, Housing and Urban Development. *Op.cit.*, page 31.
13. *ibid.*
14. Dar-Es-Salaam Sewerage and Sanitation Master Plan 1980.
15. Kulaba, S.M. *Urban Growth and Management of Urban Reform in Tanzania:* A Research Project Jointly Financed by International Development Research Center, Ottawa, Canada and the Government of the United Republic of Tanzania (second report), Ardhi-Institute, Dar-Es-Salaam, Tanzania 1985, page 47.

16. *ibid.*
17. *ibid.*
18. *ibid.*
19. This data was collected from the Health Office of the Dar-Es-Salaam City Council at the Arnautoglu Hall Building on 8th. March, 1988.
20. *ibid.*
21. *ibid.*
22. Data derived from the research findings.
23. Kulaba, S.M. *op.cit.*, page 49.
24. *ibid.*
25. Ntukula M. *Social Problems of Squatters: A Case Study of Kinondoni-Moscow, Dar-Es-Salaam, Tanzania.*, B.A. (Degree) Dissertation (Unpublished), University of Dar-Es-Salaam, March 1984, pages 50-51.
26. Kulaba, S.M. *op.cit.*, page 97.
27. Ministry of Lands, Housing and Urban Development: *op.cit.*, page 30.
28. *ibid.*
29. Kulaba, S.M. *op.cit.*, page 100.
30. Banyikwa, W.F. *The Nature of Urban Passengers Transport Services in Dar-Es-Salaam*, (Unpublished Paper), University of Dar-Es-Salaam 1986, page 143.
31. *Daily News Paper,* 3/9/87.
32. *ibid.*
33. Banyikwa, W.F. *op.cit.*, page 153.
34. *ibid.*, page 158.
35. The arguments together with the data have been borrowed from Banyikwa, W.F. *op.cit.*
36. *ibid.*, page 21.
37. *ibid.*, page 22.

Chapter 6

1. The Data as well as the analysis has been borrowed from, International Labor Office (ILO), *Basic Needs in Danger, A Basic Needs Oriented Development Strategy for Tanzania,* Jobs and Skills Program for Africa Addis Ababa, 1982, page 273.
2. Mapunda, S. "Peasants Left Out", in *Sunday News Paper,* 12/1/85.
3. ILO *op.cit.*, pages 341-342.
4. Bagachwa, M.S.D. Structure and Policy Problems of the Informal Manufacturing Sector in Tanzania, University of Dar-Es-Salaam, *Economic Research Bureau Paper No. 1983.1.*
5. ILO, page 341-342.
6. This schedule has been quoted from Bagachwa, M.S.D. *op.cit.*, page 4, the same schedule appears also in ILO, *op.cit.*, page 342.
7. Bagachwa, M.S.D. *op.cit.*, page 6.
8. *ibid.*, page 12.

9. *ibid.*
10. *ibid.*, page 23.
11. *ibid.*
12. Rossett, C. "Perus's New Economic Order", in The Informal Economy, *CUSO Journal, December 1987,* page 4.
13. Smart, J. "Street Hawking in Hong Kong", in *ibid.*, page 13.
14. *ibid.*
15. Ntukula, M. *Social Problems of Squatters: A Case Study of Kinondoni,* Moscow, Dar-Es-Salaam, Tanzania, B.A. (Degree) Dissertation, University of Dar-Es-Salaam, 1984.
16. Ishumi, A.G.M. *The Urban Jobless in Eastern Africa,* Scandinavian Institute of African Studies, Uppsala 1984.
17. *Sunday News Paper,* 12/22/85
18. *ibid.*
19. *ibid.*
20. *ibid.*
21. Ishumi, A.G.M. *op.cit.*, page 78.
22. Ishumi, A.G.M. *op.cit.*, page 73.
23. *ibid.*, page 74.
24. *ibid.*
25. Rossett, C. *op.cit.*, page 6.
26. The definition of corruption has been borrowed from Gould, J.D. *The Effects of Corruption on Administrative Performance: Illustrations from Developing Countries.* World Bank Staff Working Papers Number 580, Management and Development Series Number 7.
27. *ibid.*
28. Quadeer, M. *Urban Development in the Third World: Internal Dynamics of Lahore,* Pakistan, Praeger Publishers, 1983, page 155.
29. Turritin, J. "Petty Trading in Rural Mali", in *CUSO Journal, December 1987,* page 24.
30. *ibid.*
31. *ibid.*
32. This argument has been raised by Turritin, J. in *ibid.*, the same situation is applicable for women in Tanzania.
33. Nelson, N. "How Women and Men get by: The Sexual Division of Labor in the Informal Sector of Nairobi Squatter Settlement", in Bromley. R. and Gerry, C. (ed.) *Casual Work and Poverty in the Third World Cities,* John Wiley and Sons, Co.Ltd., 1979, pages 283-302.
34. *ibid.*, page 289.
35. Nelson, N. in *op.cit.* has observed a similar problem in Nairobi.

Chapter 7

1. Legal Aid Committee Pamphlet: *Essays on Law and Society,* Faculty of Law University of Dar-Es-Salaam, 1985, page 74.

2. *ibid.*
3. *ibid.*
4. *ibid.* page 75.
5. *ibid.*
6. *ibid.*
7. *ibid.*
8. *ibid.*
9. *ibid.* page 76.
10. Armstrong, A. *Urban Control Campaigns in the Third World: The Case of Tanzania.* Occasional Paper Series No. 19, Department of Geography, University of Glasgow, 1987, pages 12-13.
11. *Tanganyika Standard,* 7/9/57, quoted from Armstrong ,A. *op.cit.*, page 13.
12. Armstrong ,A. *op.cit.*, page 13.
13. Martin,R. *Personal Freedom and The Law in Tanzania: A Study of Socialist State Administration,* Oxford University Press (OUP), Nairobi,1971, page 100.
14. *ibid.*, page 102.
15. *Tanganyika Standard,* 7/9/57.
16. *Tanganyika Standard,* 7/9/57, Yeager, R. "Demography and Development Policy in Tanzania", *Journal of Developing Areas, 16 (4),* pages 589-610, Armstrong, A. *op.cit.* page 13.
17. *Tanganyika Standard,* ibid.
18. Labor Division of Tanganyika 1957, quoted from Armstrong, A. *op.cit.*, page 13.
19. Nyerere, J. *The Arusha Declaration: 10 years after,* Dar-Es-Salaam Government Printers, 1977 page 46.
20. See also in Ishumi, A.G.M. *The Urban Jobless in Eastern Africa,* Scandinavian Institute of African Studies, Uppsala, 1984, pages 25-26.
21. *ibid.*
22. Jamhuri ya Muungano wa Tanzania: Hotuba ya Waziri Mkuu Ndugu Edward Moringe Sokoine (Mbunge) kuhusu makadirio ya fedha kwa mwaka 1983/84, Government Printers, 1983 pages 10-11.
23. Miti, K. *Issues Raised by "Nguvu-Kazi" and its implementation in Dar-Es-Salaam,* (mimeo), University of Dar-Es-Salaam, 1983 page 3.
24. *ibid.*, page 4.
25. *ibid.*
26. Armstrong, A. *op.cit.*, page 14.
27. *ibid.*
28. *Tanganyika Information Services,* 3/13/64.
29. Armstrong, A. *op.cit.*, page 14.
30. *Reporter,* 4/27/64.
31. *Tanganyika Weekly News* 8/31/62, Armstrong, A. *op.cit.*, page 15.
32. Armstrong, A. *op.cit.*, page 15.
33. *Reporter,* 5/22/64, Armstrong, A. *op.cit.*, page 15.
34. *Tanganyika Standard,* 10/20/64, Armstrong, A. *ibid.*

35. _____, 10/9/64, _____.
36. Armstrong, A. *op.cit.*, page 16.
37. *Sunday News Paper,* 4/5/70.
38. Armstrong, A. *op.cit.*, page 17, Martin, R. *op.cit.*, page 78.
39. Armstrong, A. *op.cit.*, page 18.
40. *ibid.*
41. Maro, P. and Mlay, W. "Population Redistribution in Tanzania", in Clarke, J. and Kasinski, L. (Ed), *Redistribution of Population in Africa.* Heinemann, London 1982, pages 176-181.
42. Armstrong, A. *op.cit.*, page 19.
43. Mlay, W. "Rural to Urban Migration and Rural Development", in *Tanzania Notes and Records, 81 (2),* 1977, page 11.
44. Armstrong, A. *op.cit.*, pages 19-20.
45. *The Human Resources Deployment Act of 1983,* Part II page 99.
46. _____, Part II (Section 8 and 9) page 101.
47. _____, Part V (Section 17 & 20) pages 103-4.
48. *ibid.*
49. *ibid.*, see also in Miti, K. *op.cit.*
50. Miti, K. *op.cit.*, page 1.
51. *ibid.*
52. *ibid.*
53. *ibid.*
54. *ibid.*,pages 1-2.
55. *ibid.*
56. *The Master and Native Servant's Ordinance of 1923.*
57. Bisanda, S.S.Z. *"Nguvu-Kazi": Its Impact and Implementation in Urban Areas: A Case Study of Dar-Es-Salaam,* Unpublished B.A. (Sociology) Degree Dissertation, University of Dar-Es-Salaam, 1985, page 7.
58. *ibid.*
59. *The Labor Utilization Ordinance of 1947,* See also in Bisanda, S.S.Z. *op.cit.*, page 7.
60. Miti,K. *op,cit.*, page 3.
61. *ibid.*
62. *ibid.*
63. *ibid.*
64. *ibid.*
65. *ibid.*
66. *ibid.*
67. *ibid.*
68. *Uhuru,* 7/20/83.
69. Miti, K. *op.cit.*, page 6.
70. *ibid.*
71. *ibid.*
72. *Daily News Paper,* 8/28/83.
73. *Daily News Paper,* 9/26/83.
74. Miti, K. *op.cit.*, page 8.

75. _____, page 9.
76. _____, page 11.
77. *Daily News Paper,* 12/20/83.
78. Miti, K. *op.cit.*, page 11.
79. *ibid.*
80. Armstrong, A. *op.cit.*, page 12.
81. *ibid.*
82. *Daily News Paper,* 10/29/83.
83. _____, 10/19/83.
84. Miti, K. *op.cit.*, pages 11-12.
85. _____, page 12.
86. Bisanda, S.S.Z. *op.cit.*, page 57.
87. Miti, K. *op.cit.*, page 57.

Chapter 8

1. Awotona, A. "The Perception of Housing Conditions in Nigeria by the Urban Poor", in *Habitat International Vol. 12 No.2, 1988* page 76.
2. Hardiman, M. and Midgley, J. *The Social Dimension of Development: Social Policy and Planning in the Third World.*, John Wiley & Sons Ltd., 1982, page 221.
3. Turner, J.F. "Barriers and Channels for Housing Development in Modernizing Countries", *Journal of American Institute of Planners.33,*1967, pages 167-181.
4. Hardiman, M. and Midgley, J. *op.cit.*, page 229.
5. Herbert, J. *Urban Development in the Third World: Policy Guidelines:* New York, Praeger Publications, 1979, page 137.
6. *ibid.*, page 141.
7. Hardiman, M. and Midgley, J. *op.cit.*, page 255.
8. Hardiman, M. and Midgley, J. *op.cit.*, page 147.
9. Herbert, J. *op.cit.*, page 192.
10. *ibid.*
11. Hardiman, M. and Midgley, J. *op.cit.*, page 149.
12. *ibid.*
13. Hardiman, M. and Midgley, J. *op.cit.*, page 23.
14. *ibid.*
15. Sanyal, B. "The Urban Informal Sector Revisited: Some Notes on the Relevance of the Concept in the 1980s", *Third World Planning Review, Vol. 10, No. 1, 1988,* page 74.
16. *ibid.*, page 75.
17. *ibid.*, page 79.
18. Quadeer, M.A. *Urban Development in the Third World: Internal Dynamics of Lahore,* Pakistan, Praeger Publishers, 1983, page 253.
19. *ibid.*

References

Andors, S. "Urbanization and Urban Government in China's Development: Towards a Political of Urban Community", in *Economic Development and Cultural Change*, Vol. 26 No.3, April 1978.

Abrams, C. *Housing in the Modern World: Man's Struggle for Shelter in An Urbanizing World*, Faber & Faber (London), 1966.

Amani, H.K.R. *A Regional and Interregional Study of Tanzania*, Economic Research Bureau, Part 1-2, University of Dar-Es-Salaam, 1987.

Amin, S."Underdevelopment and Dependence in Black Africa: Origins and Contemporary Forms", in *Journal of Modern African Studies, Vol X, No. 4,* 1972

Amis, S."Squatters or Tenants: The Commercialization of Unauthorized Housing in Nairobi", in *World Development, Vol .12 No.1,* 1984.

Armstrong, A. "Urban Control Campaigns in the Third World: The Case of Tanzania". *Occasional Paper Series No. 19*, Department of Geography, University of Glasgow, 1987.

Armstrong, A."Tanzania's Expert-Lead Planning: An Assessment", in *Public Administration and Development (London), Vol.7 No. 3,* 1987.

Armstrong, A."Foreign Experts in Planning: Recent Experiences in Aid Assisted Regional Planning in Tanzania", in *The African Review, Vol.11, No.2,* 1984.

Armstrong, A."Urban Planning in Developing Countries", in *Singapore Journal of Tropical Geography, Vol.7 No.1,* 1986.

Awiti, A."Ismani and the Rise of Capitalism", in Cliffe, L. and Saul, J.(Eds), *Socialism in Tanzania:An Interdisciplinary Reader, Vol. 1.* EAPH, 1972.

Awatona, A. "The Perception of Housing Conditions in Nigeria by the Urban Poor", in *Habitat International Vol.12, No.2,* 1988.

Bagachwa, M.S.D. Structure and Policy Problems of the Informal Manufacturing Sector in Tanzania, *Economic Research Bureau Paper 1983*. University of Dar-Es-Salaam.

Bagachwa, M.S.D. and Maliyamkono,T.A.L. *The Second Economy in Tanzania,* James Curry, 1990.

Bannerjee, N. "Survival of the Poor", in Safa,H.(Ed.), *Towards a Political Economy of Urbanization in the Third World,* OUP, 1982.

Banyikwa,W.F. *The Nature of Urban Passengers Transport Services in Dar-Es-Salaam,* (Unpublished Paper) University of Dar-Es-Salaam, 1986.

Banyikwa,W.F. "How to Formulate a Hierarchy of Service Centers of a Region in Tanzania: The Case Study of Mwanza", in *The Journal of Geographical Association of Tanzania, No.23,* 1984.

Banyikwa,W.F. "Salient Characteristics of Urbanization in Tanzania", in *Journal of Geographical Association of Tanzania, No.24,* 1985.

Barkan, J.(ed), *Politics and Public Policy in Kenya and Tanzania,* HEB, Nairobi, 1984.

Barnes, S.T. "Public and Private Housing in Urban West Africa: The Social Implications", in Morrison, M.K.C. and Gutkind P.C.W.(ed), *Housing the Urban Poor In Africa,* Maxwell School of Citizenship and Public Affairs, Syracuse University, 1982.

Barnum, H.N. and Sabot, R.H. *Migration, Education and Urban Surplus Labor: The Case Study of Tanzania,* Paris, OECD, 1976

Barton, S.E. "The Urban Housing Problem: Marxist Theory and Community Organizing", in *Review of Radical Political Economics, Vol.9,* 1977.

Berg, E.J. "The Development of a Labor Force in Sub-Saharan Africa", in *Economic Development and Cultural Change, 13(4),* July, 1965.

Berman, B.J. "The Concept of Articulation and the Political Economy of Colonialism", in *Canadian Journal of Africa Studies, Vol.2,* 1984.

Bernstein, H.(ed), *Underdevelopment and Development: Third World Today,* Penguin, 1973.

Berry, B.J.L. *Urbanization and Counter Urbanization:* Sage Publication, 1976.

Bienefeld. M.A. and Sabot, R.H. *The National Urban Mobility, Employment and Income Survey of Tanzania (NUMEIST),* Ministry of Economic Affairs and Development Planning/Economic Research Bureau, University of Dar-es-Salaam, 1971.

Bienefield, M.A. and Binhammer, H.H. "Tanzania Housing Finance and Housing Policy", *Economic Research Bureau Paper 69.19,* University of Dar-Es-Salaam, 1969.

Bienefeld, M.A. "The Informal Sector and Peripheral Capitalism:The Case of Tanzania", in *Bulletin of the Institute of Development Studies, Vol.6, No 3,1975.*

Bienefeld, M.A. *A Longterm Housing Policy for Tanzania.* Economic Research Bureau, University of Dar_es-Salaam,1970.

Bienefeld, M.A. "The Self-Employed of Urban Tanzania", *Economic Research Bureau Paper, No.75.11,* University of Dar-es-Salaam,1975.

Birkbeck, C. "Garbage Industry and The "Vultures" of Cali in Colombia", in Bromley, R. and Gerry, (eds.), *Casual Work and Poverty in the Third World Cities.* John Wiley and Sons Co. Ltd, paged 161-183.

Bisanda, S.S.Z. *"Nguvu-Kazi":Its impact and implementation in urban areas: A case study of Dar_es-Salaam,* Unpublished B.A.(Sociology) Degree Dissertation, University of Dar-es-Salaam,1985.

Boesen, J. (et al), *Tanzania: Crisis and struggle for Survival,* Scandinavian Institute of African Studies,1986.

Booshan, B.S.(et.al), "Shelter: People's needs and government response", in *Ekistics, No.48.286,*1981.

Boukhemis, K. (et al), "Appraisal of Rural_Urban Migration Determinants: A case study of Constraints, Algeria", in *Third World Planning Review, Vol.10.February 1988.*

Brain, A. *The Political Economy of Urbanization in Tanzania,* Unpublished Ph.D Thesis, University of British Columbia,1979.

Breese, G. *The Human Consequences of Urbanization,* MacMillan Press,1973.

Breese, G. *Urbanization in Newly Developing Countries*, Prentice Hall Inc.1966.
Brennan, E.M.& Harry, W.R. "Urbanization and Urban Policy in Sub-Saharan Africa", in *African Urban Quarterly, Vol.1 No.1*,(Nairobi),1986.
Bromley, R.& Gerry, C. "Small-Scale Manufacturing and Repairs in Dakar: A Survey of Market Relations within the Urban Economy" in Bromley, R. & Gerry, C. *op. cit.*
Bromley, R. "Introduction-The Urban Informal Sector: Why is it worth discussing?", *In World Development. Vol6.No.9/10,1978.*
Bryan, R. *Cities of Peasants,* Edward Arnold Co. Ltd. (London),1978.
Bureau of Statistics: *Statistical Abstracts,* 1984.
Bureau of Statistics in Dar-es-Salaam: *The Household Budget Survey of 1976.*
Bryant, C. *Health and the Developing World,* Cornell University Press,1969.
Campbell,J.& Pons, V. *Urbanization, Urban Planning and Urban Life in Tanzania: An annotated bibliography,* Occasional Paper, Department of Sociology and Social Anthropology, University of Hull (U.K.),1987.
Capital Development Authority (C.D.A.) Pamphlet, Government Printer, 1973.
Capital Development Authority (CDA), *Low Cost Housing Unit Project,* Social Economic Survey in Dodoma, 1987.
Castells, M.E. "Squatters and Politics in Latin America: A comparative analysis of urban social movements in Chile, Peru and Mexico", in Saffa, H. *op.cit.*
Castells, M. *The Urban Questions: A Marxist Approach* , Edward Arnold, 1972.
Castells, M.E. *City, Class and Power,* MacMillan Press, 1978.
Chachage, S.L.C. *Urban Capitalism in Tanzania: An Example of Arusha Town,* Unpublished M.A. Degree Thesis, University of Dar-es-Salaam 1983.
Collier, P.(et al), *Labour and Poverty in Rural Tanzania: Ujamaa and Rural Development in the United Republic of Tanzania,* Clarendon 1986.
Comoro,C.J.B. *Two Shantytowns in Dar-es-Salaam: A Study of Housing Process.* Unpublished .M.A. (Degree) Thesis-Department of Sociology, University of Carleton, 1984.
Comoro,C.J.B. *Urban Housing Provision for Low Income Population in Mbeya.* Unpublished M.A. (Degree) Thesis, Deparment of Sociology, University of Dar-es-Salaam.1981.
Conyers ,D. "Decentralization for Regional Development : A Comparative Study of Tanzania, Zambia and Papua New Guinea", in *Public Administration and Development Vol.1. No.2,* John Wiley and sons (U.K.) 1981.
Cornelius, W.A. *Urbanization and Inequality: The Political Economy of Urban and Rural Development in Latin America,* Sage Publications, 1975.
Correa, C. " Third World Housing: Space as a resource", in *Ekistics. Vol.41 No.242.* 1976.
Coulson, A. *African Socialism in Practice,* Spokesman, Nottingham, 1979.
Coulson, A. *Tanzania: A Political Economy,* Clarendon Press.1982.
Cowi-Consult Dar-es-Salaam, *Urban Passenger Transport Study, Final Report for National Transport Corporation, Dar-es-Salaam.*1983.
Dar-es-Salaam Sewerage and Sanitation Master Plan. 1980.

Dar-es-Salaam Sewerage and Sanitation Department: *Ventilated Improved Pit Latrines (VIP) Project-* Buguruni Dar-es-Salaam.
Dix, G. "Small Cities in The World System", in *Habitat International.Vol.10.No.1/2,* Pergamon Press (Oxford), 1986.
Doherty, J. *Ideology and Town Planning in Tanzania* (Mimeo) University of Dar-es-Salaam, 1975.
Drakakis, S.D. *Urbanization, Housing and the Development Process* , Croom Helm (London) 1981.
Drakakis, S.D. "Urban Renewal in an Asian Context: A case study in Hongkong", in *Urban Studies No.13.* 1976.
Drakakis, S.D. *The Third World City,* Methuen & Co. 1987.
Dwyer, D.J. *People and Housing in the Third World Cities.* Longman (London) 975.
Dwyer, D.J. *The City in the Third World,* MacMillan,1974.
Fimbo,G.M. *Double allocation of urban plots: A legal Labyrinth, Citizen's puzzlement and nightmare,* Public lecture,The Law Association of Tanzania. 1988.
Frank, A.G. *Capitalism and Underdevelopment in Latin America,* Monthly Review Press, 1969.
French,R.A.& Hamilton,F.E .(eds) *The Socialist City,* John Wiley and sons, 1979.
Freyhold, Von,M. "The Post-Colonial State and its Tanzanian Version: Contribution to a Debate", in Othman,H.(ed) *The state in Tanzania:Who controls it and whose interests does it serve ?* Dar-es-Salaam University Press. 1980.
Freyhold, Von M. *Ujamaa Villages in Tanzania: An analysis of a Social Experiment,* HEB. (London) 1979.
Friedmann, J. "The role of cities in national development", in Bourne,L.S.& Simmons, J.W.(eds) *Systems of Cities,* OUP, 1978.
Friedmann J. "A general theory of polarized development " in Manson N. (ed), *Growth centres in regional economic development.* The Free Press, New York 1972.
Fuller,T.D.(et al), "Housing, Stress, and Physical Wellbeing:Evidence from Thailand", in *Social Science and Medicine, Vol.36,No.11,1993.*
Gambishi, B.N.J. *Industrialization and Urban Development in Tanzania, 1969-1981 : The case study of Arusha and Morogoro Towns,* Unpublished M.A. (Thesis), University of Dar-es-Salaam. 1983.
Geertz, C. *Peddlers and Princes: Social Development and Economic Change in two Indonesian Towns,* Chicago University Press, 1963.
Gibb, A. *A plan of Dar-es-Salaam, 1949.*
Gibbon, P. *Background report on development in Dodoma Capital District and design for future research,* Department of Sociology, University of Dar-es-Salaam,1980.
Gilbert, A.& Gugler, J. *Cities, Poverty and Development: Urbanization in the Third World,* OUP,1982.

Gilbert,A. "The spatial allocation of education and health facilities in less developed nations", in Helleiner, F.M. and Stohr, W.B. (eds). *Proceedings of the Commission on Regional Aspects of Development of the International Geographical Union.II: Spatial Aspects of Development Process*, Allister, Toronto,1974.

Gould J.D. *The effects of corruption on administrative performance:Illustrations from developing countries*, World Bank Staff Working Papers No.580, Management and Development Series No.7.

Greble, R.E. *Urban growth problems of Mwanza Township*.Unpublished Ph.D. Thesis University of Boston 1971.

Green, R. "Tanzania's political economy: Goals, Strategies and Results", in Mwansasu,B.& Pratt,C. *Towards Socialism in Tanzania*,TPH, Dar-es-Salaam.

Green,J.A. *A Socio-Economic History of Moshi Town: A Case Study of Urbanization*, M.A. Degree (Thesis), University of Dar-es-Salaam 1979.

Grimes,O.F. *Housing for Low Income Urban Families*, John Hopkins University Press 1976.

Grohs,G." Slum clearance in Dar-es-Salaam", in Hutton, J. (ed) *Urban challenge in East Africa*, EAPH,1970.

Gugler,J.& Flanagan,W. *Urbanization and Social Change in West Africa.* Cambridge University Press.1978.

Gugler, J. "Overurbanisation Reconsidered", in *Economic Development and Cultural Change, Vol. 31, No.1*.1982.

Gugler,J. "Urbanization in East Africa", in Hutton,J.(ed) *Urban Challenge in East Africa*, EAPH,1970.

Gugler,J. *The Urbanization of the Third World*, OUP, 1988.

Gutkind,P.C.W. "The Political Economy of Housing", in Morrison, K.C.M.& Gutkind,P.C.W.(eds) *Housing the Urban Poor in Africa*, Maxwell School of Citizenship and Public Affairs, University of Syracuse, 1982.

Hance,W.A. *Population Migration and Urbanization in Africa*, Columbia University Press, 1970.

Hardiman,M.& Midgley,J. *The Social Dimension of Development:Social Policy and Planning in the Third World*, John Wiley & Sons Ltd. 1982.

Hardoy,J.E.(et al), *The Poor Die Young:Housing and Health in the Third World*.Earthscan Publications Ltd. London, 1990.

Hart,K. "Informal Income Opportunities and Urban Employment in Ghana", in *Journal of Modern African Studies Vol. 11, 1973*.

Harvey,D. *Social Justice and the City*, London, Edward Arnold, 1973.

Hay,R.Jr. "Patterns of Urbanization and Socio-Economic Development in the Third World:An Overview", in Abu-Lughod,J.& Hay,R.Jr.(eds) *Third World Urbanization*, Maaroufa Press Inc. Chicago, 1977.

Hayuma,A.M. *Urban and Rural Planning in Tanzania*, Seminar Paper on Living in the Cities, Goethe Institute, Dar-Es-Salaam, July 1987.

Hayuma,A.M. "Financial and Economic Constraints in the implementation of the 1968 Dar-Es-Salaam Master Plan from 1969-1979", *International Conference on Plan Implementation and Human Settlements Administration*, Centre for Housing Studies, Ardhi Institute, Dar-Es-Salaam, 1981.

Hayuma,A.M. "The Growth of Population and Employment in Dar-Es-Salaam City Region in Tanzania", in *Ardhi Journal of Land and Development*, Vol.2 No.2, 1983.

Hayuma,A.M. "A review and assessment of the contribution of internal and bilateral aids to urban development policies in Tanzania", in *Ekistics, 1979*.

Heirich,T.J. *Technologietransfer in der Stadtplanung:Master Planung in Dar-Es-Salaam/Tansania durch Internationale Consultings*, Verlag fuer Wissenschaft(Darmstadt),1987.

Hemker,C. "*Probleme der Wohnungsversorgung durch housing cooperatives am Beispiel Mwenge in Tanzania*", Seminarbeitrag am Fachbereich Architektur, SS.81, Fachgebiet Planen und Bauen in Entwicklungslaendern, Darmstadt, 1982.

Heuer,P.(et al), *Urbanization and Housing in Tanzania*, Technical University of Berlin,1979.

Hinderink,J.& Sterkenburg,J. *Anatomy of an African Town*, State University of Utrecht, 1975.

Hodd,M.(ed), *Tanzania after Nyerere*, London, 1988.

Honey,M. "Asian industrial activities in Tanganyika", in *Tanzania Notes and Records 1975*.

I.L.O. "Women's Employment Patterns, Discrimination and Promotion of Equality in Africa:The case Tanzania",in *I.L.O. Jobs and Skills Programme for Africa(JASPA), Addis Ababa, 1986*

Iliffe, J. *Tanganyika under German rule 1905-1912*, Cambridge University Press,1969.

Iliffe, J. *Agricultural change in modern Tanzania*, East African Publishing House,1971.

Iliffe,J. "Wage labour and urbanization" in Kaniki, M.H.Y. (ed) *Tanzania under Colonial rule*, Longman,1979.

International Labour Office: *Employment, Income and Equality:A Strategy for Increasing Productive Employment in Kenya, 1972*.

International Labour Office: *Basic Needs in Danger: A Basic Needs Orientated Development Strategy for Tanzania*, Jobs and Skills Programme for Africa, Addis Ababa.1982.

Ishumi ,A.G.M. *The Urban Jobless in Eastern Africa*, Scandinavian Institute of African Studies, Uppsalla,1984.

Jambiya,J.L.K. *Industrial Location in Tanzania:A study of the Spatial Dimension Decision Making.*Unpublished M.A. Thesis University of Dar-es-Salaam, 1987.

Kahama, G.C. (et al) *The challenge for Tanzania'a Economy*, James Curry, and TPH Dar-es-Salaam,1986.

Kang, G.E.& Kang, T.S. "The Korean urban shoeshine gang:A minority community", in *Urban Anthropology. Vol.7, 1978*.

Kim, K.S. (et al) *Papers on the Political economy of Tanzania,* Economic Research Bureau, University of Dar-es-Salaam, HEB 1979.

Kiros, F.G.(ed). *Challenging rural poverty: Experiences in institution building and popular participation for rural development in Eastern Africa,* Africa World Printer, 1985.

Kisege, H.S. *The impact of capital development on housing in Dodoma Town,* Unpublished Diploma (Dissertation) in Land Management and Evaluation, Ardhi Institute, Dar-es-Salaam 1979.

Kleemier, L. "Integrated rural development in Tanzania", in *Public Administration and Development Vol.8 No.1, 1988.*

Kleemier, L. " Regional planning in Tanzania, 1961-1972", in *The African Review (Dar-es-Salaam) Vol. 10. No.1 1983.*

Kulaba, S.M." An integrated development approach to housing cooperatives in Tanzania", in *Ekistics Vol.50, 1983.*

Kulaba, S.M. *The provision and management of housing in urban areas: A case study of Dar-es-Salaam,* Seminar on living in the cities, Goethe Institute, Dar-es-Salaam, July 1987.

Kulaba, S.M. *Urban growth and management of urban reform in Tanzania.* A research project report jointly financed by the international development research centre, Ottawa, Canada and the United Republic of Tanzania (second report). Centre for Housing studies, (CHS), Ardhi Institute, Dar-es-Salaam, 1985.

Kulaba, S.M. *Housing, Socialism and National Development in Tanzania: A Policy framework,* Occasional Paper, Centre for Housing Studies, Ardhi Institute, Dar-es-Salaam, 1981

Kulaba, S.M. "Managing rapid urban growth through Sites and Services and Squatter upgrading in Tanzania, Lessons and Experiences", in Crooke, P.(ed), *Management of Sites and Services and Squatter Upgrading Housing Areas,* Occasional Paper, CHS. Tanzania, May 1985.

Kulaba, S.M. *Urban management and the delivery of urban services in Tanzania:* Final report of a research jointly financed by International Development Research Centre, Ottawa, Canada and the Government of the United Republic of Tanzania January 1989.

Kulaba, S.M. *The Ten Commandments and Self-Reliance in Housing and Urban Development in Africa,* CHS. Ardhi Institute, Dar-es-Salaam, 1985.

Laquian, A.A. "Whither site and services?" in *Habitat International No.2. 1977.*

Leeds, A. "The significant variables determining the character of squatter settlements", in *America Latina, No.12.* 1969.

Legal Aid Committee Pamphlet: *Essays on Law and Society,* Faculty of law, University of Dar-es-Salaam, 1985.

Leishman, A.D.H. " A Regional Approach to the Capital City transfer", in *Tanzania Notes and Records, No. 84. 1980.*

Leslie, J.A.K. *A survey of Dar-es-Salaam,* OUP. 1963.

Leys, C. "Interpreting African Underdevelopment: Reflections on the ILO report on Employment, Incomes and Equality in Kenya", in *African Affairs, Vol. 72, No.289, 1973.*

Lipton,M. *Why Poor People Stay Poor:A Study of Urban Bias in World Development*, Temple Smith (London), 1977.

Lipumba,N.H.I.(et al), *Economic stabilization policies in Tanzania*, Economics Department & Economic Research Bureau, University of Dar-Es-Salaam, 1984.

Lloyd,P. *Slums of hope? Shanty Towns of the Third World*, Manchester University Press, 1979.

Lomnitz,L. "Mechanisms of articulation between Shanty Town Settlers in the Urban System", in *Urban Anthropology Vol.7, 1978*.

Lomnitz,L. "The Social and Economic Organization of a Mexican Shanty Town", in Cornelius,W.A.& Trueblood,F.D. (eds), *Latin American Urban Research Vol.4*. Anthropological Perspectives on Latin American Urbanization, Sage Publications, 1974.

Lugalla,J.L.P. "Is Dodoma, The Capital City of Tanzania a Socialist City?", in *African Urban Quarterly Vol.2.No.2,May 1987*.

Lugalla,J.L.P. "Conflicts and Politics in Urban Planning in Tanzania", in *African Study Monographs Vol.9. No.4. 1989*.

Lugalla,J.L.P. "The State, Law and Urban Poverty in Tanzania", in *Journal of Law and Politics in Africa, Asia and Latin America, Vol.22.No.2. 1989*.

Lugalla,J.L.P. *The Structural Adjustment Programmes (SAPS) and the Education Sector in Tanzania.* A State of the Art Paper presented at the Workshop on Social and Political Impact of SAPS in Subsaharan Africa, Harare, Zimbambwe, March 1992.

Lugalla,J.L.P. *Poverty and Adjustments in Tanzania:Grappling with Poverty Issues During Adjustment Period.* An Unpublished Research Report, Department of Sociology, University of Dar-Es-Salaam, March, 1993.

Lugalla,J.L.P. *Cost of Education, Willingness to Pay and Ability of Parents to Share Costs.* An Unpublished Research Report, Department of Sociology, University of Dar-Es-Salaam, August,1993.

Magubane,B. "The City in Africa: Some Theoretical Issues", in Obudho,R.A.& El-Shakhs,S.(eds), *Development of Urban Systems in Africa,1979*.

Maro,P.& Mlay,W. "Population Redistribution in Tanzania", in Clarke,J.& Kasinski,L.(ed), *Redistribution of Population in Africa*, HEB, London 1982

Marris,P. "African City Life", in *Nkanga Editions No.1*, Institute of Social Research, University of Makerere,Kampala, Uganda.

Martin,R. *Personal Freedom and the Law in Tanzania: A Study of Socialist State Administration*, OUP, Nairobi,1971.

Mascarenhas,A.C. "Urban Housing in Tanzania", in Egero,B.& Henin,R.(eds), *The population of Tanzania: An Analysis of the 1967 Population Census, 1973*.

Mascarenhas,A.C. "The Port of Dar-Es-Salaam", in Dar-Es-Salaam: City, Port and Region, *Tanzania Notes and Records,No.71, 1970*.

Mascarenhas,A.C. *Urban Development in Dar-Es-Salaam*, M.A. Thesis,University of California, Los Angeles, 1966.

Materu,J. "Sites and Services Projects in Tanzania", in *Third World Planning Review, Vol.8.No.2,1986*.

Mayer,P. "Migrancy and the study of Africans in Towns", in *American Anthropologist 64*.

Mazumdar,D. "The Urban Informal Sector", in *World Development No.4, 1976*.

Mbah,F.U. *Prostitution in Tanzania: A Case Study of Dar-Es-Salaam*, Unpublished B.A.(Sociology) Degree Dissertation, University of Dar-Es-Salaam, 1980.

McCarthy,D.M.P. *Colonial Bureaucracy and Underdevelopment:Tanganyika 1919-1940*, Iowa State University Press 1982.

McGee,T.G. *The Urbanization Process in the Third World:Exploration in search for a Theory*. London: G.Bell,1971.

Mgullu,F.P. *Housing: A Study of Nationalities and Services Schemes*, Unpublished LL.M. Thesis, University of Dar-Es-Salaam, 1978.

Ministry of Lands, Housing and Urban Development: *The National Housing Development Policy, 1982*.

Ministry of Planning and Economic Affairs:*Structural Adjustment Programme for Tanzania, June 1982*.

Miti,K. *Issues raised by "Nguvu-Kazi" and its implementation in Dar-Es-Salaam*, (mimeo) University of Dar-Es-Salaam, 1983.

Mlay,W.F.I. *Recent Rural-Urban Migration in Tanzania with reference to movements o Arusha and Moshi Towns*, Unpublished Ph.D. Thesis, London University, 1974.

Mlay,W.F.I. "Rural to Urban Migration and Rural Development", in *Tanzania Notes and Records No. 81 & 82, 1977*.

Moser,C.O.N. "Informal Sector and Petty Commodity:Dualism or Dependence in Urban Development?" in *World Development No.6 1978*.

Nelson,N. "How Women and Men get by: The Sexual Division of Labour in the Informal Sector in Nairobi Squatter Settlement", in Bromley,R.& Gerry,C.(eds), *op. cit.*

Ntukula,M. *Social Problems of Squatters: A Case Study of Kinondoni-Moscow in Dar-Es-Salaam*, Tanzania. Unpublished B.A.(Degree) Dissertation, University of Dar-Es-Salaam, 1984.

Nyerere,J.K. *The Arusha Declaration*, Government Printer, Dar-Es-Salaam, 1967.

Nyerere,J.K. *Decentralization Policy*, Government Printer, Dar-Es-Salaam,1972.

Nyerere,J.K. *Villagization Policy*, Government Printer, Dar-Es-Salaam, 1972.

Nyerere,J.K. *The Arusha Declaration:Ten Years after*, Government Printer,1977.

Nyerere,J.K. *Freedom and Socialism*, OUP, 1968.

Obudho,R.A. "National urban policy in East Africa", in *Regional Development Dialogue, Vol.4.No.2, 1983*.

Papanek,G. "The Poor of Jakarta", in *Economic Development and Cultural Change Vol.24,1975*.

Parliamentary Act No.45 of 1962:*The National Housing Corporation of Tanganyika Act*, Government Printer, Dar-Es-Salaam, 1962.

Payne,G. *Urban Housing in the Third World*, Routledge and Kegan Paul Co.Ltd. 1977.

Peil,M.& Sada,P.O. *The African Urban Society,*John Wiley & Sons Ltd. 1984.

Peil,M. *Cities and Suburbs: Urban Life in West Africa,* Africana Publishing, 1981.

Peil,M. "African Squatter Settlements: A Comparative Study, in *Urban Studies Vol.13, 1976.*

Perlman,J.E. *"Myth of Marginality": Urban Poverty and Politics in Rio de Janeiro,* University of California Press, 1976.

Pons,V.(et al), *Urban Social Research:Problems and Prospects,* Routledge & Paul Kegan, 1983.

Portes,A. "Housing Policy, Urban Poverty and the State:The Favelas of Rio de Janeiro, 1972-1976", in *Latin America Research Review No. 14, 1979.*

Portes,A. "Rationality in the Slum: An Essay on Interpretative Sociology", in *Comparative Studies on History and Society, No. 14, 1972.*

Qadeer,M.A. "Successful housing planning for Third World countries must be indigenous", in *Journal of Housing, Vol. 37, No.3.1980.*

Qadeer,M.A. *Urban Development in the Third World:Internal Dynamics of Lahore,* Pakistan, Praeger Publishers, 1983.

Raikes,P. *"Differentiation and Progressive Farmer Policies",* Paper presented to the East African Agriculture Economics Society, June 1972.

Ramachandran, P. *Pavement Dwellers in Bombay,* Tata Institute of Social Science, Bombay, 1974.

Redmond,P. *A Political History of the Songea Ngoni from the Mid-19th. Century to the rise of TANU,* Unpublished Ph.D. Thesis, University of London, 1972.

Roberts,B. *Cities of Peasants:The Political Economy of Urbanization in the Third World,* Edward Arnold,1978.

Rodney,W. *How Europe Underdeveloped Africa,* TPH, Dar-Es-Salaam, 1972.

Rondinelli,D.A. "Integrated Regional Development Planning:Linking urban centres and rural areas in Bolivia", in *World Development Vol.11,No.1. 1983.*

Rweyemamu,J.F. *Underdevelopment and Industrialization in Tanzania:A Study of perverse capitalist development,* OUP, 1973.

Sabot,R.H. *Economic Development and Urban Migration in Tanzania 1900-1971,* Clarendon Press, 1979.

Sabot,R.H. *Open Unemployment and Employed Compound of Urban Surplus Labour,* Economic Research Bureau, University of Dar-Es-Salaam, 1974.

Sandbrook,R. & Stren,R.E. "Notes Towards the Political Economy of Third World Urban Policy", Department of Political Science, University of Toronto, *Working Paper, No.B.2. 1983.*

Sandbrook,R. *The Politics of Basic Needs:Urban Aspects of Assaulting Poverty,* HEB. 1982.

Sanyal, B. "The Urban Informal Sector Revisited: Some Notes on the relevance of the concept in the 1980s", in *Third World Planning Review, Vol. 10.No.1. 1988.*

Saunders,P. *Social Theory and the Urban Question,* Hutchinson & Co. Ltd. 1981.

Saylor,G. Variation in Sukumaland Cotton Yields and Extension Service, *Economic Research Bureau Paper No. 70.5,* University of Dar-Es-Salaam, 1970.
Schmetzer,H. "Housing in Dar-Es-Salaam", in *Habitat International, Vol. No.4. 1982.*
Second Five Year Development Plan for Tanzania, 1969-1974.
Shao,J. "The Villagization program and the disruption of the ecological balance in Tanzania", in *Canadian Journal of African Studies(Toronto), Vol.20.2,1986.*
Sheriff,F. "Housing policies and strategies in Tanzania", in *Trialog, Vol. 6. 1985.*
Shivji,I. *Class Struggle in Tanzania,* TPH. 1967.
Shivji,I. *Law, State and the Working Class in Tanzania,* James Curry,HEB & TPH 1986.
SIDA, *Health Centres in Need of Treatment,* SIDA Evaluation Report, Health, Tanzania, No.4, 1987.
Simonic,J.M. *Citizens in Conflict:The Sociology of Town Planning,* Hutchinson, London, 1974.
Sinclair,S.W. "Bibliography on the Informal Sector", in *Bibliography Services No.10,* Centre for Developing Areas Studies, McGill University, 1978.
Skarstein,R. & Wangwe,S.W. *Industrial Development in Tanzania:Some Critical Issues,* Scandinavian Institute of African Studies/Tanzania Publishing House,1986.
Soja,E.W. & Weaver,C.E. "Urbanization and Underdevelopment in East Africa", in Berry,B.J.L.(ed), *Urbanization and Counterurbanization* Sage Publications, 1976.
Soja, E.W. and Tobin, R.J. "The Geography of Modernization: Paths, Patterns, and Processes of Social Change in Developing Countries", in Abu-Lughod, J. and Hay, R.Jr. (eds.), *Third World Urbanization,* Maaroufa Press, 1977.
Souza, P.R. and Tokman, V. "The Informal Urban Sector in Latin America", in *International Labour Review No. 114,* 1976.
Sparpston, M.J. "Uneven Geographical Distribution of Medical Care: A Ghanaian Case Study", in *Journal of Development Studies, Vol. 9,* 1972.
Spengler, F. "Die Agrarpolitik Tansanias", in *KAS -Auslandsinformationen - Sankt Augustin - Bonn, Vol.1, No.2,* 1985.
Stohr, W. and Taylor, D.R.F. *Development from above or below? The dialectics of Regional planning in developing countries,* John Wiley & Sons, 1981.
Stren, R.E. *Urban inequality and housing policy in Tanzania: The problem of squatting,* University of California, Berkeley, 1975.
Stren, R.E. "Urban Policy", in Okumu, J.J. *Politics and Public Policy in Kenya and Tanzania,* Heineman Educational Books (HEB), Nairobi, 1979.
Sutton, J.E.G. "Dar-Es-Salaam: A sketch of a hundred years", in *Tanzania Notes and Records, No.71,* 1970.
Svendsen, K.E. "The Creation of Macroeconomic Imbalances and a Structural Crisis", in Boesen, J. (et al), *Tanzania: Crisis and Struggle for Survival,* Scandinavian Institute of African Studies, Uppsala, 1986.

Swantz, M.L. *The City, Town and Village,* Paper presented at the International Workshop "Urban Development in Rural Context in Africa", Scandinavian Institute of African Studies, Uppsala, September 14th.-17th., 1989.

Szelenyi, I. *Urban Inequalities under State Socialism,* OUP, 1983.

Tanganyika: *Town Development Control Ordinance Cap. 103 of 1956,* Government Press, Dar-Es-Salaam.

Tanzania Housing Bank: *Annual Report and Accounts, Dar-Es-Salaam, 1977.*

Tanzania: *The Land Acquisition Act, Act No.47 of 1967.*

Tanzania: *The National Capital Master Plan for Dar-Es-Salaam,* The Project Planning Associates of Canada, 1969.

Tanzania: *Local Government (Urban Authorities) Act 1982, No.8 of 1982,* Government Printers, Dar-Es-Salaam, 1982.

Tanzania: *Town and Country Planning Ordinance, Cap. 378,* Government Press, Dar-Es-Salaam.

Tanzania: *The Constitution of the United Republic of Tanzania, 1984.*

Tanzania: *The Land Registration Ordinance, Cap. 334.*

Tanzania: *Mpango wa Maendeleo wa mwaka 1984/85,* Printpak, Dar-Es-Salaam, 1984.

Tanzania: *Annual Manpower Report to the President 1979,* Ministry of Manpower, Development and Administration, 1982.

Tanzania: *The National Capital Master Plan, Dodoma,* Tanzania, Vol.1-8, The Project Planning Associates of Canada, 1976.

Tanzania: *Survey of Employment and Earnings 1977-78,* Bureau of Statistics, Ministry of Planning and Economic Affairs, Dar-Es-Salaam, 1981.

Tanzania: *Statistical Abstract 1984 & 1991,* Bureau of Statistics, Ministry of Finance, Planning and Economic Affairs, Dar-Es-Salaam, 1986 & 1993.

Tanzania: *Economic Indicators of Tanzania,* Bureau of Statistics, Ministry of Finance, Planning and Economic Affairs, Dar-Es-Salaam, October, 1986.

Tanzania: *Survey of Industrial Production 1980-1981,* Bureau of Statistics, 1986.

Tanzania: *Basic Data: Agriculture and Livestock Sector (1981/82-1985/86),* Planning and Marketing Division, Ministry of Agriculture and Livestock Development, 1987.

Tanzania: *Hali ya Uchumi wa Taifa Katika Mwaka 1985,* Wizara ya fedha, Uchumi na Mipango, Dar-Es-Salaam, Tanzania, Government Printer, 1986.

Tanzania: *National Accounts of Tanzania 1976-1985,* Bureau of Statistics, Ministry of Finance, Economic Affairs and Planning, Dar-Es-Salaam, September, 1986.

Tanzania: *Transport Statistics 1985,* Bureau of Statistics, Ministry of Finance, Planning and Economic Affairs, Dar-Es-Salaam, January, 1987.

Tanzania: *Dar-Es-Salaam Sewerage and Sanitation Study: Existing Foul Sewerage System,* Ministry of Lands, Housing and Urban Development.

Tanzania: *Second Five Year Plan for Economic and Social Development 1969-1974,* Government Printers, Dar-Es-Salaam, 1969.

Tanzania: *The Government Decentralization Act, No.27 of 1972,* Government Printers, Dar-Es-Salaam, 1972.

Tanzania: *The Third Five Year Plan for Economic and Social Development, 1976-1981,* Government Printer, 1976.
Tanzania: *Urban Councils (Interim Provisions) Act No.11 of 1978.*
Tanzania: *1985/86 Budget for Urban Authorities,* Prime Minister's Office, 1985.
Tanzania: *Sensa 1988: 1988 Population Census: Preliminary Report,* Bureau of Statistics, Ministry of Finance, Economic Affairs and Planning, Dar-Es-Salaam, 1989.
Tanzanian Industrial Studies and Consulting Organization (TISCO), *Industrial Directory, 1983.*
Temu, A.J. "The Rise and Triumph of Nationalism", in Kimambo, I. and Temu, A.J. (eds.) *A History of Tanzania.*
THB, *Report and Statement of Accounts for the Period July 1983 to June 1984.*
THB, *Masharti ya Kupata Mkopo, 1985.*
The Economic Sabotage and Organized Crime Act of 1984.
The Penal Code of Tanzania.
The Human Resources Deployment Act of 1983.
The Master and Native Servant's Ordinance of 1923.
The Labour Utilization Ordinance of 1947.
The Development Plan for Tanganyika, Government Printers, Dar-Es-Salaam 1962.
Thiele, G. "The state and rural development in Tanzania: The village administration as a political field", in *The Journal of Development Studies (London), Vol.22, No.3,* 1986.
The Rent Restriction Act of 1984.
Tibaijuka, J. *Property Rent in Urban Areas in Tanzania Mainland,* Advanced Diploma in Land Management and Evaluation (unpublished), Ardhi Institute, Dar-Es-Salaam, 1987.
Todaro, M.P. "Income expectations, Rural-Urban Migration and Employment in Africa", in *International Labour Review, Vol.104, No.5,* 1971.
Tripp, A.M. *"Defending the Right to Subsist:The State Versus The Urban Informal Economy in Tanzania",* Paper presented at the African Association Annual Meeting in Chicago, Illinois, USA, October, 1988.
Tungaraza, F.S.K. *Notwendigkeit und Möglichkeit von Sozialpolitik in Tansania,* Universität Augsburg, Fachbereich Wirtschafts- und Sozialwissenschaften, 1988.
Turner, J.F. "Barriers and Channels for Housing Development in Modernizing Countries", *Journal of American Institute of Planners.33,* 1967.
Turner, J. F. C. "Uncontrolled Urban Settlements: Problems and Policies", in Breese, G. (ed.) *The City in Newly Developing Countries: Readings on Urbanism and Urbanization,* Prentice Hall, 1969.
Turner, J. "Uncontrolled Urban Settlements. Problems and Policies", Breese, G. *The City in Newly Developing Countries,* Englewood Cliffe, N.J. Prentice-Hall, 1969.
Turnham, D. *The Employment Problem in Less Developed Countries: A Review of Evidence,* OECD Development Centre, 1970.

Turritin, J. "Petty Trading in Rural Mali", in *CUSO Journal, December 1987*.

Turshen, M. *The political ecology of disease in Tanzania*, New Brunswick, Rutgers University Press, 1984.

Urquidi, V.L. "The Underdeveloped City", in Hardoy, J.E. (ed.) *Urbanization in Latin America: Approaches and Issues,* Anchor Books, 1976.

Valentine, T.R. "Government Wage Policy, Wage and Employment Trends, and Economic Instability in Tanzania since independence", *Economic Research Bureau Paper, 81.1,* University of Dar-Es-Salaam, 1981.

Weeks, J. *Employment and Growth of Towns,* a paper presented to the British African Studies Association, September 1972.

Weisner, T.S. "Kariobangi: The Case History of a Squatter Resettlement Scheme in Kenya", 1976, in Arens, W. (ed.) *A Century of Change in East and Central Africa,* Monton, 1976.

White, A. "Squatter Settlements, Politics and Class Conflict", University of Glasgow, Institute of Latin American Studies, *Occasional Paper no. 17,* 1975.

Wilson, F.B. "Urban Ecology: Urbanization and Systems of Cities", in *Annual Review of Sociology, Vol.10,* 1984.

Wirth, H. *Aspekte des Zusammenhangs von Entwicklungshilfe und Entwicklungsplanung in Tanzania,* Bonn, 1985.

World Bank: Tanzania: *The Second National Sites and Services Project,Report No.1513-TA, World Bank, 1977.*

Yeager, R. "Demography and Development Policy in Tanzania", *Journal Of Developing Areas, 16 (4).*

Yeung, Y.M. *Hawkers in South East Asian Cities,* Ottawa, International Development Research Centre, 1977.

Zakaria, M.L. *The Politics Of Housing in Tanzania, A Case Study of Sinza Area in Dar-ES-Salaam,* Unpublished B.A. Degree Dissertation, University of Dar-Es-Salaam, 1982.

Index

A

affluent classes 129
after office hours prostitutes 151
Agha-Khan 97
agricultural extension 6
Ardhi Institute 47, 48, 50, 54
area Commissioners 170, 171
Armstrong 158, 162, 163, 165, 166, 172, 173, 174, 176, 193, 199, 200, 201
Arusha 7, 11, 12, 14
Arusha Declaration xvii, xviii
Asians 13
Awiti 7, 191
Awotona 201

B

Bagachwa 119, 129, 130, 131, 197
bank 109, 118
Bantje 99
Banyikwa 113, 114, 192, 197
barmaids 149, 150, 151
Barnes 88, 196
Basic Necessary Income 123
begging xxi
Berg 10, 192
bhang 138, 153
bikinis 149
Bisanda 200, 201
black-marketing 120, 122, 138, 147, 148, 154
born-here-here 140
born-town 140
Brain 4, 11, 12, 13, 14, 18, 191, 192, 195
Bremen xv
bribes 124, 128, 144, 154
British Mandate 1, 4
Bromley 198
Buguruni 38
Building Research Unit 50, 52, 60
Burundi xvii

C

capital city 22, 33, 34
Capital Development Authority 66
Carnegie xv
cash-crops 1, 3, 11
cashew nuts xvii
Center for Housing Studies 50, 54
Chachage xv, 194, 195
Chaduru 43, 66
Chama Cha Mapinduzi 29, 128
Chang 43, 66
Changanyikeni 105
Chibuku 127
Chinang 66
cholera 106, 109
class polarization 129
Cliffe 191
coffee xvii, xviii, 1, 2, 3, 5, 8, 9
Collinson 6, 191
colonial economy 1, 2, 3, 7, 8, 10, 11, 12, 14, 17
colonial state 1, 2, 5, 9, 11, 13
colonial towns 12, 13, 18
commercialized sex 138, 140, 149, 152
Comoro, Christopher xv
Congo Street 145
consumption patterns 126, 128
copra 3, 5
Cornelius 196
corruption 124, 147, 148, 153
cotton xvii, 3, 5, 6, 8
Coulson 3, 5, 6, 8, 9, 191, 192
craftsmen 127
crisis 181, 185, 189

D

Dalla-Dalla 96, 114, 115, 116
danguro 150, 153
Dar-Es-Salaam 21, 22, 24, 27, 29, 30, 32, 33, 34, 35, 36, 37, 38, 39
Dar-Es-Salaam City Council 100, 107, 117
decentralization 28

Delpos, Manuela xv
Demographic and Health Survey 99
detention 175
Deutsch Ostafrika 1
diarrhea 109
director generals 128
directors 128
Disease Prevention Act 137
Dodoma 22, 29, 32, 33, 34, 35, 36, 37, 38, 39
Doherty 35, 193
domestic servants 126, 130, 148
drainage xxi, 95, 97, 101, 106, 111

E

East African community xviii
economic activity 12
Economic and Organized Crime Control Act 147
economic crisis 119, 120, 125, 126, 137, 149, 154
Economic Recovery Program One xix
economic sabotage 147
economic structure 2, 4, 7, 13, 17
education 95, 97, 99, 100, 101, 102, 118
Education for Self-Reliance 24
education system 2
electricity 95, 96, 97, 103, 104
employment 19, 23, 24, 25, 26, 32
Employment Ordinance 170
entertainment industry 149
environmental conditions 98

F

Fitzgerald, Anne xv

G

Gambishi 193
Gangilonga 14
garbage pickers 146
general managers 128
generative 18

Gerezani 130
German colonialism 4
German colony 1
Germany xv
Gerry 198
Geza-Ulole 164
Gibb, Alexander 27, 37, 38, 39
Gibbon 193
Goba 171
Gongo La Mbotto 63
Good, Byron xv
Gould 198
Green 23
Growth Pole Centers 28, 29, 32
Growth Pole Strategy 28, 33, 34
Gutkind 196
Gymkhana 102

H

HABITAT 189
Hardiman 183, 188, 201
Haussermann, Hartmut xv
hawkers 126, 130, 131, 132, 133, 134, 135, 136, 144, 145, 154
hawking 131, 133, 145
Hayuma 193
health 95, 97, 98, 99, 101, 103, 106, 108, 118
health education 22
Heggenhhougen, Kris xv
Herbert 184, 186, 201
Heuer 194
high standard areas 38
high-income class 39
Hoffman, Helmut xv
Honey 9, 192
household heads 74, 79, 82
housing conditions 44, 45, 47
housing market 48, 71
housing policies 49, 57, 72
Human Resources Act 172
Human Resources Deployment 151
hygiene education 23

I

ideology 24, 37
ideology of assistance 90, 92
idle and disorderly persons 140
Ilala 98, 100, 108
Iliffe 3, 15, 16, 191, 192
illegal business 174
illicit activities xxi
impoverization 134
imprisonment 156, 158, 170
independence 1, 3, 5, 7, 8, 10, 17, 18
industrial development 26, 29, 31, 32
industrialization 8, 9, 10
informal manufacturing 129
informal sector 120, 126, 127, 129, 130, 131, 134, 137, 144, 145, 146, 148, 154
institutional approach 42, 50
International Development Agency 54
Iringa 14
Ishumi 198, 199
Ismani 7
ivory 3

J

Jalala Kuu 139
Jangwani Street 17
Japan 34
job security 101
jobless corners 138
jobless youths 111

K

Kahama 99, 102
Kangara 127
kanga 125, 149, 152
Kariakoo 15, 16, 130, 139, 145, 149
Katibu Kata 87
Keko-Machungwa 63
Keko-Magurumbasi 63
Keko-Mwanga 63
Kibugumo 164
kickbacks 124, 128, 147, 148
Kigamboni 142
Kigoma 3, 11
Kihesa 64, 65
Kijitonyama 55
Kimara 63
Kimara Stop-Over 63
Kimara-Mavurunza 63
Kimbiji 164, 165
Kimpumu 85, 127
Kinondoni 44, 69, 130, 131, 171
Kirapa 143
Kisege 195
Kisutu 65, 66
kitenge 125, 152
Kiwalani 38
Kjaerby 191
komoni 85
kufa na kupona 127
Kulaba 62, 68, 194, 195, 196, 197
kuuza wajibu 124

L

labor-intensive industries 181
landlords 65, 71, 72
Legal Aid Committee 157
legislation method 50
Lindi 32
Little, Arthur D. 34
local brew 127
Loleza 14
Lomnitz, Larissa 73, 196
low standard areas 38
Lugalla 12

M

Mabibo 124, 126
Mabwe-Pande 171
magangwe 140
magenges 149
Magomeni 98
Maili Mbili 43, 66
majani 138

Makonde 85
malaria 15, 109
Malawi xvii
Maliyamkono 119
Mama Nitilie 149
Mantu 171
Manzese 56, 64, 65, 126, 130, 131, 134, 149
mapapai 96
Mapunda 197
marginalization 134
marijuana 138
Marino, Nyasi 139
Maro 200
Marris 73, 196
Martin 199, 200
Masaki 38, 69
mashimo 117
Mason 10
Master and Native Servant 169, 170
master plan 27, 34, 35, 37, 38
MAWASILIANO 112
Mayer 196
Mbah 186
Mbeya 14, 100, 109, 112
Mbezi 38
Mbulu 5
Mbuyuni 32
medium standard areas 38
medium-income class 39
Mergner, Gottfried xv
Mfanyakazi 137
Mgullu 195
Midgley 183, 201
migration 13
mihogo 96
Mikocheni 38
mikokoteni 111, 117, 118
military officers 128
Milles, Dietrich xv
Ministry of Education 24
miscellaneous amendments 156
mishikaki-nyama choma 131
misokoto 138
Mitchell 34

Miti 169, 171, 172, 173, 174, 176, 199, 200, 201
mitumba 125, 127
Mkalama 124
Mkita 137
Mlalakua 63
Mlandizi 105
Mlay 23, 25, 192, 193, 200
Morrison 196
Mozambique xvii
Mponezya, Hamisi 107
Msasani 38
Msewe 83
Msogola 171
Mtoni Kwa Azizi 63
Mtwara 30
Muchiri, Lucy xv
Mueller, Rainer xv
Muhimbili 65
Mukhandi 145
Mwadui 11
Mwami, Abunuwas xvi
Mwana-Dilatu 164, 165
Mwananyamala 98
Mwangi, Christina xv
Mwanjelwa 32
Mwansasu 192
Mwanza 6, 11, 12, 14
Mwinyi 144, 145

N

National Economic Survival Plan xix
National Housing Corporation 50, 60
national population census 20
National Price Commission 122
National Sites and Service Scheme 54, 62
Ndjovu 48
Ndosi, Noah xv
Nelson 150, 153, 198
Nguvu-Kazi Act 151, 157, 161, 165, 166, 169, 170, 175, 178

Njombe 3
Ntukula 109, 197, 198
Nunge 142, 143
nutrition 23
NUWA 105
Nyakato 32
Nyerere 15, 199

O

odd jobs 127, 138, 139
Oldenburg xv
Oyster Bay 44, 67

P

paper planning 181
parasitic 18
Pare 5
parking boys 126, 138
Parkipuny 6, 191
peddlers 131, 132
Perlman 195
Permanent Housing Finance
  Company of Tanzania 50, 51
physical infrastructure 97, 103
pick-pocketers 140
pick-pocketing 138, 139
political dimension 87
poor low-income class 39
population census 20, 21
post-colonial state 41, 49
potholes 111, 117
principal secretaries 128
Priority Social Action Plan xix
private hospitals 98, 99
professors 128
Project Planning Associates 27, 34, 37
Project/Program Approach 50, 54
Prostitutes
  hard-core 151
  stationed in guest houses 150
  street-loitering 150
prostitution xxi, 127, 131, 137, 138, 147, 148, 150, 151, 152, 153

Puja 101
pyrethrum xvii

Q

Quadeer 147, 198, 201

R

recreation 95, 97, 102
Redmond 3
regent estate 44
regional commissioner 161, 162, 171, 173, 175
Registrar of Buildings 50, 52, 60
Rent Restriction Act ix
rogue 156, 172
Ross 149
Rossett 198
rubber 3, 5
rural development 186, 187
rural-urban migration 19, 23, 25
Rwanda xvii

S

Saaty 34
Sabot 2, 13, 191, 193
sanitation 95, 97, 106, 107, 109
Sanya-Sanya 114, 115
Sanyal 188
Savei 63
Saylor 191
Schmetzer 44, 56, 195
secondary education 24
semi-skilled 127
Serikali ya Tanzania 128
sesame 3
settlement schemes 161, 162
Shina 87
Shinyanga 6, 11
Shirika la Umma 128
Simba 17
Singida 32
Sinza 55, 62, 63, 70
sisal xvii, 1, 3, 5, 8, 9
Sittig, Elizabeth xv

Skutsch 47
slum clearance ix, 42, 50, 51, 54, 57, 65, 68
smuggling 147
Social Action Plan xix
social dimension 82, 92
social networks 86, 88, 89, 90
social organization 92, 93
Social Service Facilities 95, 97
social service facilities 95
social services 25, 26
social structure 2, 13
Social Welfare 159, 163, 166, 170
Songea 3
squatter settlements 43, 45, 47, 48, 63, 64, 66, 70, 72
Squatter Upgrading Program ix
street boys 137, 139, 140, 146
street children 140, 141
street vendors 126, 130, 131, 132, 134, 136, 144, 145, 154
Stren 193, 194, 195
structural adjustment ix, xix, xx
Sukuma 6
Sukuma Development Scheme 5
Sumbawanga 32
survival tactics xx, xxi
Swahili 85

T

Tabata 38
Tabora 13
Tambuka-Reli 66
Tandika 126, 130, 131, 149
TANESCO 104, 105
Tanga 4, 11, 12
TANU 16, 18
Tanu Youth League 162
Tanzania Housing Bank 50, 51, 53
Tanzania ni Nchi ya Bongo 153
TAZARA 3
tea xvii
Tegeta 164, 165
Teksi Bubu 115

telephone 96, 109, 110, 118
Tembo 127
Temeke 98, 100, 108, 173
Temu 192
tenants 48, 71, 72
Thumni-Thumni 114
tobacco xvii
town planning 19, 27, 35, 37, 39
trade liberalization 128
truants 138
Trueblood 196
tuberculosis 15, 109
Tuliani 137
Tume ya Bei 122
Tungaraza, Felician xvi
Turner 182, 201
Turritin 148, 198
typhoid 109

U

Ubungo Kisiwani 38
Ubungo-Kibangu 63
ugali 143
Uhindini 14
Uhuru 160
Ujamaa xviii
Ukimwi 152
Ukonga 63
Uluguru 5
unemployment 19, 25, 26, 28
Unga Limited 31, 32
University of Dar-Es-Salaam xv
Uraka 127
urban civic 95, 97
urban crisis 96, 101, 106, 115, 118
urban development 26, 27, 28, 30, 33, 34, 37, 38
urban dwellers 41, 48, 49, 71
urban economy 177
urban growth 19, 20, 22, 23, 28
urban housing 41, 42, 47, 48, 49, 52, 62, 68, 69, 72
    problems 49, 62
urban infrastructure 95, 118

urban planning 19, 37, 38, 39, 182, 186
urban poor 122, 129, 134, 137, 145, 153, 154, 155, 157, 161, 165, 166
urban population xi, xxi, 20, 21, 22, 23, 25, 26, 30, 31, 32
urban poverty 181, 188, 189
urban sanitation xxi
urban social classes 126
urban system 126, 128, 129, 146
urban transportation 96, 97, 110, 114, 115
urban workers 13
urbanization 181, 186, 187
Usafiri Dar-Es-Salaam 96, 112
Usambara 5
Uzunguni 14

V

vagabond 156, 172
vendoring 131, 145
vibaka 126
Vienna xv
vilabu 85
Vingunguti 38
Von Freyhold, Michaela xv

W

wachomoaji 140
wadokozi 140
wahujumu 147
wahuni 140
wateja 149
watemi 140
water supply xxi, 97, 103, 105
widi 138
World Bank 54, 56
worm infection 109

Y

Yanga 17
Yeager 193, 199

Z

Zaire xvii
Zakaria 195
Zambia xvii, 3
Zanzibar Declaration xviii

About the Author

Dr. Joe L.P. Lugalla is a Tanzanian Sociologist/Anthropologist who works as a senior lecturer in the Department of Sociology at the University of Dar-Es-Salaam. After training as a teacher, he taught in both primary and secondary schools in Tanzania before joining the University of Dar-Es-Salaam in 1979 where he pursued his Bachelor of Arts and a Master of Arts degrees in Sociology. Between 1984 and 1990, he stayed in the Federal Republic of Germany where he did his doctoral studies in Sociology and Anthropology at the University of Bremen. Since then he has been lecturing at the University of Dar-Es-Salaam. Dr. Lugalla has also worked as a researcher at the Center of African Studies at Bremen University, a visiting researcher at the University of Vienna, and visiting fellow at the Harvard Medical School in Boston. He has published a variety of articles in scholarly international journals and his main areas of specialization are urban sociology/anthropology, medical sociology/anthropology, social policy, health, culture, and development, environmental sociology, and political sociology. Dr. Lugalla also holds a post-doctoral diploma in Education and International Development. He will be joining the University of New Hampshire in 1995 where he will be an assistant professor in the Anthropology program in the Department of Sociology and Anthropology.